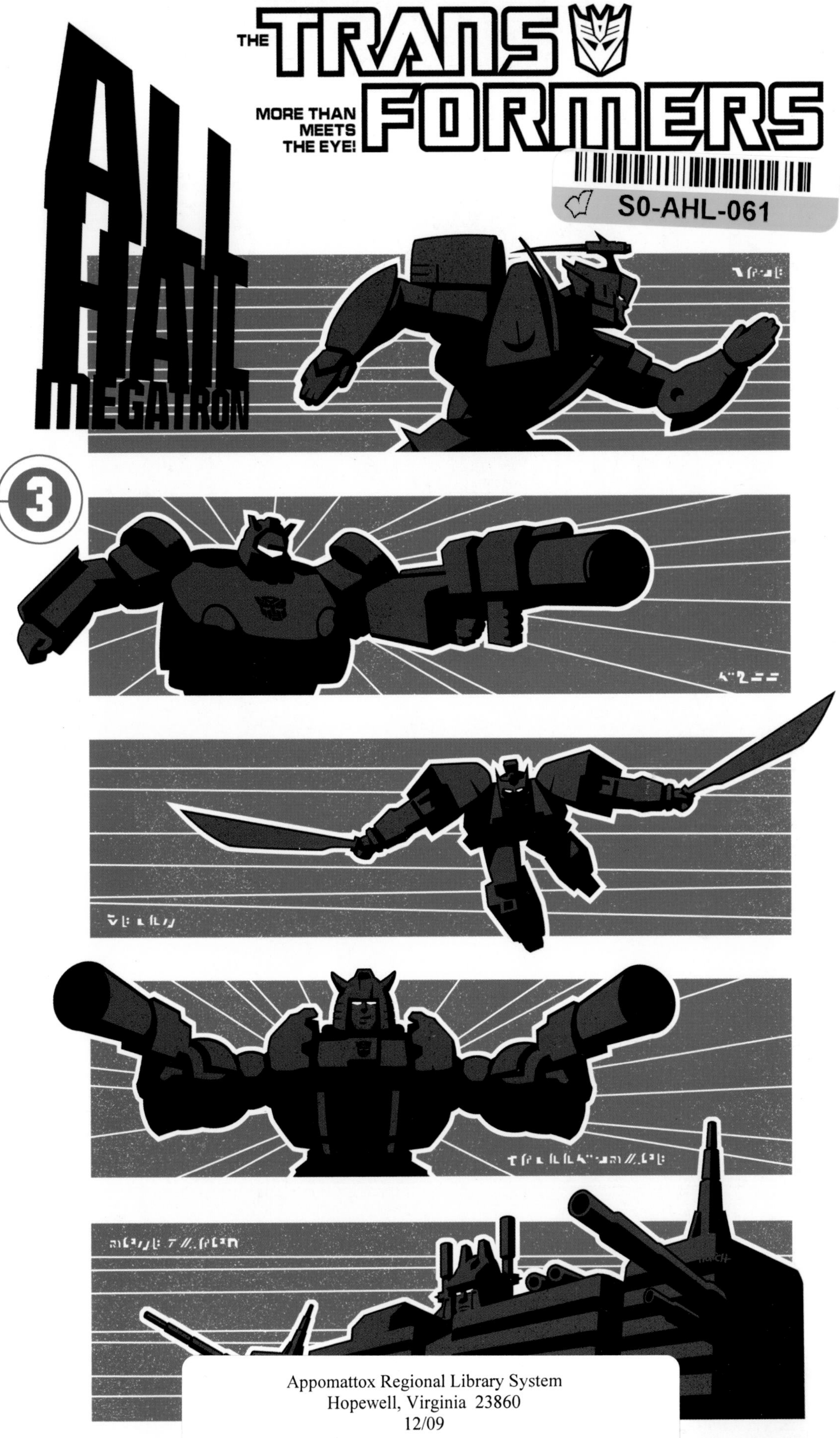
THE TRANSFORMERS
MORE THAN MEETS THE EYE!
ALL HAIL MEGATRON
3

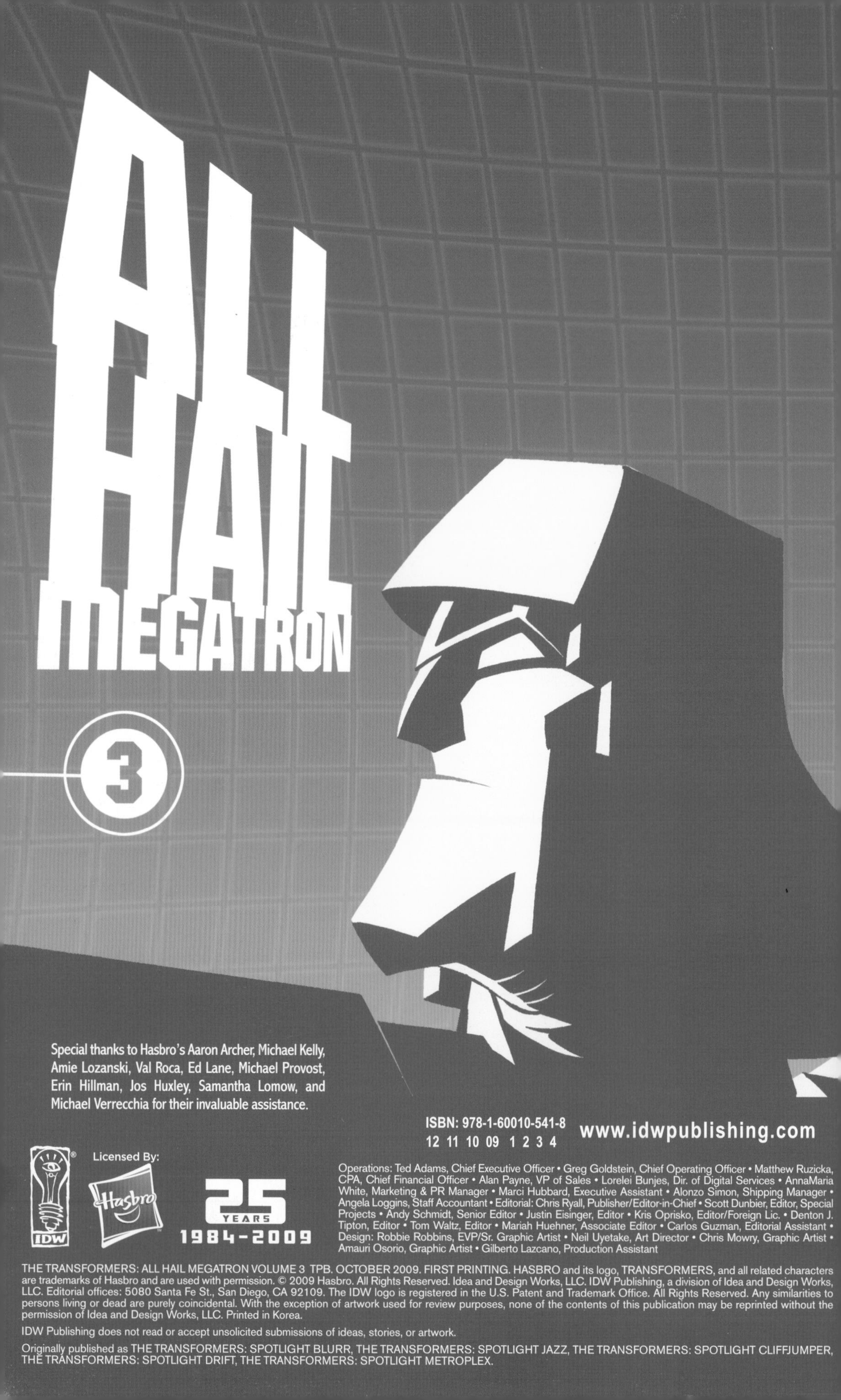
ALL
HAIL
MEGATRON
3

Special thanks to Hasbro's Aaron Archer, Michael Kelly, Amie Lozanski, Val Roca, Ed Lane, Michael Provost, Erin Hillman, Jos Huxley, Samantha Lomow, and Michael Verrecchia for their invaluable assistance.

ISBN: 978-1-60010-541-8
12 11 10 09 1 2 3 4

www.idwpublishing.com

Licensed By:

25 YEARS 1984-2009

Operations: Ted Adams, Chief Executive Officer • Greg Goldstein, Chief Operating Officer • Matthew Ruzicka, CPA, Chief Financial Officer • Alan Payne, VP of Sales • Lorelei Bunjes, Dir. of Digital Services • AnnaMaria White, Marketing & PR Manager • Marci Hubbard, Executive Assistant • Alonzo Simon, Shipping Manager • Angela Loggins, Staff Accountant • Editorial: Chris Ryall, Publisher/Editor-in-Chief • Scott Dunbier, Editor, Special Projects • Andy Schmidt, Senior Editor • Justin Eisinger, Editor • Kris Oprisko, Editor/Foreign Lic. • Denton J. Tipton, Editor • Tom Waltz, Editor • Mariah Huehner, Associate Editor • Carlos Guzman, Editorial Assistant • Design: Robbie Robbins, EVP/Sr. Graphic Artist • Neil Uyetake, Art Director • Chris Mowry, Graphic Artist • Amauri Osorio, Graphic Artist • Gilberto Lazcano, Production Assistant

Originally published as THE TRANSFORMERS: SPOTLIGHT BLURR, THE TRANSFORMERS: SPOTLIGHT JAZZ, THE TRANSFORMERS: SPOTLIGHT CLIFFJUMPER, THE TRANSFORMERS: SPOTLIGHT DRIFT, THE TRANSFORMERS: SPOTLIGHT METROPLEX.

Original Series Edits by Denton J. Tipton and Andy Schmidt

Collection Edits by Justin Eisinger
Editorial Assistance by Mariah Huehner
Collection Design by Chris Mowry

He is the fastest Cybertronian alive. He is glorious, unbeaten, and adored by millions. His capacity for victory is matched only by his overwhelming sense of self belief and his all-encompassing ego. His celebrity threatens to reach heights that heretofore have never been seen. Yet, deep down, he is plagued by a need for something more...

...his name is BLURR.

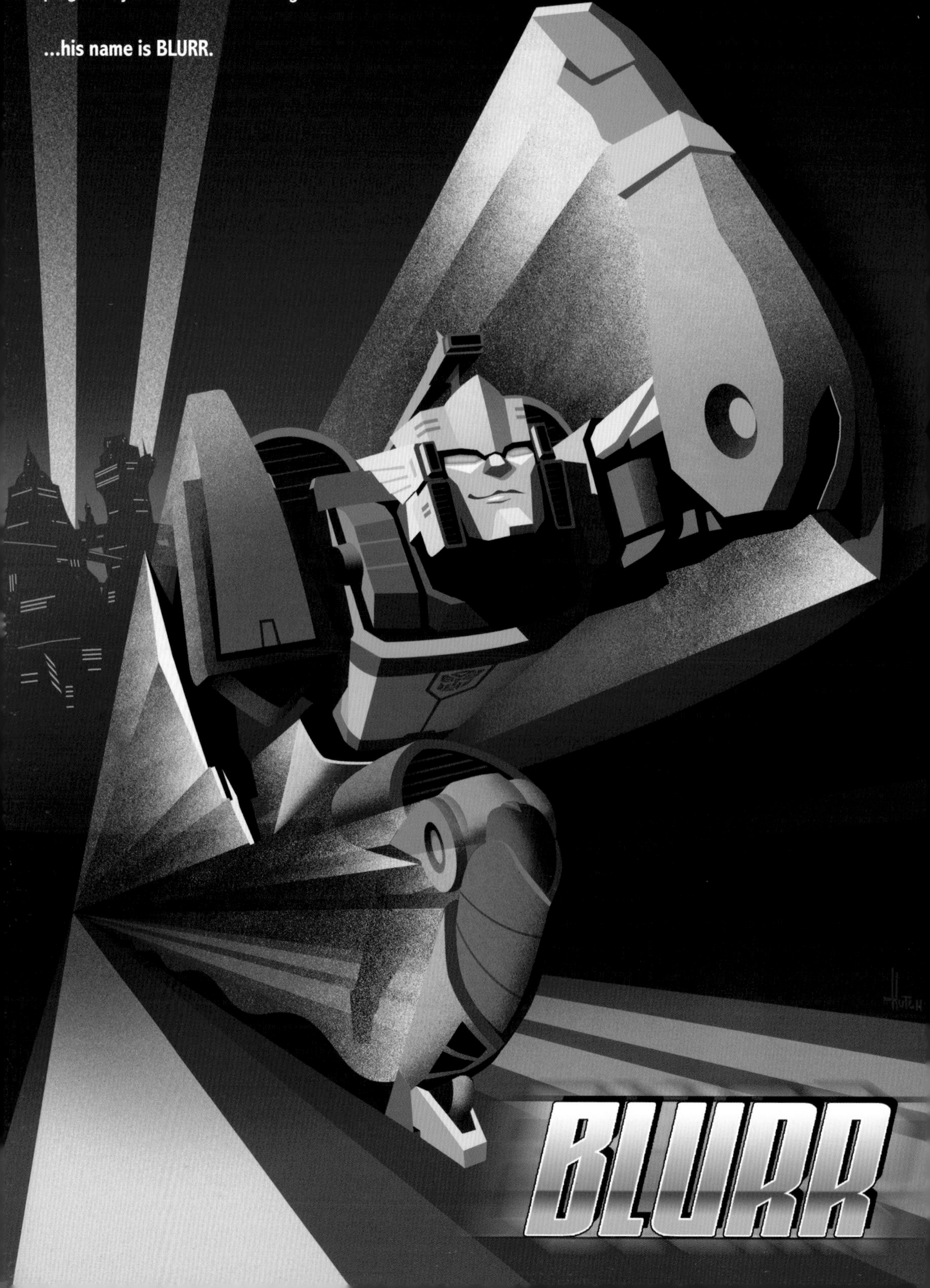
BLURR

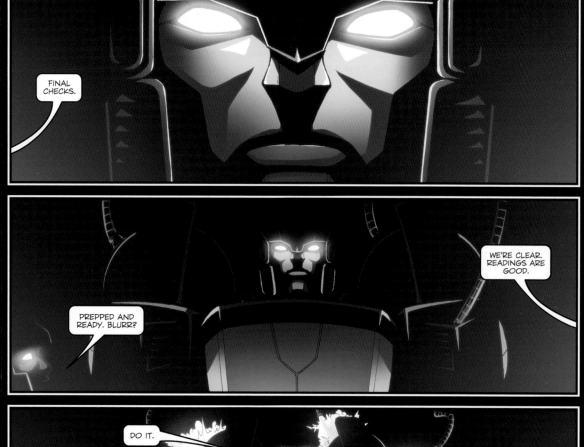

FINAL CHECKS.
PREPPED AND READY. BLURR?
WE'RE CLEAR. READINGS ARE GOOD.
DO IT.
DISENGAGE. SET FOR LAUNCH.

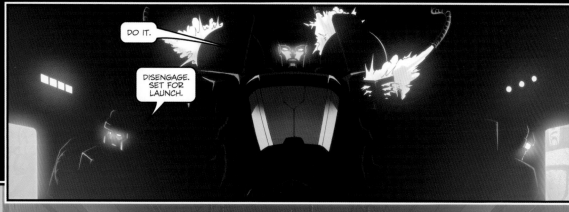

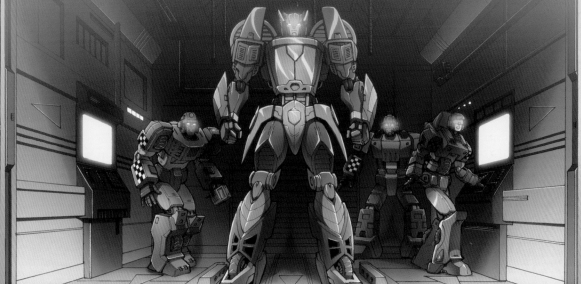

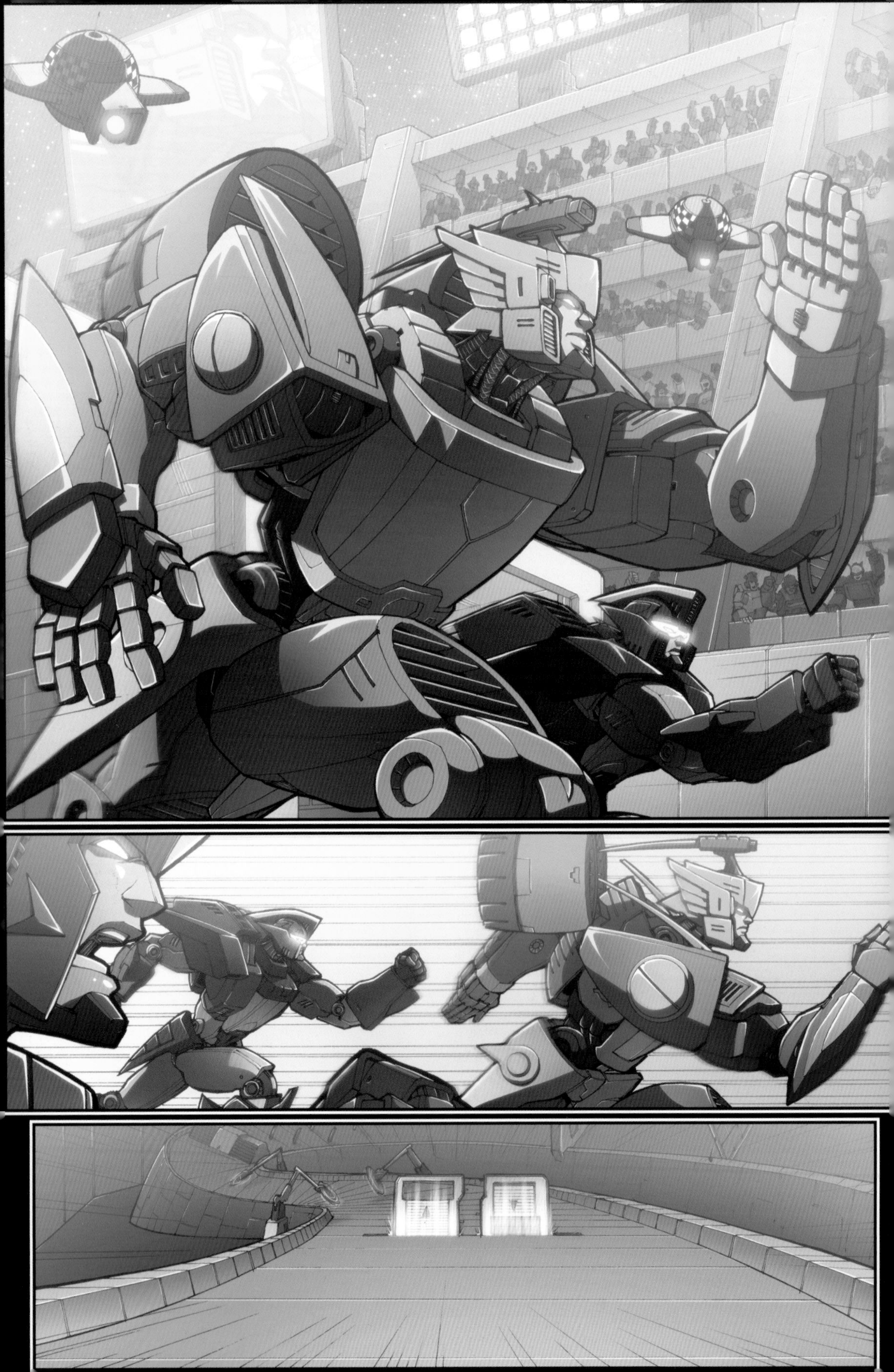

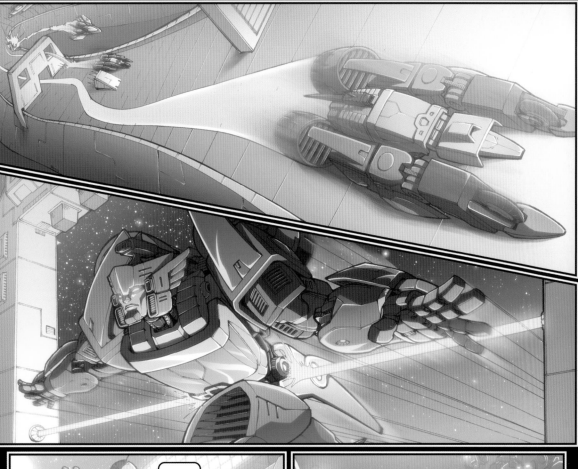

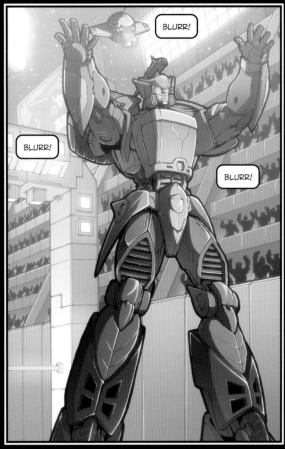

BLURR!

BLURR!

BLURR!

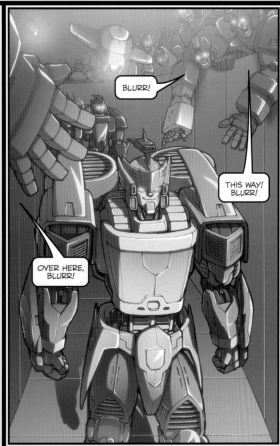

BLURR!

THIS WAY! BLURR!

OVER HERE, BLURR!

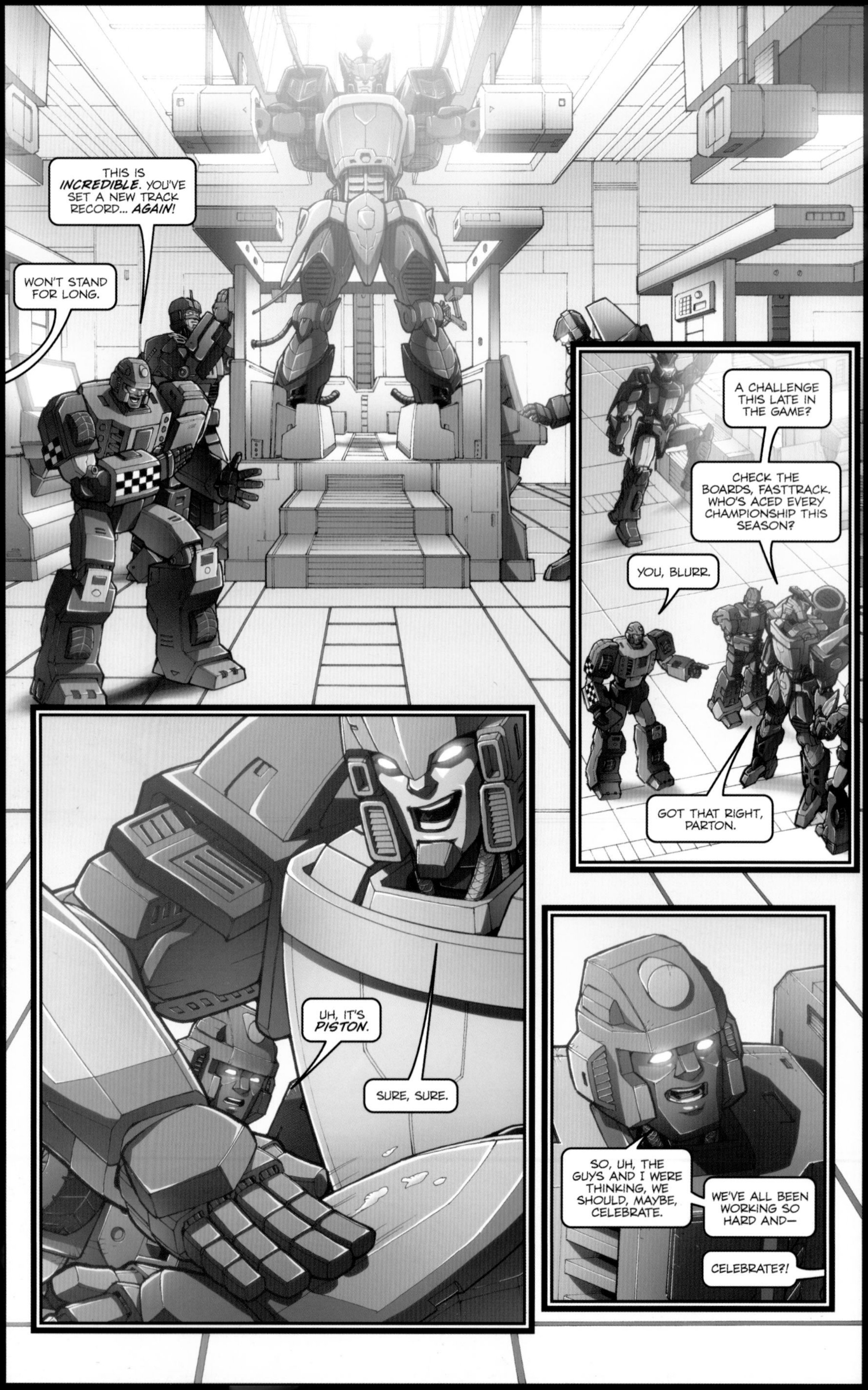
THIS IS *INCREDIBLE*. YOU'VE SET A NEW TRACK RECORD... *AGAIN*!
WON'T STAND FOR LONG.
A CHALLENGE THIS LATE IN THE GAME?
CHECK THE BOARDS, FASTTRACK. WHO'S ACED EVERY CHAMPIONSHIP THIS SEASON?
YOU, BLURR.
GOT THAT RIGHT, PARTON.
UH, IT'S *PISTON*.
SURE, SURE.
SO, UH, THE GUYS AND I WERE THINKING, WE SHOULD, MAYBE, CELEBRATE.
WE'VE ALL BEEN WORKING SO HARD AND—
CELEBRATE?!

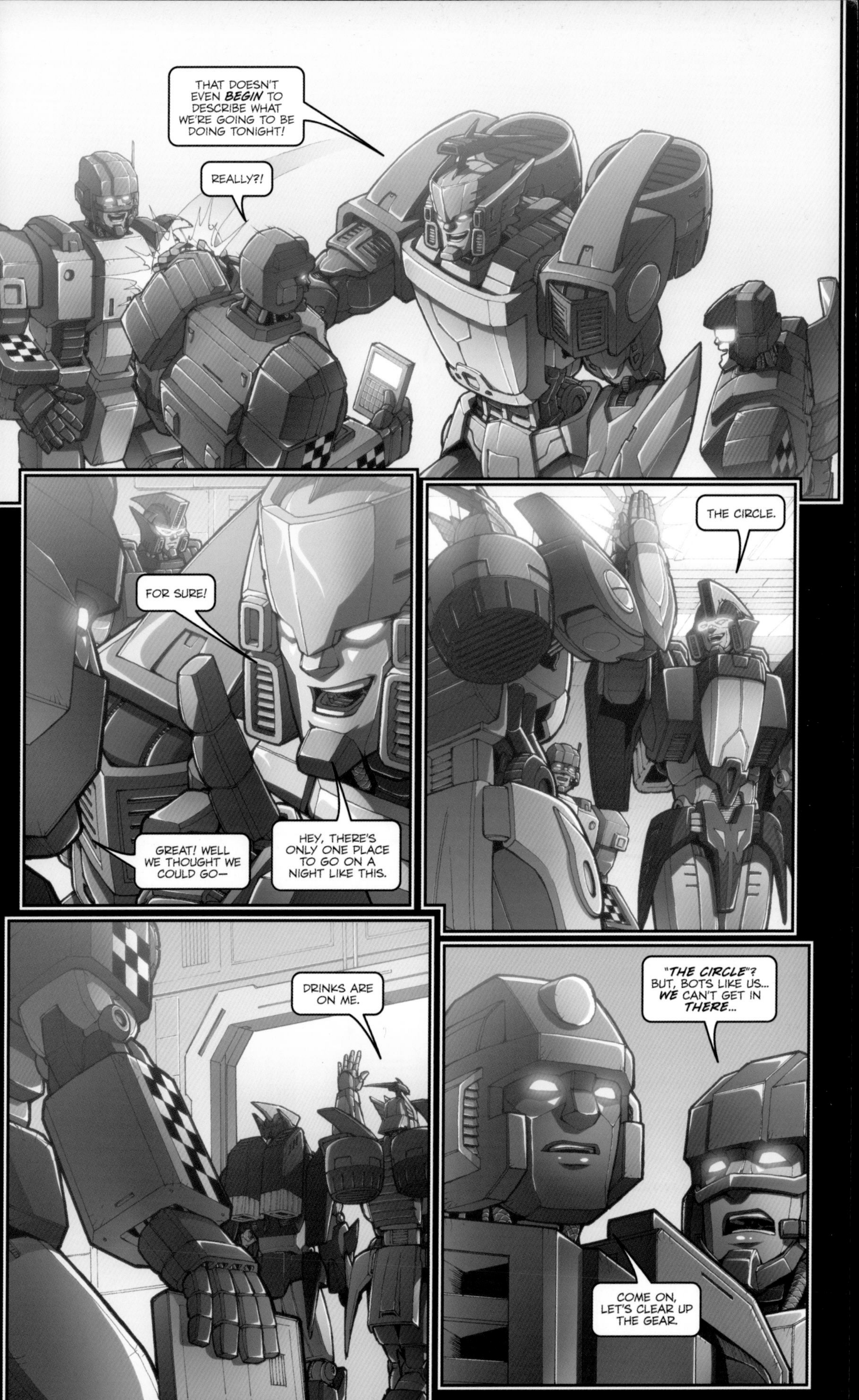
THAT DOESN'T EVEN *BEGIN* TO DESCRIBE WHAT WE'RE GOING TO BE DOING TONIGHT!
REALLY?!
FOR SURE!
GREAT! WELL WE THOUGHT WE COULD GO—
HEY, THERE'S ONLY ONE PLACE TO GO ON A NIGHT LIKE THIS.
THE CIRCLE.
DRINKS ARE ON ME.
"*THE CIRCLE*"? BUT, BOTS LIKE US... *WE* CAN'T GET IN *THERE*...
COME ON, LET'S CLEAR UP THE GEAR.

HE'S HERE!

BLURR!

BLURR, OVER HERE!

CAN YOU BELIEVE HE GETS *DRIVEN* AROUND?

LOOK AT HIM!

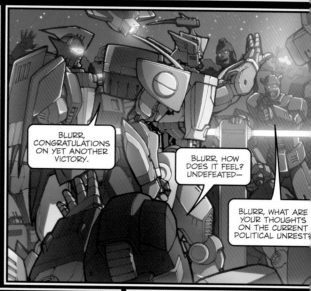

BLURR, CONGRATULATIONS ON YET ANOTHER VICTORY.

BLURR, HOW DOES IT FEEL? UNDEFEATED—

BLURR, WHAT ARE YOUR THOUGHTS ON THE CURRENT POLITICAL UNREST?

EXCUSE ME?

WHAT IS YOUR STANCE ON THE CURRENT POLITICAL UPHEAVAL ON CYBERTRON AND WHAT IT MEANS TO THE—

POLITICAL WHAT NOW?

SURELY YOU KNOW WHAT'S BEEN HAPPENING... YOU *DO* WATCH THE NEWS...

PAL, I DON'T *WATCH* THE NEWS, I *AM* THE NEWS.

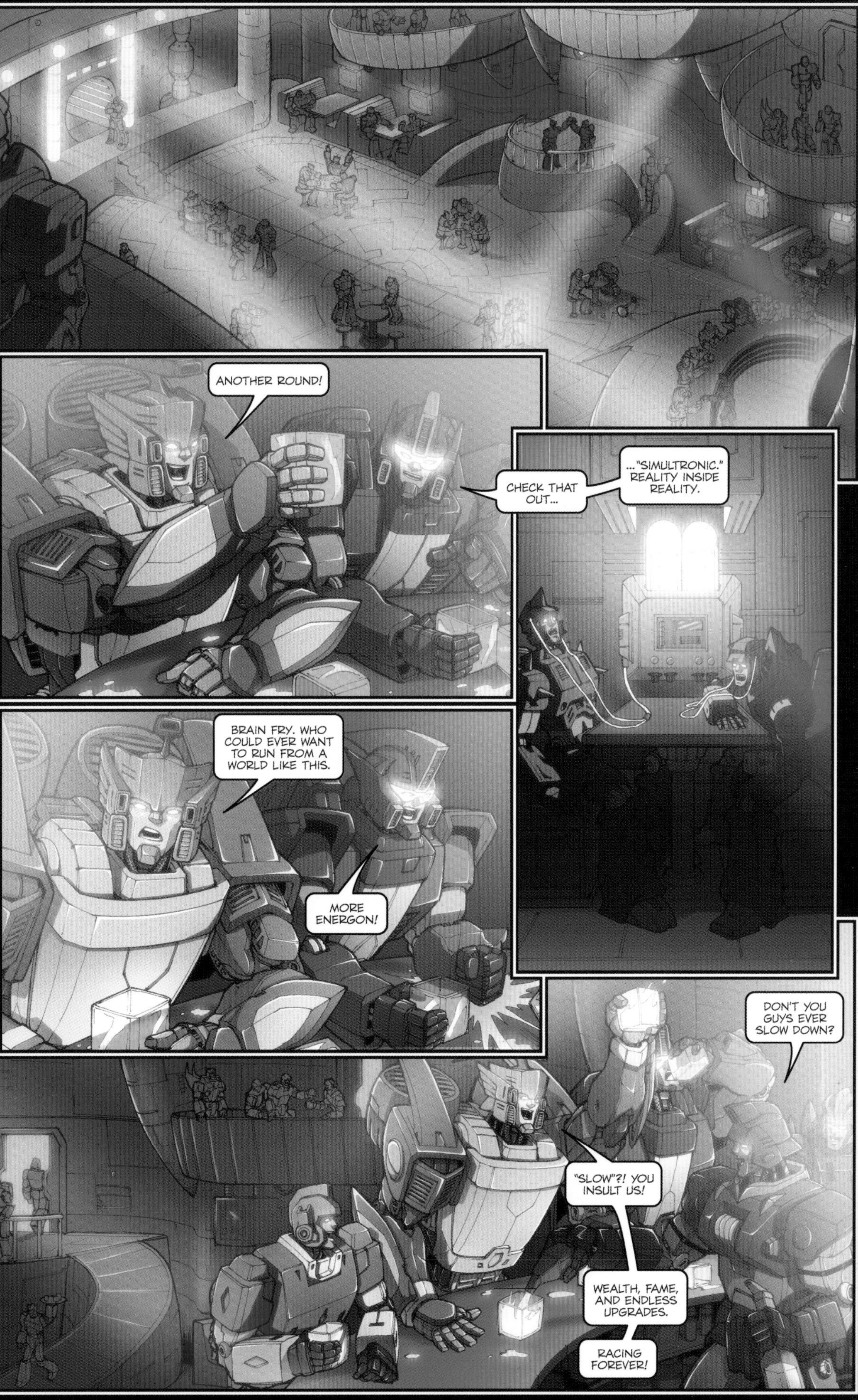
ANOTHER ROUND!
BRAIN FRY. WHO COULD EVER WANT TO RUN FROM A WORLD LIKE THIS.
MORE ENERGON!
CHECK THAT OUT...
..."SIMULTRONIC." REALITY INSIDE REALITY.
DON'T YOU GUYS EVER SLOW DOWN?
"SLOW"?! YOU INSULT US!
WEALTH, FAME, AND ENDLESS UPGRADES.
RACING FOREVER!

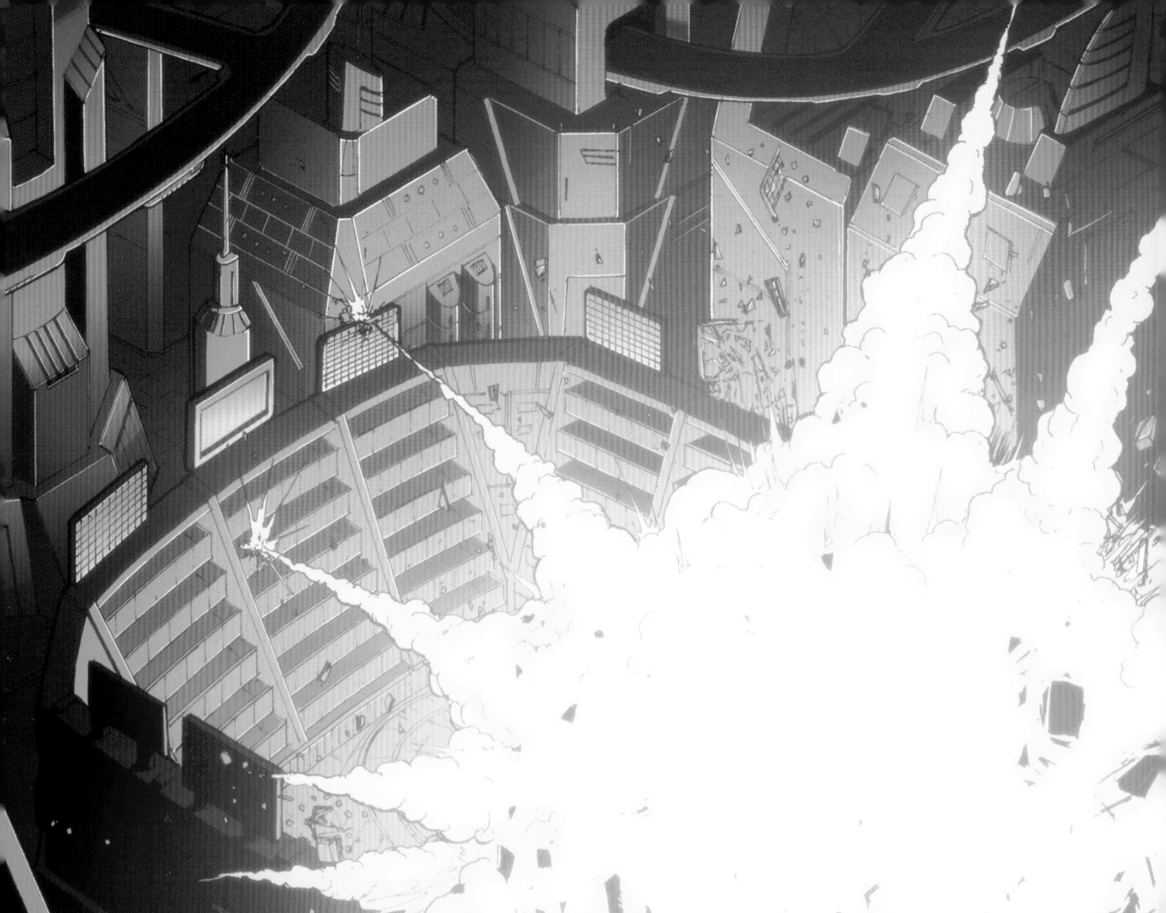

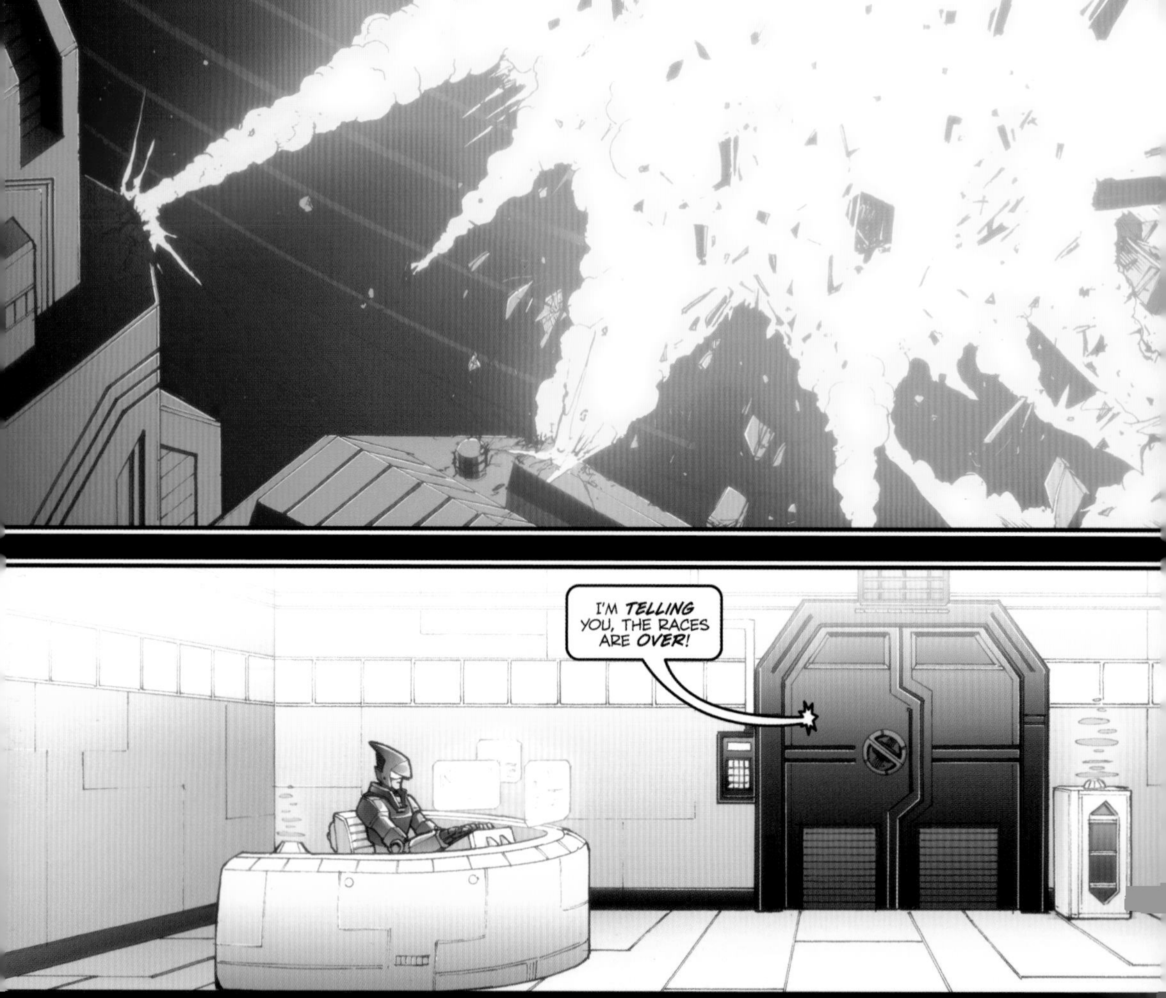
I'M TELLING YOU, THE RACES ARE OVER!

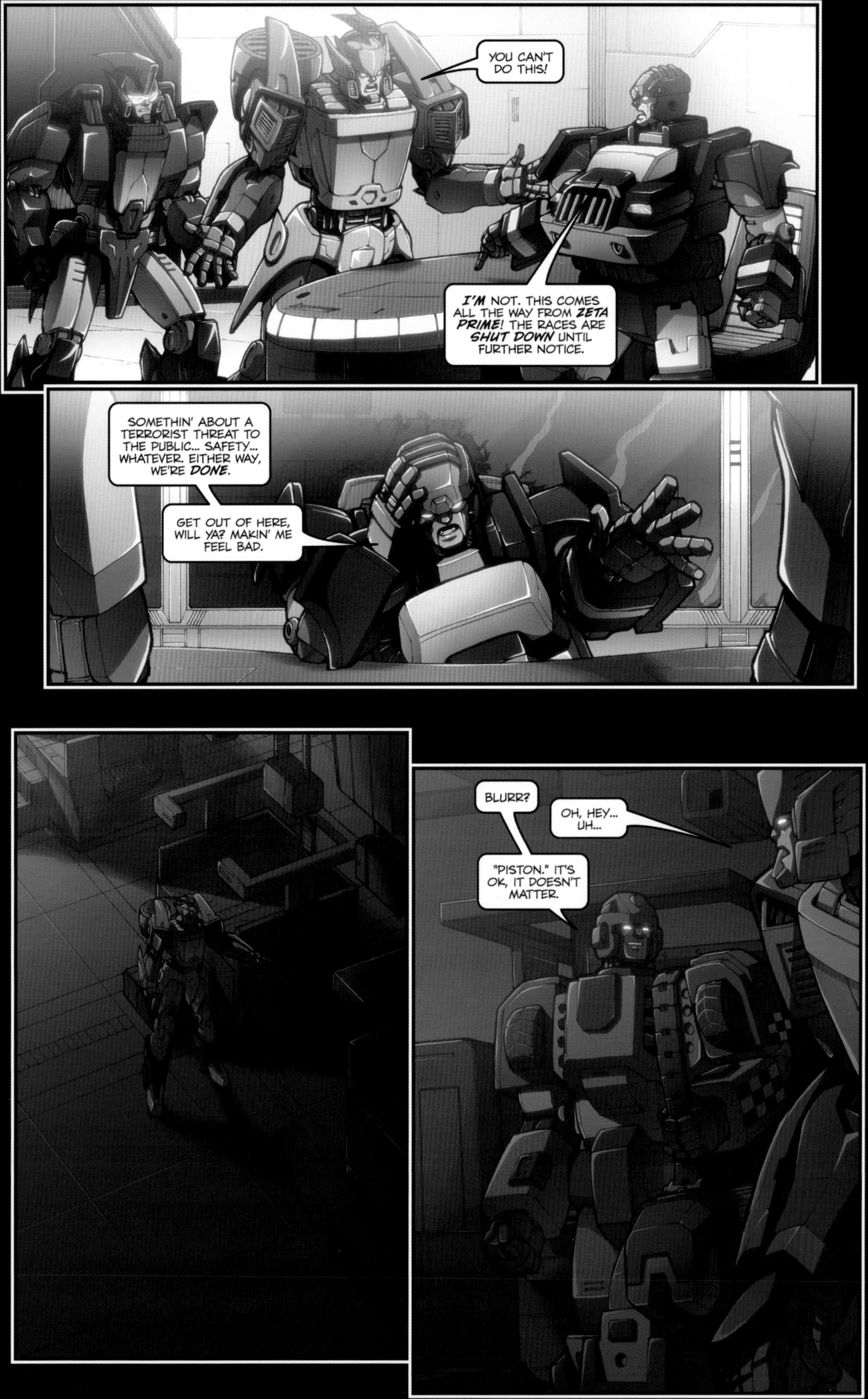
YOU CAN'T DO THIS!
I'M NOT. THIS COMES ALL THE WAY FROM ZETA PRIME! THE RACES ARE SHUT DOWN UNTIL FURTHER NOTICE.
SOMETHIN' ABOUT A TERRORIST THREAT TO THE PUBLIC... SAFETY... WHATEVER. EITHER WAY, WE'RE DONE.
GET OUT OF HERE, WILL YA? MAKIN' ME FEEL BAD.
BLURR?
OH, HEY... UH...
"PISTON." IT'S OK, IT DOESN'T MATTER.

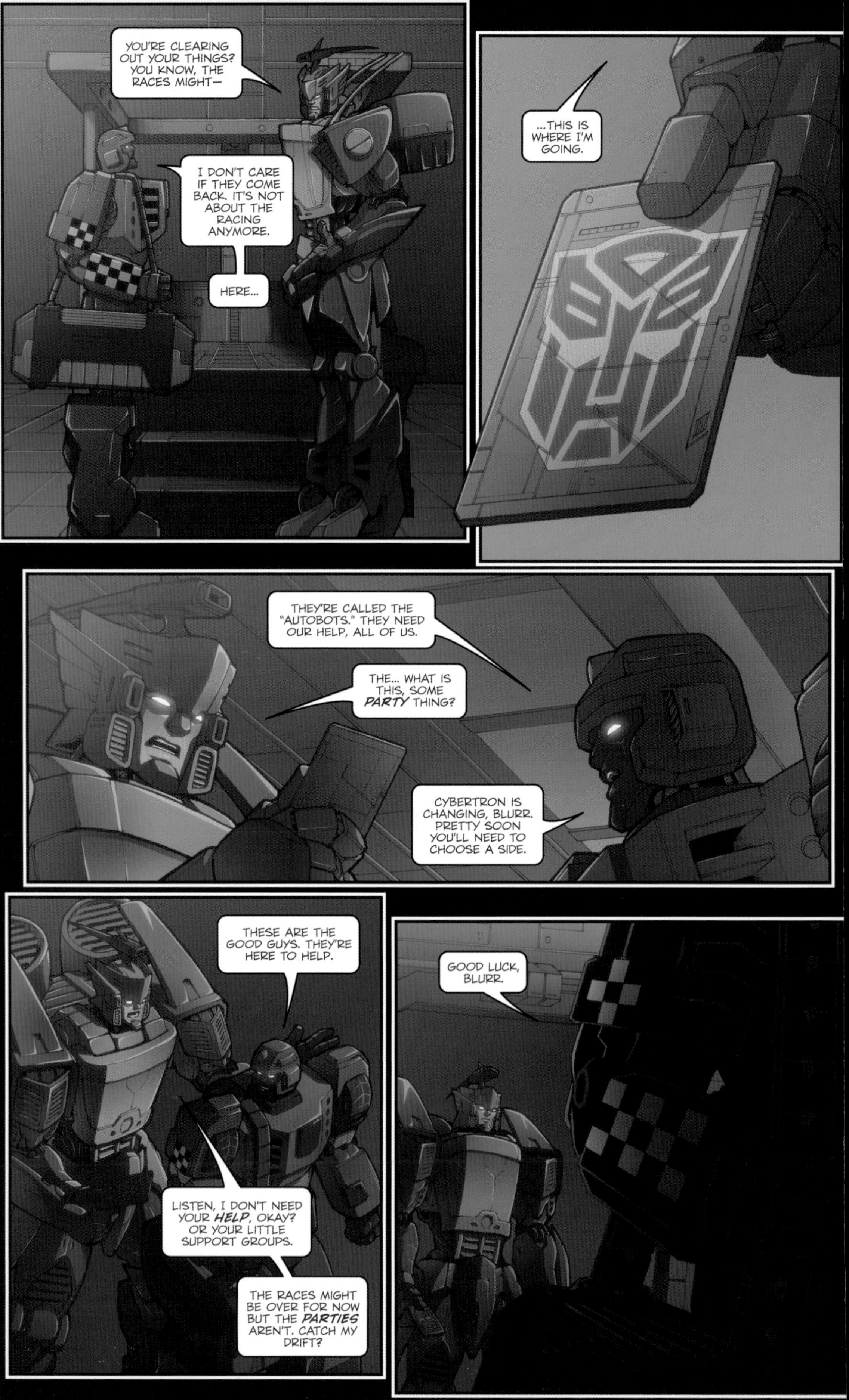
YOU'RE CLEARING OUT YOUR THINGS? YOU KNOW, THE RACES MIGHT—
I DON'T CARE IF THEY COME BACK. IT'S NOT ABOUT THE RACING ANYMORE.
HERE...
...THIS IS WHERE I'M GOING.
THEY'RE CALLED THE "AUTOBOTS." THEY NEED OUR HELP, ALL OF US.
THE... WHAT IS THIS, SOME *PARTY* THING?
CYBERTRON IS CHANGING, BLURR. PRETTY SOON YOU'LL NEED TO CHOOSE A SIDE.
THESE ARE THE GOOD GUYS. THEY'RE HERE TO HELP.
LISTEN, I DON'T NEED YOUR *HELP*, OKAY? OR YOUR LITTLE SUPPORT GROUPS.
THE RACES MIGHT BE OVER FOR NOW BUT THE *PARTIES* AREN'T. CATCH MY DRIFT?
GOOD LUCK, BLURR.

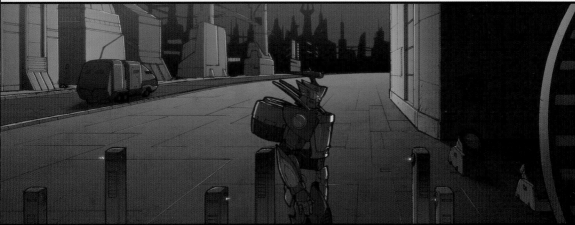

THIS PLACE *STILL* DEAD?

IT'S A *WAR ZONE* OUT THERE. HAVEN'T YOU *NOTICED?*

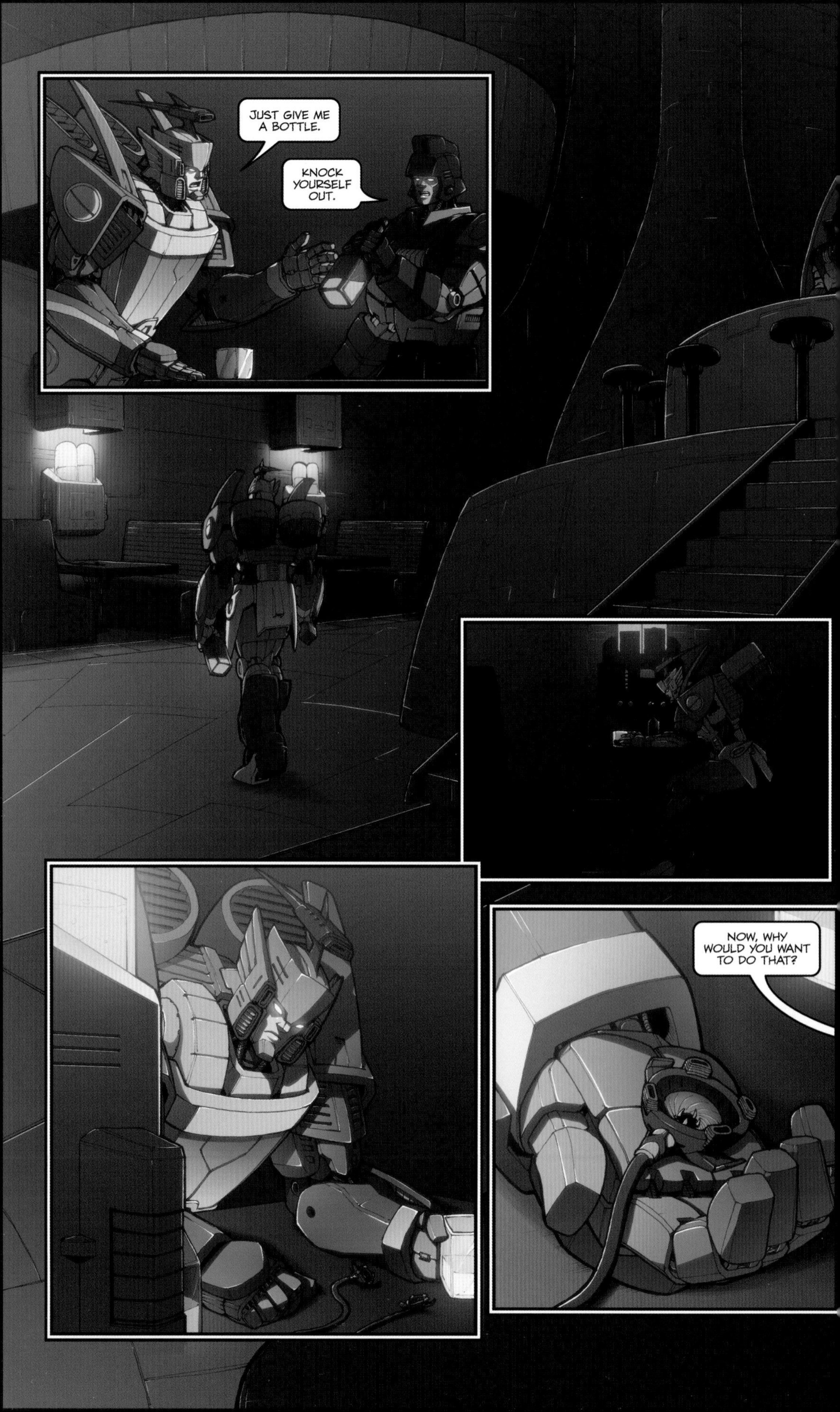
JUST GIVE ME A BOTTLE.
KNOCK YOURSELF OUT.
NOW, WHY WOULD YOU WANT TO DO THAT?

I ALWAYS FELT *THAT* WAS THE PROVINCE OF THE WEAK, NOT THE STRONG.

WHO ARE YOU?

A FRIEND.

TELL ME, HAVE YOU EVER *REALLY* FELT REMORSE? LOSS?

LET ME PUT IT THIS WAY, HOW MUCH DO YOU *REALLY* CARE ABOUT THOSE AROUND YOU?

IF THIS IS GOING TO BE *ANOTHER* CONVERSATION ABOUT HOW *COLD* AND *ARROGANT* I AM, TRUST ME, I'VE HEARD IT *ALL* BEFORE.

FROM PEOPLE SCARED OF YOUR GIFTS, NO DOUBT.

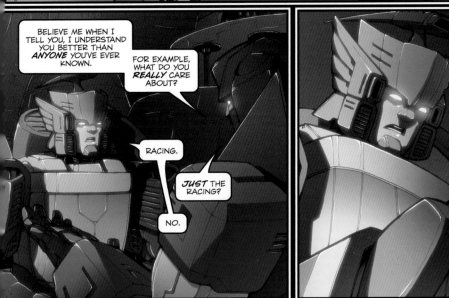

BELIEVE ME WHEN I TELL YOU, I UNDERSTAND YOU BETTER THAN *ANYONE* YOU'VE EVER KNOWN.

FOR EXAMPLE, WHAT DO YOU *REALLY* CARE ABOUT?

RACING.

JUST THE RACING?

NO.

THE CROWDS. WHEN I CAN FEEL THEM BEHIND ME.

THE LIGHTS. THE *ROAR*.

AND THAT ONE MOMENT, THAT ONE *SINGLE* MOMENT WHEN I KNOW WHAT I'M DOING REALLY MATTERS.

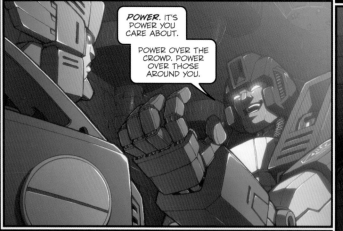

POWER. IT'S POWER YOU CARE ABOUT.

POWER OVER THE CROWD. POWER OVER THOSE AROUND YOU.

YOU HAVE A SINGLE-MINDED DEVOTION TO *ACHIEVE*.

YOU HAVE LITTLE TIME FOR THOSE AROUND YOU AND CARE *ONLY* FOR WHAT *YOU* WANT, WHAT *YOU* CAN GET.

OTHERS WOULD HAVE YOU BELIEVE THESE TO BE ABHORRENT QUALITIES. *NOT* US.

WHAT WE BELIEVE IS SIMPLE. ONLY THE STRONG SHOULD RULE.

YOU ARE STRONG, BLURR. YOU'RE SUPERIOR TO *EVERYONE* AROUND YOU.

I REPRESENT A GROUP THAT EXISTS TO BRING FREEDOM TO THOSE LIKE YOURSELF.

FREEDOM FROM A REGIME THAT SEEKS TO DEPRIVE US OF WHAT WE *TRULY* DESERVE. ONE THAT TOOK AWAY YOUR DREAM—

WAIT A MINUTE, YOU'RE THOSE *AUTOBOTS*.

MY GROUP COULD REALLY *USE* SOMEONE WITH YOUR GIFTS, BLURR. SOMEONE WITH YOUR *CLARITY*.

ALL THOSE RACES, ALL THOSE VICTORIES, AND YOU *STILL* FELT HOLLOW, DIDN'T YOU?

RULE... OR SERVE.

YOU'LL KNOW WHAT TO DO.

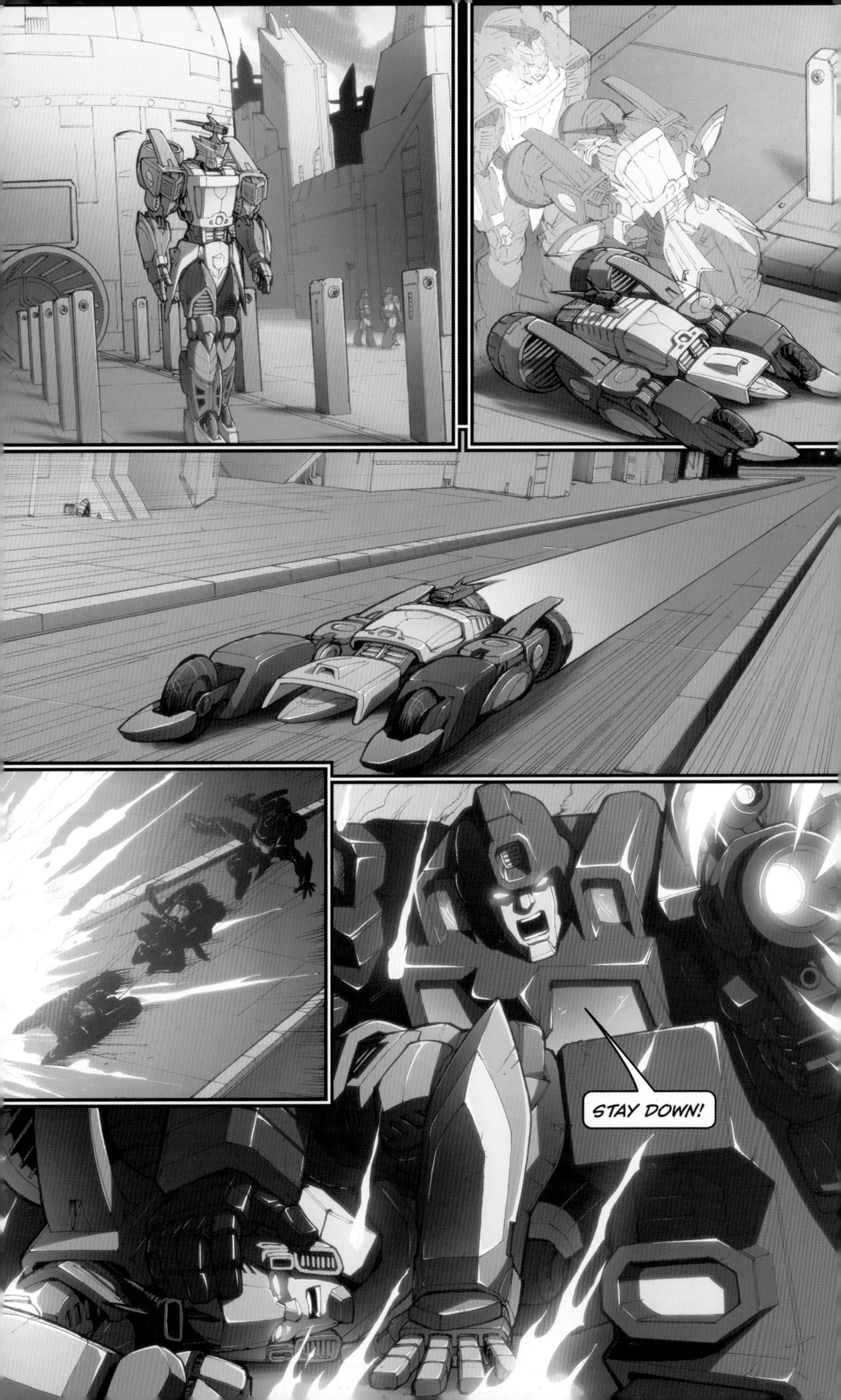
STAY DOWN!

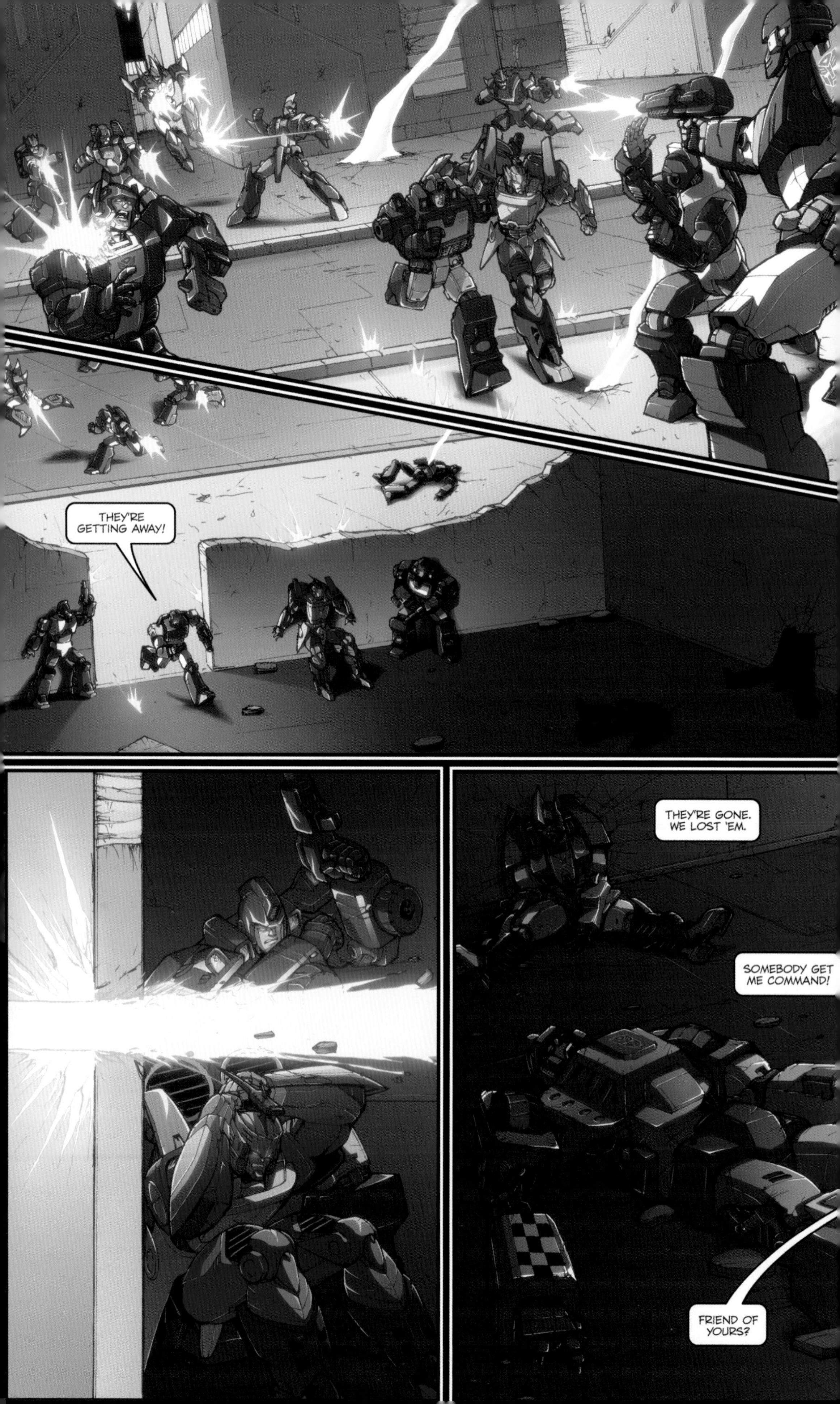
THEY'RE GETTING AWAY!
THEY'RE GONE. WE LOST 'EM.
SOMEBODY GET ME COMMAND!
FRIEND OF YOURS?

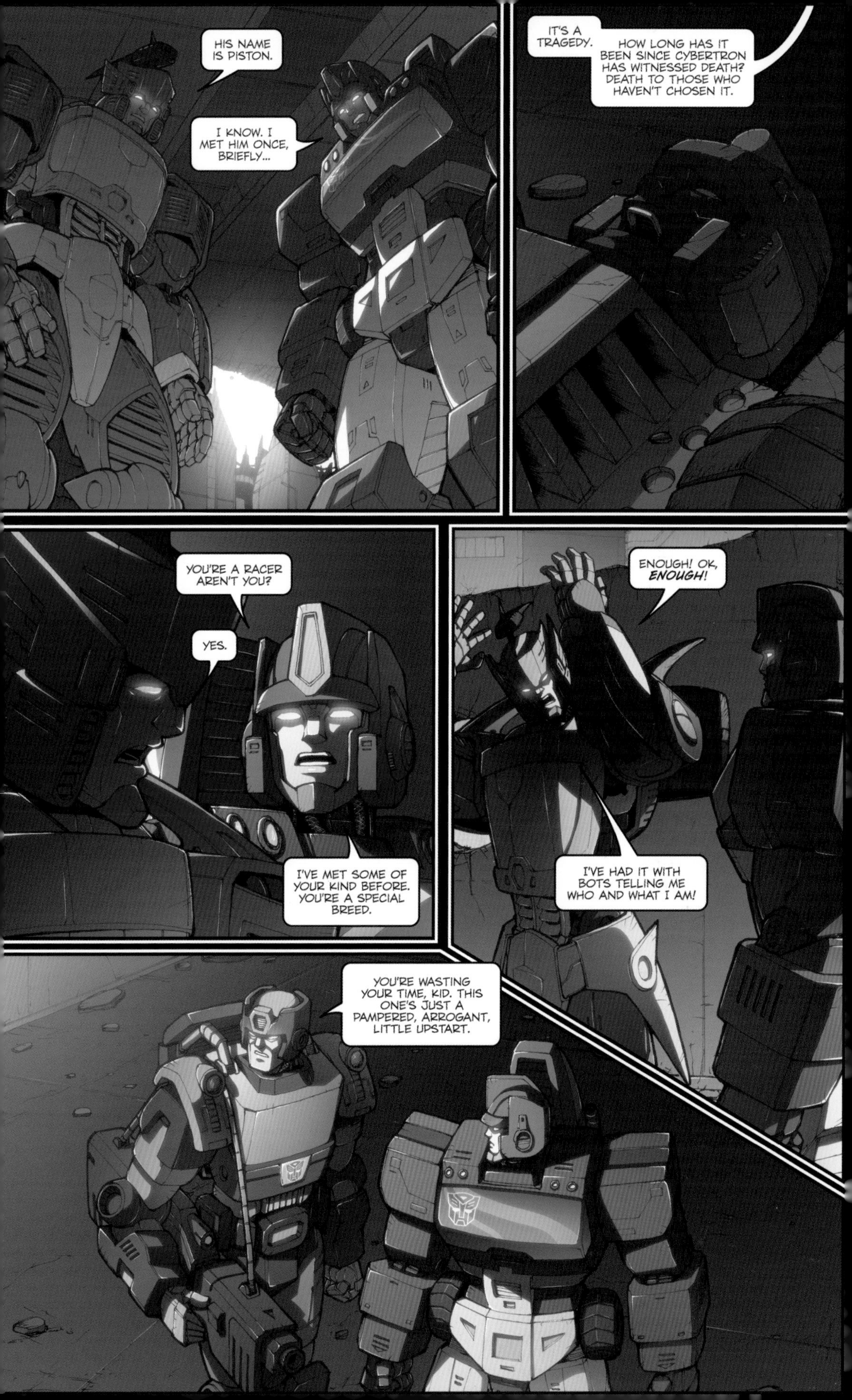
HIS NAME IS PISTON.
I KNOW. I MET HIM ONCE, BRIEFLY...
IT'S A TRAGEDY.
HOW LONG HAS IT BEEN SINCE CYBERTRON HAS WITNESSED DEATH? DEATH TO THOSE WHO HAVEN'T CHOSEN IT.
YOU'RE A RACER AREN'T YOU?
YES.
I'VE MET SOME OF YOUR KIND BEFORE. YOU'RE A SPECIAL BREED.
ENOUGH! OK, **ENOUGH!**
I'VE HAD IT WITH BOTS TELLING ME WHO AND WHAT I AM!
YOU'RE WASTING YOUR TIME, KID. THIS ONE'S JUST A PAMPERED, ARROGANT, LITTLE UPSTART.

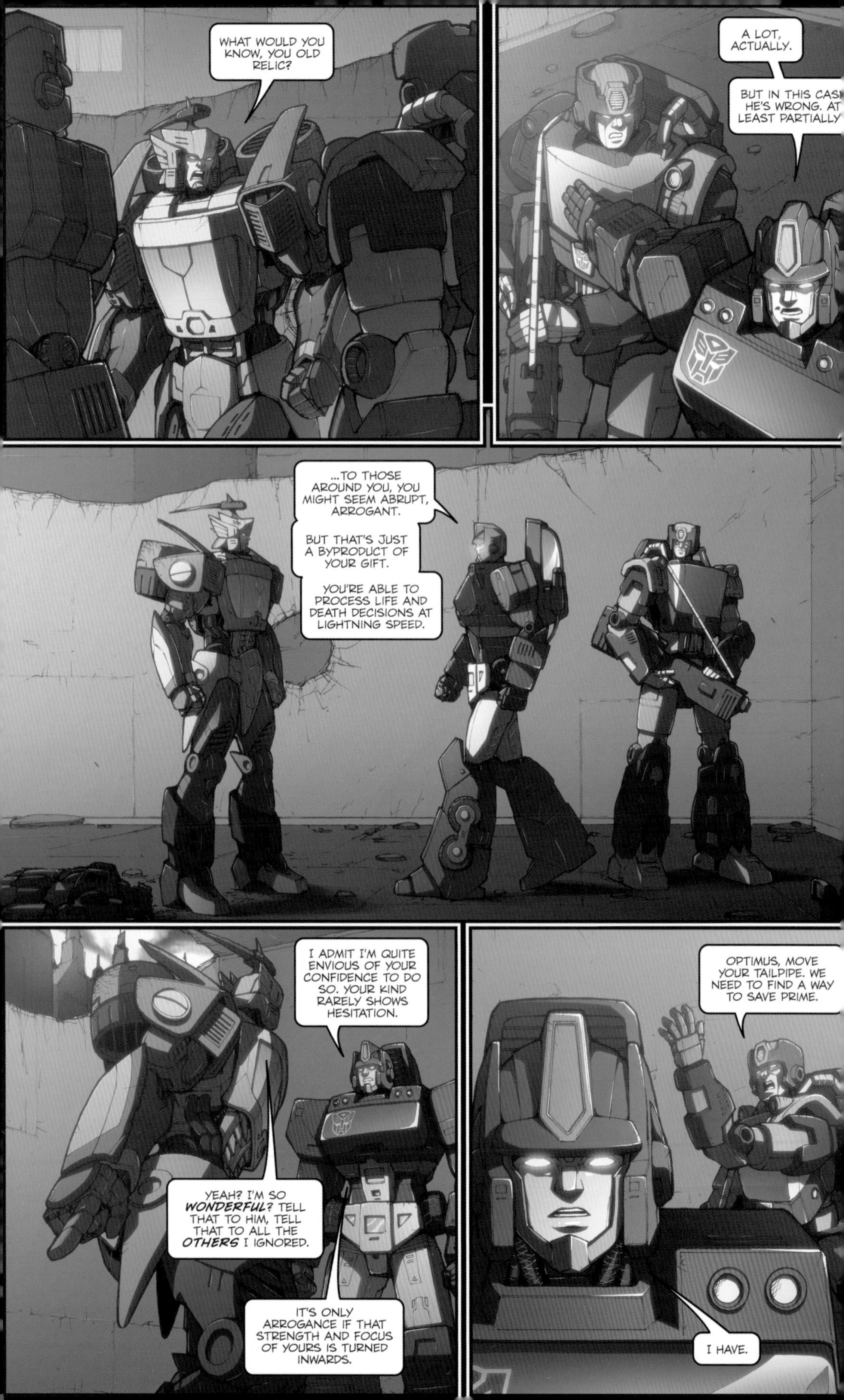
WHAT WOULD YOU KNOW, YOU OLD RELIC?
A LOT, ACTUALLY.
BUT IN THIS CAS HE'S WRONG. AT LEAST PARTIALLY
...TO THOSE AROUND YOU, YOU MIGHT SEEM ABRUPT, ARROGANT.
BUT THAT'S JUST A BYPRODUCT OF YOUR GIFT.
YOU'RE ABLE TO PROCESS LIFE AND DEATH DECISIONS AT LIGHTNING SPEED.
I ADMIT I'M QUITE ENVIOUS OF YOUR CONFIDENCE TO DO SO. YOUR KIND RARELY SHOWS HESITATION.
YEAH? I'M SO ***WONDERFUL***? TELL THAT TO HIM, TELL THAT TO ALL THE ***OTHERS*** I IGNORED.
IT'S ONLY ARROGANCE IF THAT STRENGTH AND FOCUS OF YOURS IS TURNED INWARDS.
OPTIMUS, MOVE YOUR TAILPIPE. WE NEED TO FIND A WAY TO SAVE PRIME.
I HAVE.

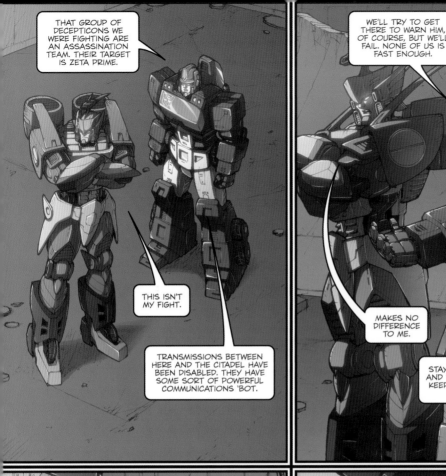

THAT GROUP OF DECEPTICONS WE WERE FIGHTING ARE AN ASSASSINATION TEAM. THEIR TARGET IS ZETA PRIME.

THIS ISN'T MY FIGHT.

TRANSMISSIONS BETWEEN HERE AND THE CITADEL HAVE BEEN DISABLED. THEY HAVE SOME SORT OF POWERFUL COMMUNICATIONS 'BOT.

WE'LL TRY TO GET THERE TO WARN HIM, OF COURSE, BUT WE'LL FAIL. NONE OF US IS FAST ENOUGH.

MAKES NO DIFFERENCE TO ME.

STAY OUT OF IT AND YOU GET TO KEEP YOUR OLD LIFE?

I *LIKE* MY OLD LIFE.

DO YOU?

CYBERTRON'S "GOLDEN AGE" AND WE'RE QUIETLY DYING A SLOW DEATH. WE'RE *LOST* AND THEY'RE TAKING *ADVANTAGE* OF IT.

ALL THOSE TIMES IN THE ARENA, WAS IT THE *VICTORIES* THAT KEPT YOU GOING?

OR WAS IT THE CHANCE TO CONSTANTLY INSPIRE OTHERS TO STRIVE FOR *MORE*?

YOU CAN *STILL* BE AN INSPIRATION, BLURR.

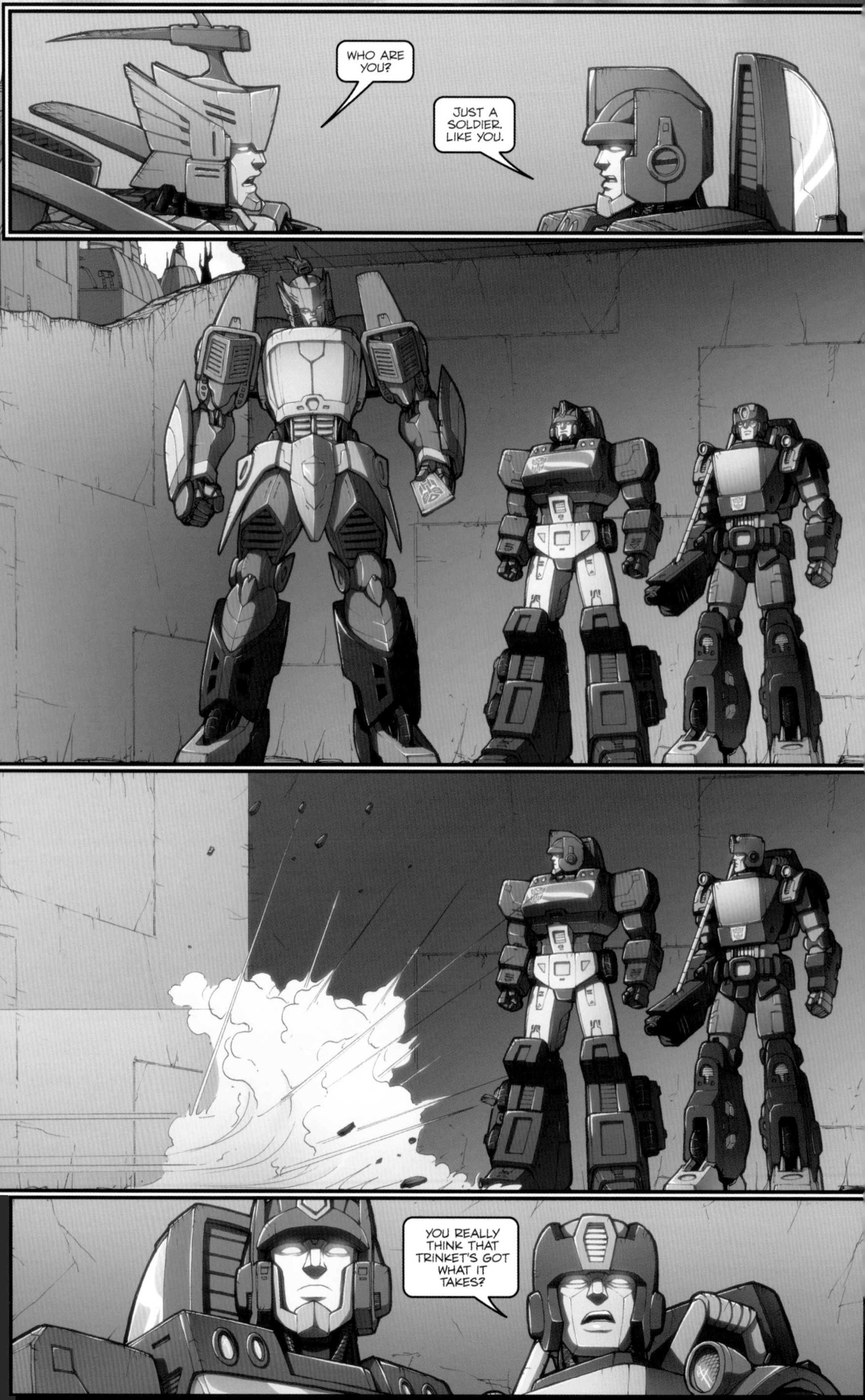
WHO ARE YOU?
JUST A SOLDIER. LIKE YOU.
YOU REALLY THINK THAT TRINKET'S GOT WHAT IT TAKES?

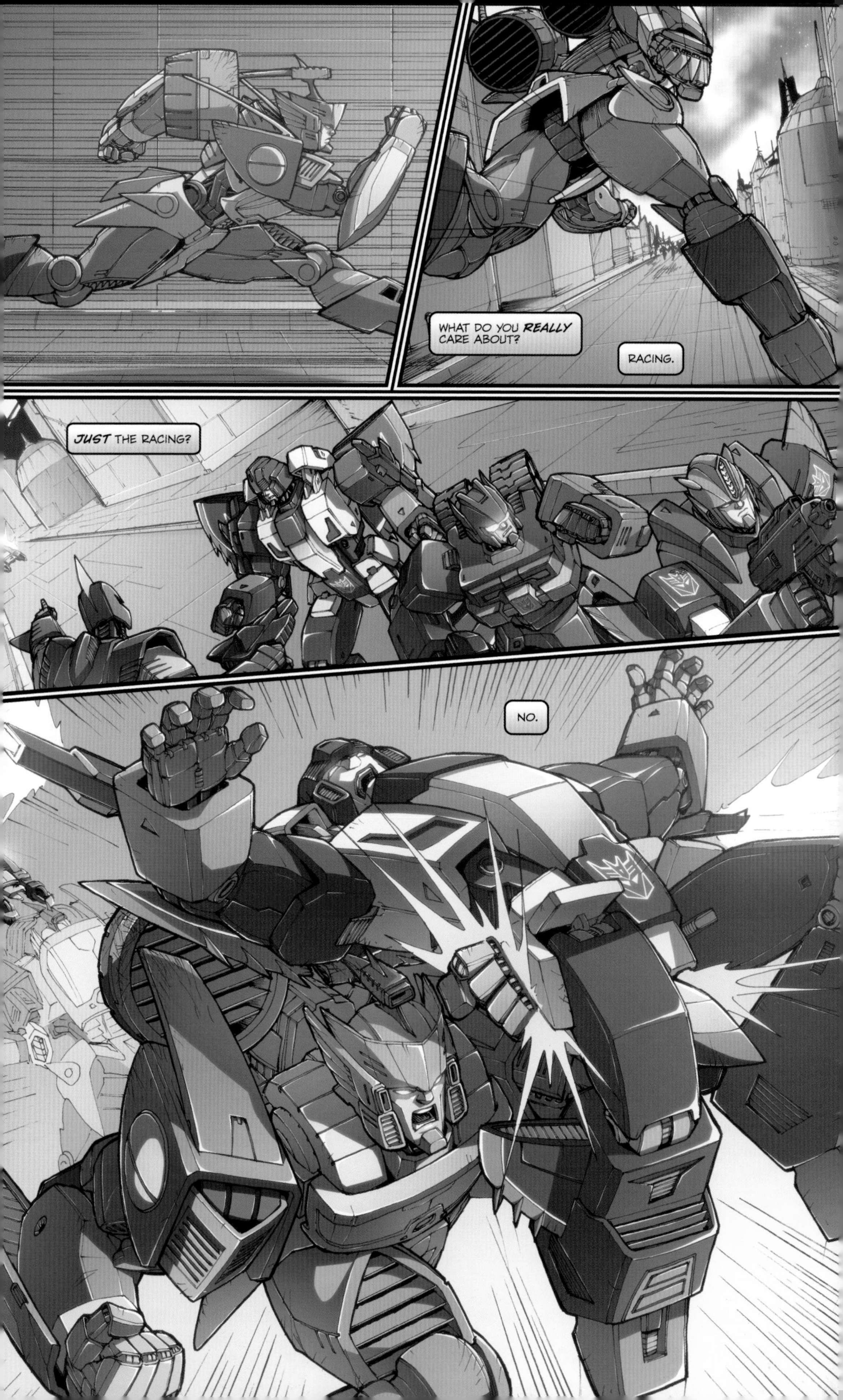
WHAT DO YOU REALLY CARE ABOUT?
RACING.
JUST THE RACING?
NO.

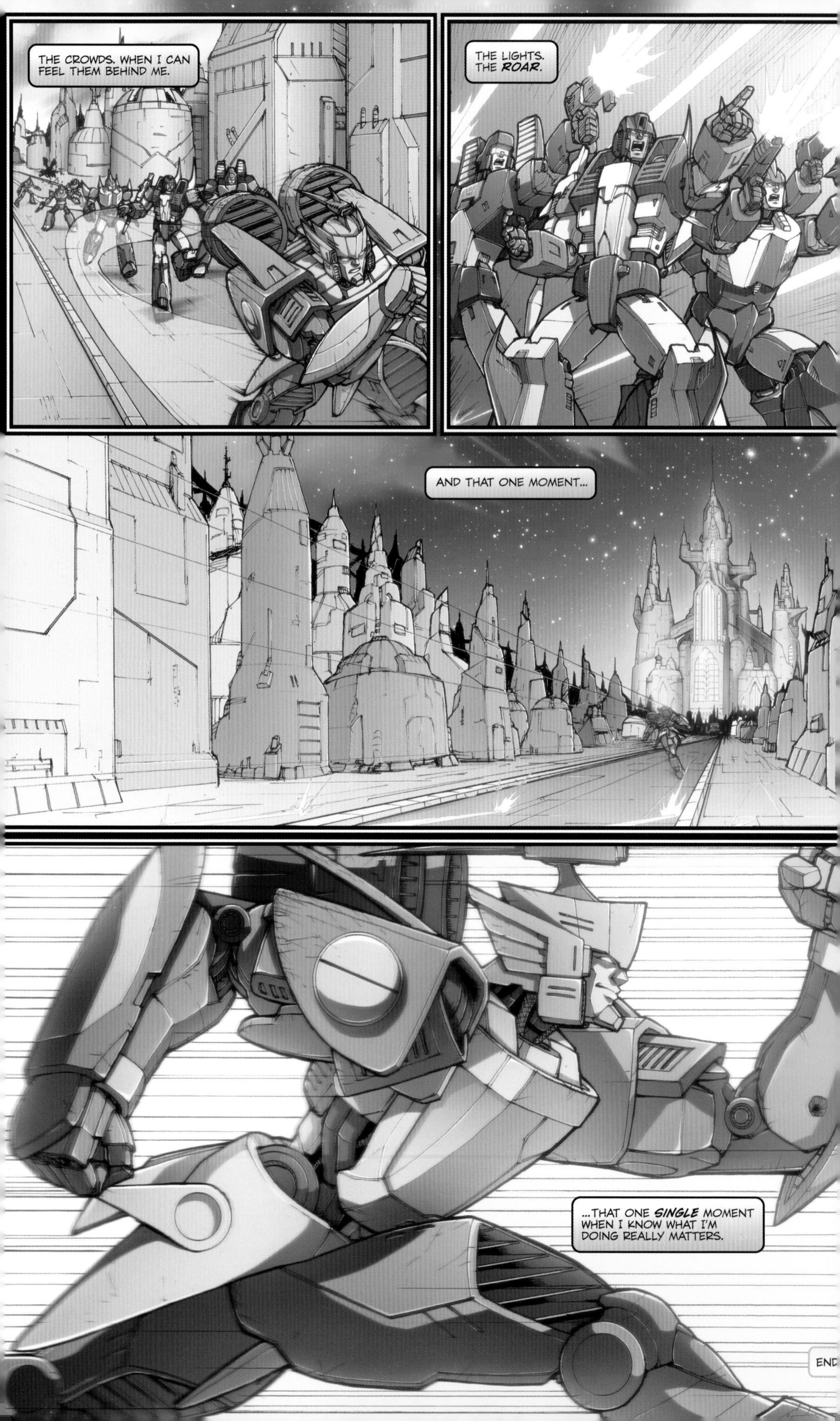
THE CROWDS. WHEN I CAN FEEL THEM BEHIND ME.
THE LIGHTS. THE *ROAR*.
AND THAT ONE MOMENT...
...THAT ONE *SINGLE* MOMENT WHEN I KNOW WHAT I'M DOING REALLY MATTERS.
END

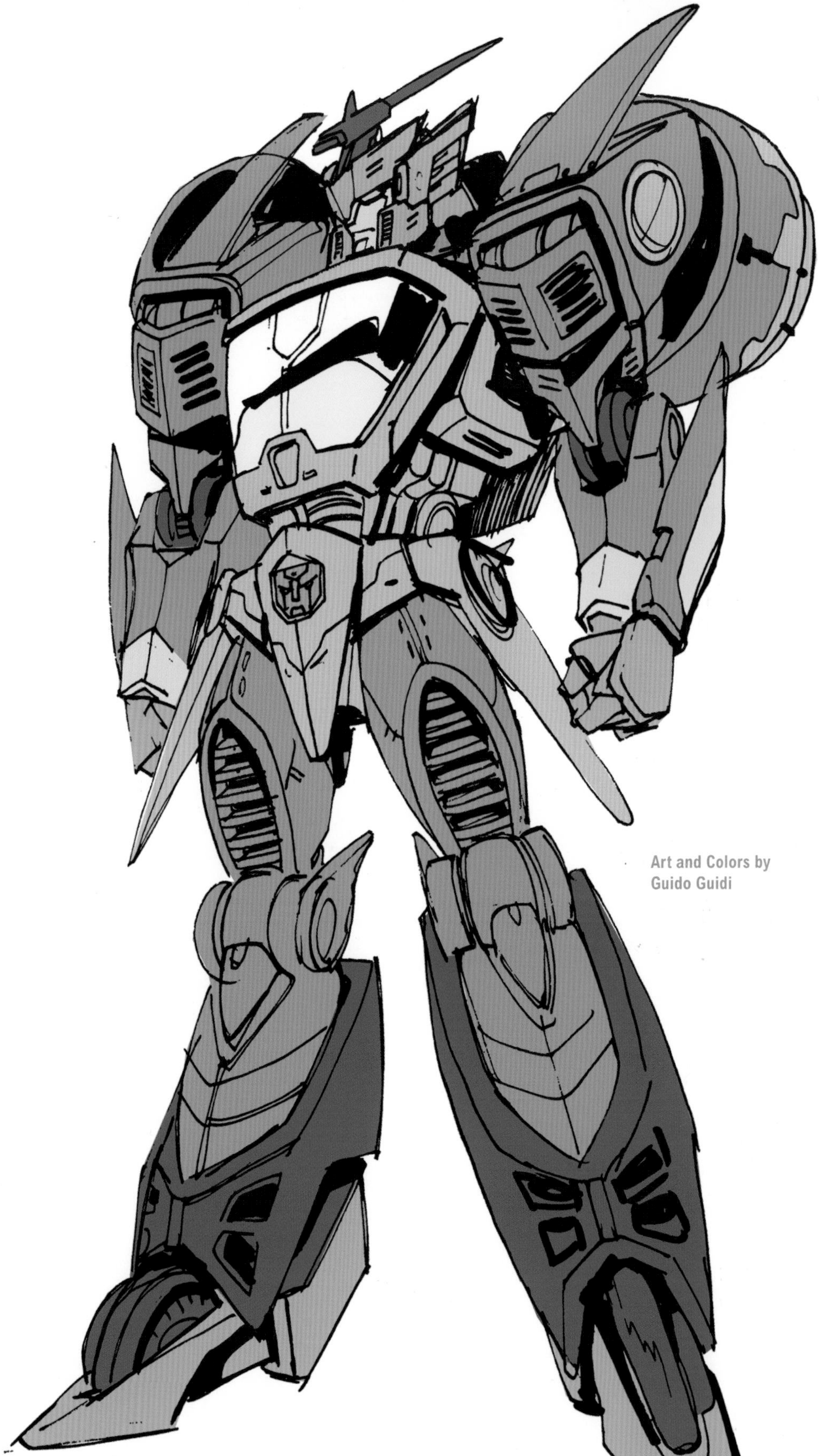

Art and Colors by
Guido Guidi

JAZZ

For most, the word "AUTOBOT" is simply a faction or title. But for one individual, it is a way of life, defining his every thought and action. Always there to lift dampened spirits, he has hope in even the darkest of times...

...his name is JAZZ.

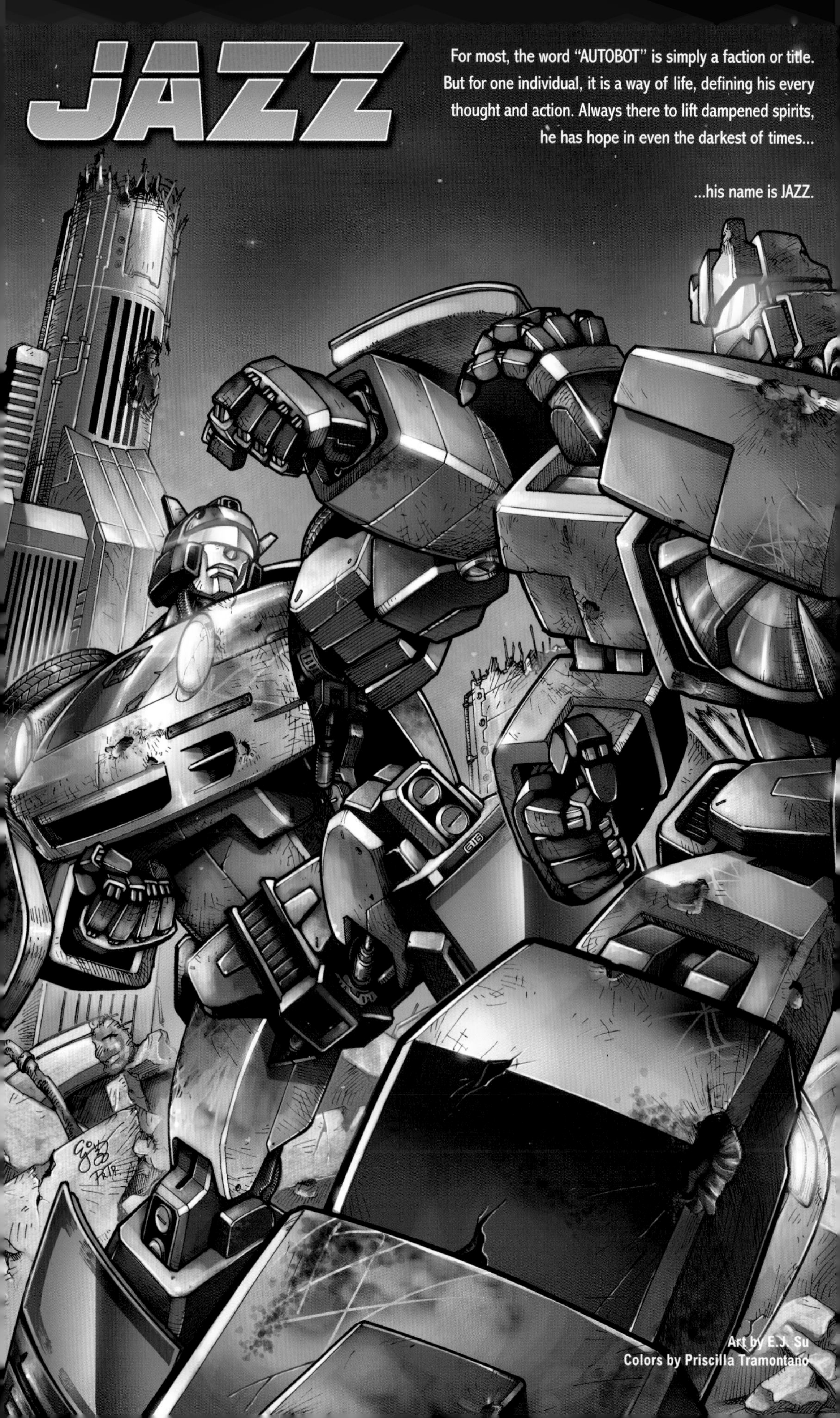

Art by E.J. Su
Colors by Priscilla Tramontano

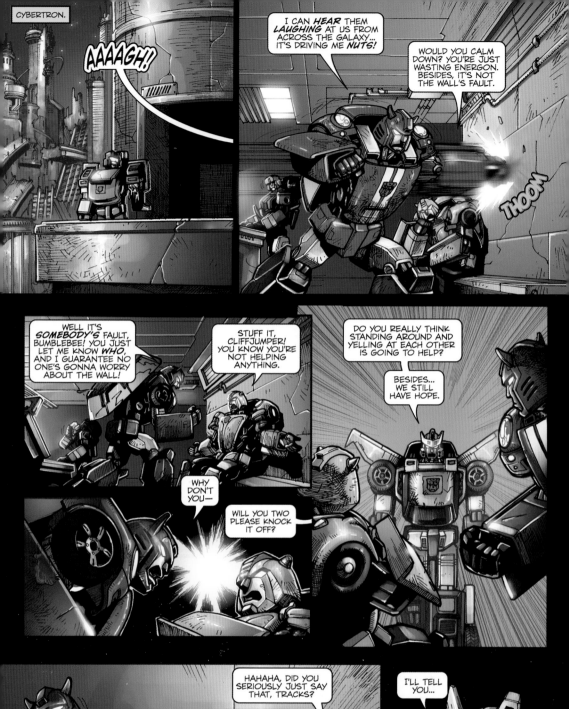

CYBERTRON.
AAAAGH!
I CAN HEAR THEM LAUGHING AT US FROM ACROSS THE GALAXY... IT'S DRIVING ME NUTS!
WOULD YOU CALM DOWN? YOU'RE JUST WASTING ENERGON. BESIDES, IT'S NOT THE WALL'S FAULT.
THOOM
WELL IT'S SOMEBODY'S FAULT, BUMBLEBEE! YOU JUST LET ME KNOW WHO, AND I GUARANTEE NO ONE'S GONNA WORRY ABOUT THE WALL!
STUFF IT, CLIFFJUMPER! YOU KNOW YOU'RE NOT HELPING ANYTHING.
WHY DON'T YOU—
WILL YOU TWO PLEASE KNOCK IT OFF?
DO YOU REALLY THINK STANDING AROUND AND YELLING AT EACH OTHER IS GOING TO HELP?
BESIDES... WE STILL HAVE HOPE.
HAHAHA, DID YOU SERIOUSLY JUST SAY THAT, TRACKS?
AND WHADDA YOU KNOW ABOUT IT, COMMANDER WAX-N-BUFF?
WHEN HAVE YOU EVER GOTTEN YOUR HANDS DIRTY?
I'LL TELL YOU...

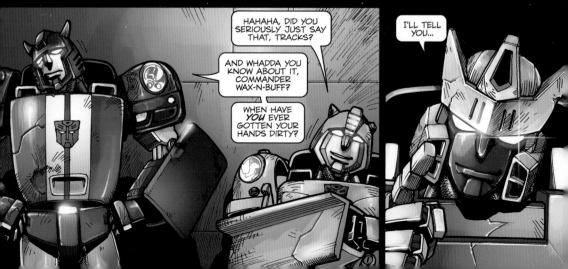

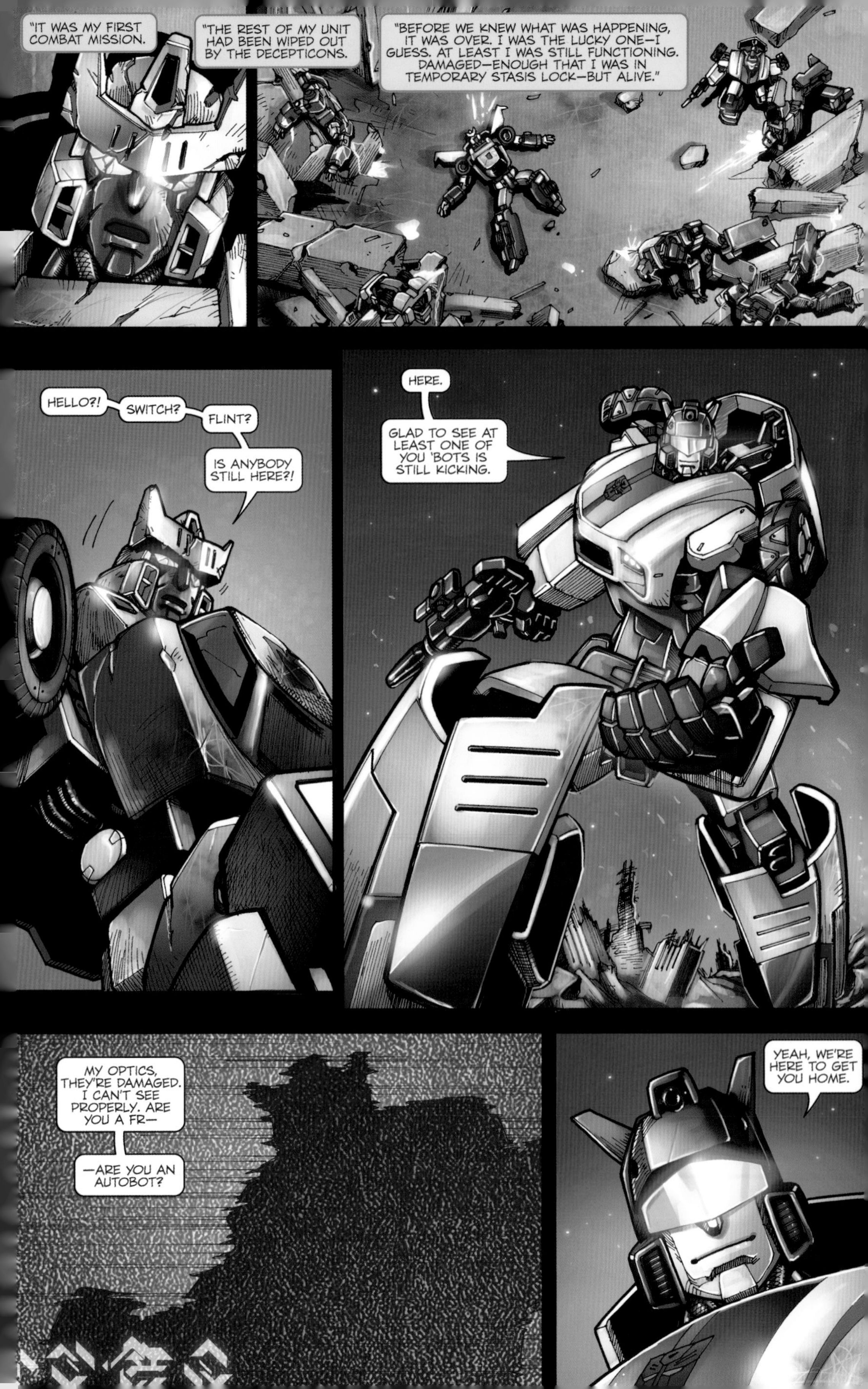
"IT WAS MY FIRST COMBAT MISSION.
"THE REST OF MY UNIT HAD BEEN WIPED OUT BY THE DECEPTICONS.
"BEFORE WE KNEW WHAT WAS HAPPENING, IT WAS OVER. I WAS THE LUCKY ONE—I GUESS. AT LEAST I WAS STILL FUNCTIONING. DAMAGED—ENOUGH THAT I WAS IN TEMPORARY STASIS LOCK—BUT ALIVE."
HELLO?!
SWITCH?
FLINT?
IS ANYBODY STILL HERE?!
HERE.
GLAD TO SEE AT LEAST ONE OF YOU 'BOTS IS STILL KICKING.
MY OPTICS, THEY'RE DAMAGED. I CAN'T SEE PROPERLY. ARE YOU A FR—
—ARE YOU AN AUTOBOT?
YEAH, WE'RE HERE TO GET YOU HOME.

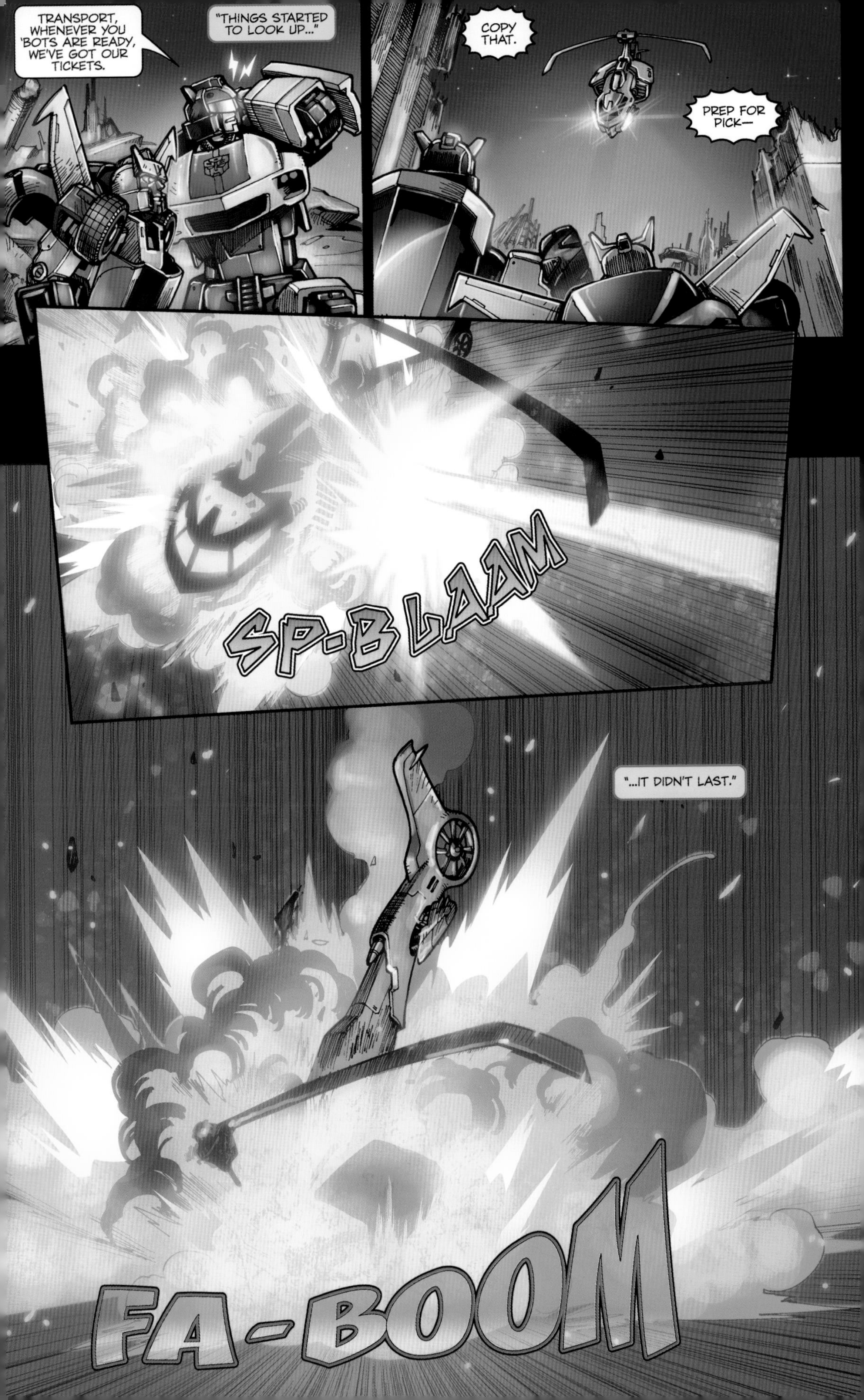
TRANSPORT, WHENEVER YOU 'BOTS ARE READY, WE'VE GOT OUR TICKETS.
"THINGS STARTED TO LOOK UP..."
COPY THAT.
PREP FOR PICK—
SP-BLAAM
"...IT DIDN'T LAST."
FA-BOOM

WHAT WAS *THAT*?

SOMETHING BAD.

CAN YOU TRANSFORM?

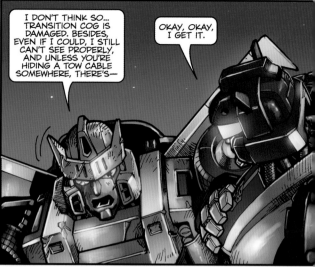

I DON'T THINK SO... TRANSITION COG IS DAMAGED. BESIDES, EVEN IF I COULD, I STILL CAN'T SEE PROPERLY, AND UNLESS YOU'RE HIDING A TOW CABLE SOMEWHERE, THERE'S—

OKAY, OKAY, I GET IT.

GUESS WE'LL DO THIS THE HARD WAY, THEN.

"TWO SURVIVORS, HEADING NORTH."

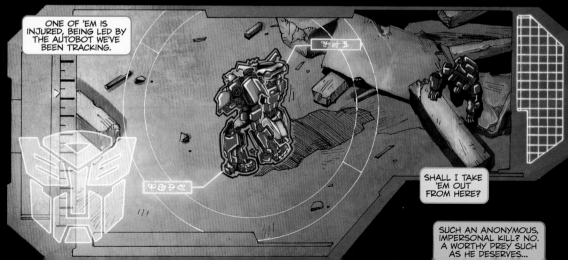

ONE OF 'EM IS INJURED, BEING LED BY THE AUTOBOT WE'VE BEEN TRACKING.

SHALL I TAKE 'EM OUT FROM HERE?

SUCH AN ANONYMOUS, IMPERSONAL KILL? NO. A WORTHY PREY SUCH AS HE DESERVES...

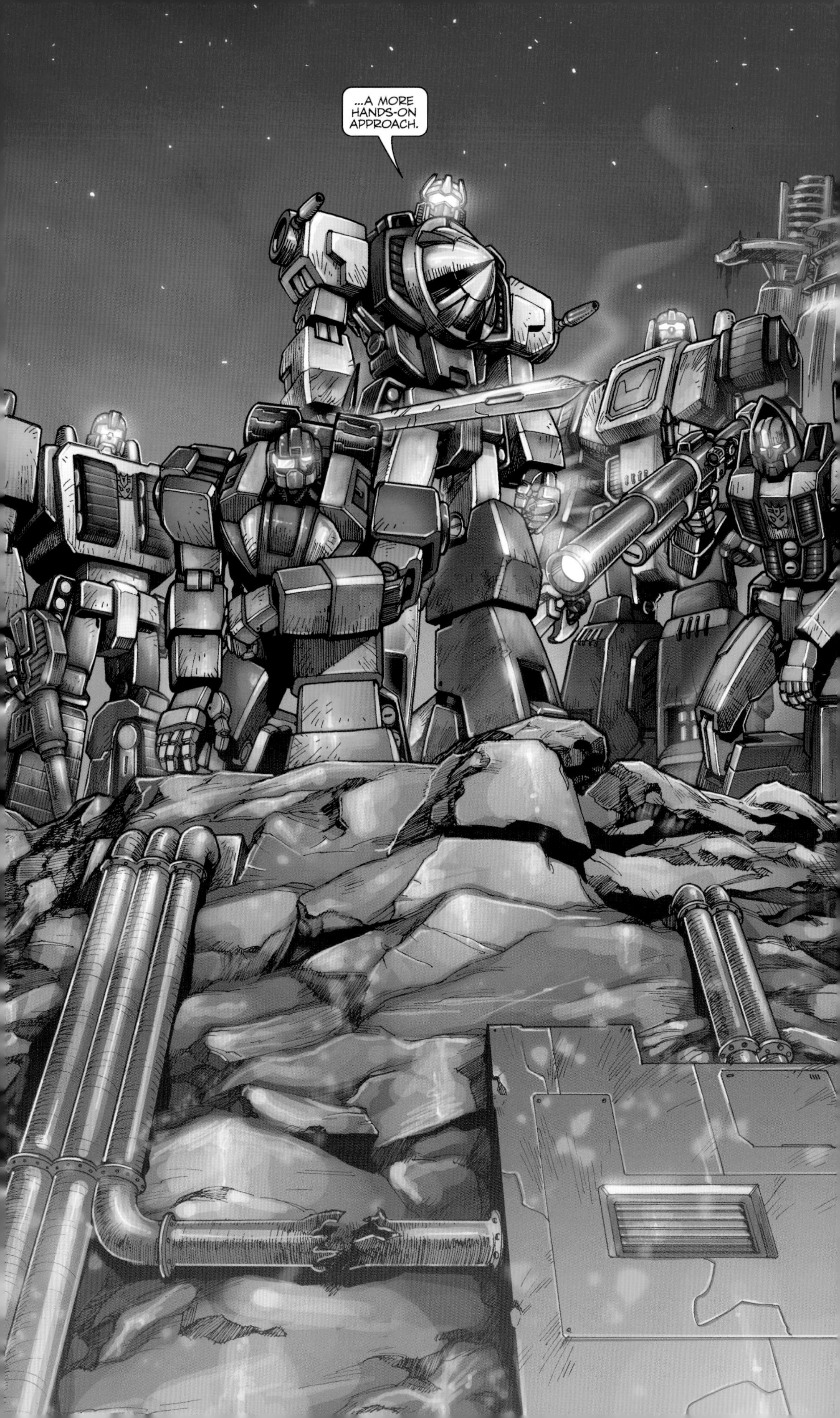
...A MORE HANDS-ON APPROACH.

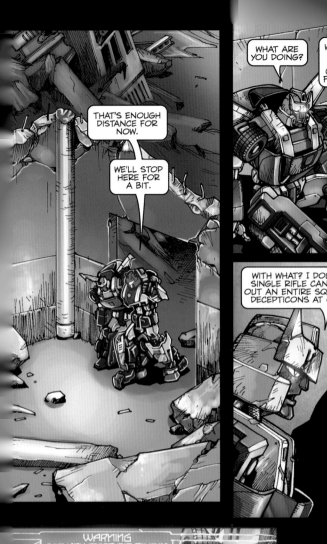

THAT'S ENOUGH DISTANCE FOR NOW.

WE'LL STOP HERE FOR A BIT.

WHAT ARE YOU DOING?

WHOEVER SHOT THE SHUTTLE DOWN MIGHT COME BACK TO FINISH THE JOB.

WE'LL NEED TO BE ABLE TO BITE BACK.

WITH WHAT? I DOUBT A SINGLE RIFLE CAN TAKE OUT AN ENTIRE SQUAD OF DECEPTICONS AT ONCE.

TRUE. SO WE TRY A LITTLE IMPROVISATION...

...WITH MY AUXILIARY ENERGON RESERVOIR.

WARNING
AUXILIARY RESERVOIR REMOVED
TIME TO STASIS LOCK: 30 CYCLES

ARE YOU *CRAZY*?

ONLY IF IT DOESN'T WORK.

I'M GONNA DIE.

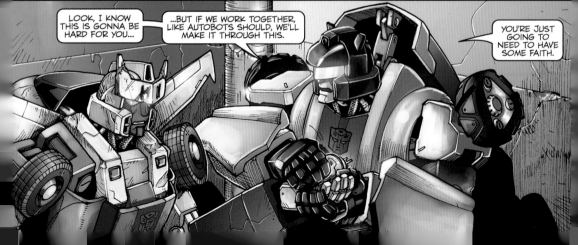

LOOK, I KNOW THIS IS GONNA BE HARD FOR YOU...

...BUT IF WE WORK TOGETHER, LIKE AUTOBOTS SHOULD, WE'LL MAKE IT THROUGH THIS.

YOU'RE JUST GOING TO NEED TO HAVE SOME FAITH.

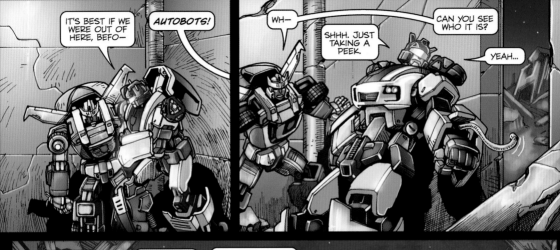

IT'S BEST IF WE WERE OUT OF HERE, BEFO—

AUTOBOTS!

WH—

SHHH. JUST TAKING A PEEK.

CAN YOU SEE WHO IT IS?

YEAH...

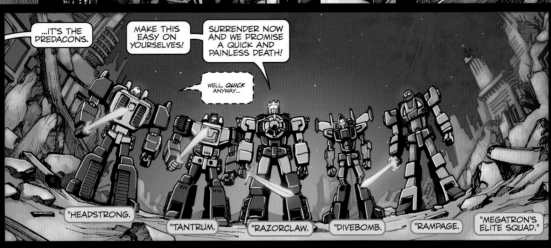

...IT'S THE PREDACONS.

MAKE THIS EASY ON YOURSELVES!

SURRENDER NOW AND WE PROMISE A QUICK AND PAINLESS DEATH!

WELL, QUICK ANYWAY...

"HEADSTRONG.

"TANTRUM.

"RAZORCLAW.

"DIVEBOMB.

"RAMPAGE.

"MEGATRON'S ELITE SQUAD."

GUESS THAT EXPLAINS WHY BOTH OUR TEAMS ARE DEAD.

YUP.

THIS IS REALLY BAD, ISN'T IT?

YUP.

DO YOU HAVE A PLAN?

YUP.

CARE TO SHARE IT?

YUP.

YOU'RE GONNA PICK A FIGHT WITH THEM.

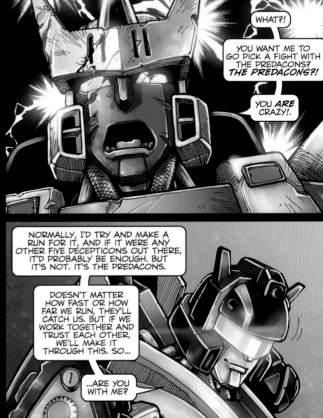

WHAT?!

YOU WANT ME TO GO PICK A FIGHT WITH THE PREDACONS? THE PREDACONS?!

YOU ARE CRAZY!.

NORMALLY, I'D TRY AND MAKE A RUN FOR IT, AND IF IT WERE ANY OTHER FIVE DECEPTICONS OUT THERE, IT'D PROBABLY BE ENOUGH. BUT IT'S NOT. IT'S THE PREDACONS.

DOESN'T MATTER HOW FAST OR HOW FAR WE RUN, THEY'LL CATCH US. BUT IF WE WORK TOGETHER AND TRUST EACH OTHER, WE'LL MAKE IT THROUGH THIS. SO...

...ARE YOU WITH ME?

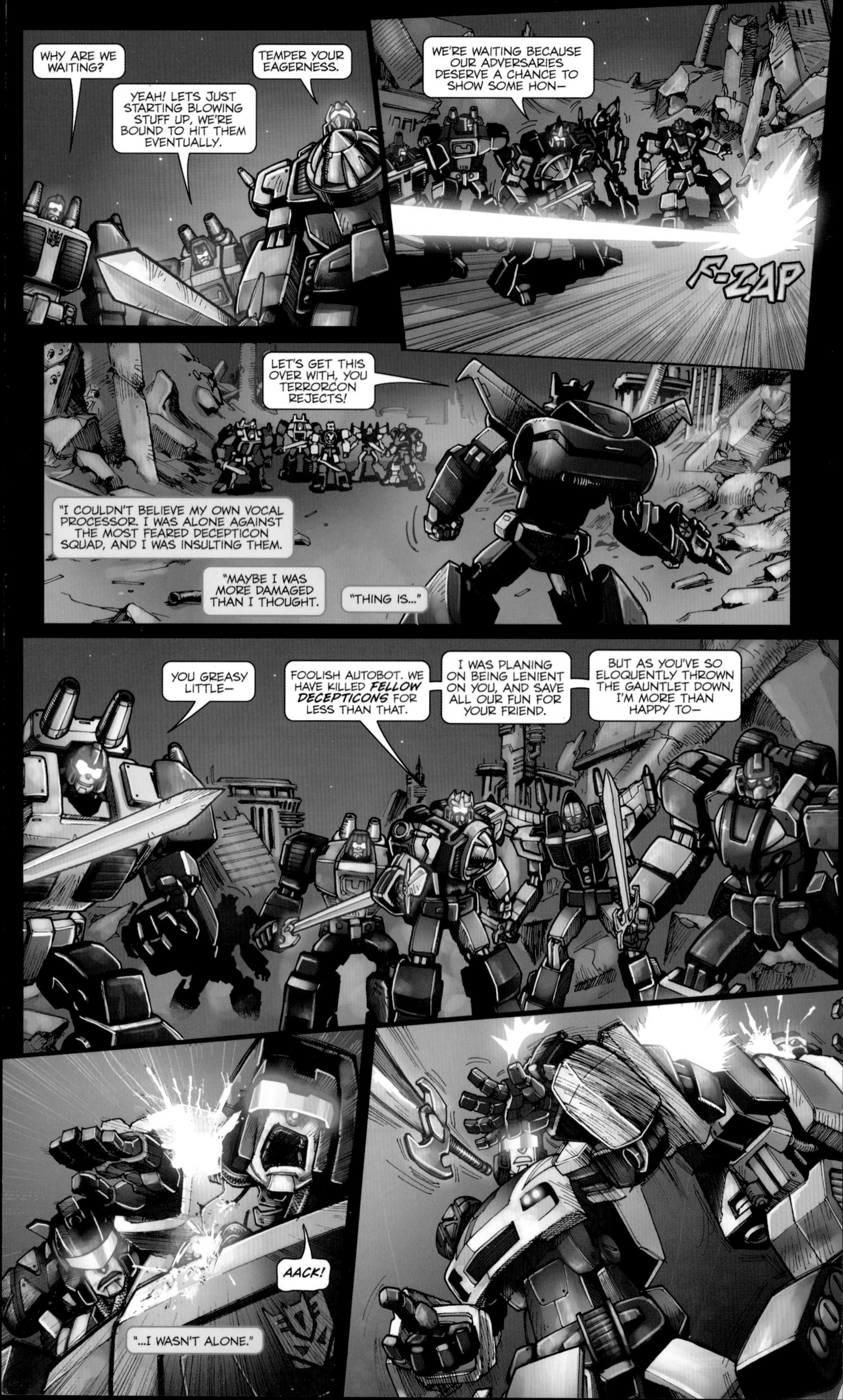
WHY ARE WE WAITING?
YEAH! LETS JUST STARTING BLOWING STUFF UP, WE'RE BOUND TO HIT THEM EVENTUALLY.
TEMPER YOUR EAGERNESS.
WE'RE WAITING BECAUSE OUR ADVERSARIES DESERVE A CHANCE TO SHOW SOME HON—
F-ZAP
LET'S GET THIS OVER WITH, YOU TERRORCON REJECTS!
"I COULDN'T BELIEVE MY OWN VOCAL PROCESSOR. I WAS ALONE AGAINST THE MOST FEARED DECEPTICON SQUAD, AND I WAS INSULTING THEM.
"MAYBE I WAS MORE DAMAGED THAN I THOUGHT.
"THING IS..."
YOU GREASY LITTLE—
FOOLISH AUTOBOT. WE HAVE KILLED FELLOW DECEPTICONS FOR LESS THAN THAT.
I WAS PLANING ON BEING LENIENT ON YOU, AND SAVE ALL OUR FUN FOR YOUR FRIEND.
BUT AS YOU'VE SO ELOQUENTLY THROWN THE GAUNTLET DOWN, I'M MORE THAN HAPPY TO—
AACK!
"...I WASN'T ALONE."

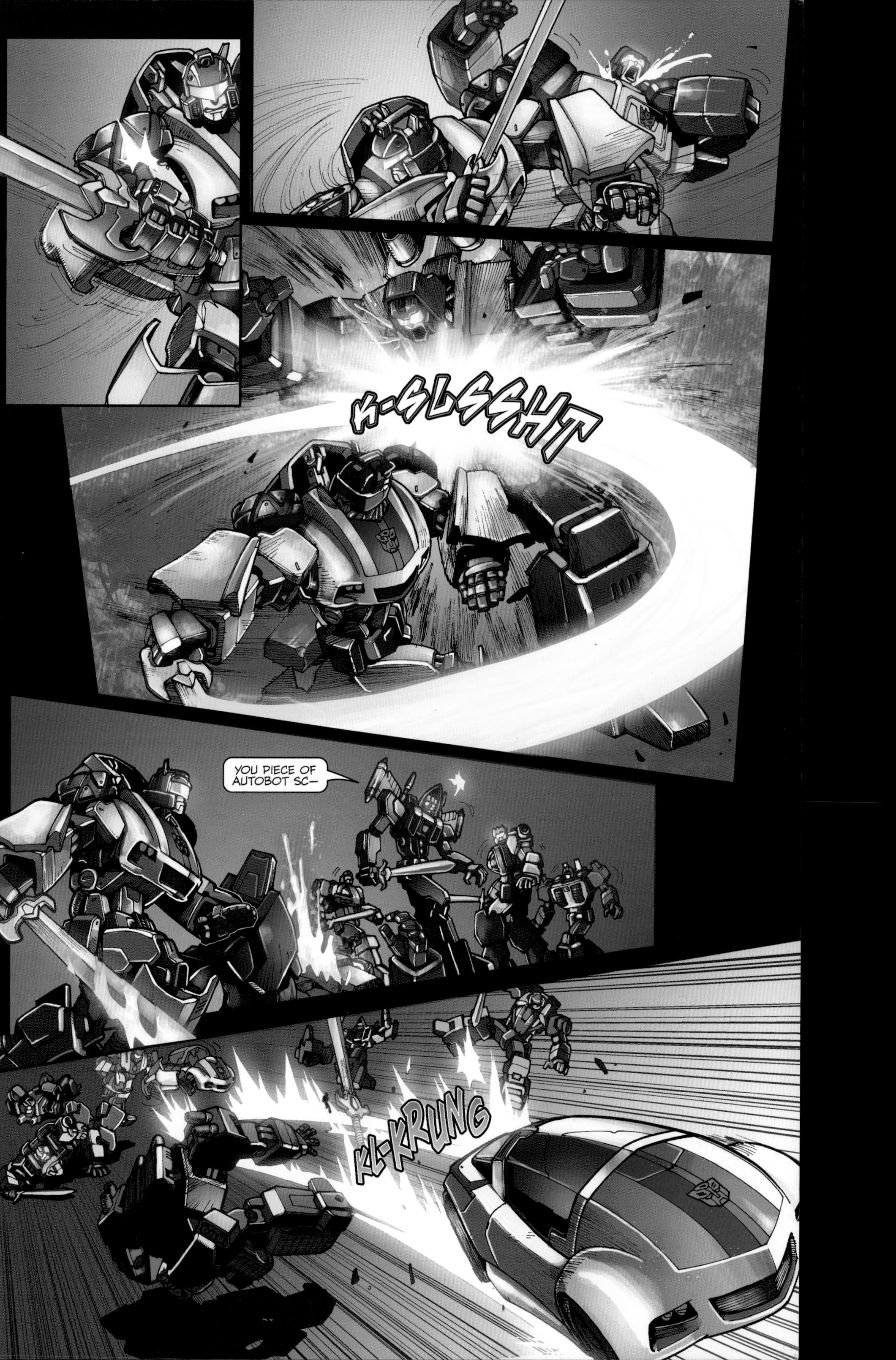
K-SLSSHT
YOU PIECE OF AUTOBOT SC—
KL-KRUNG

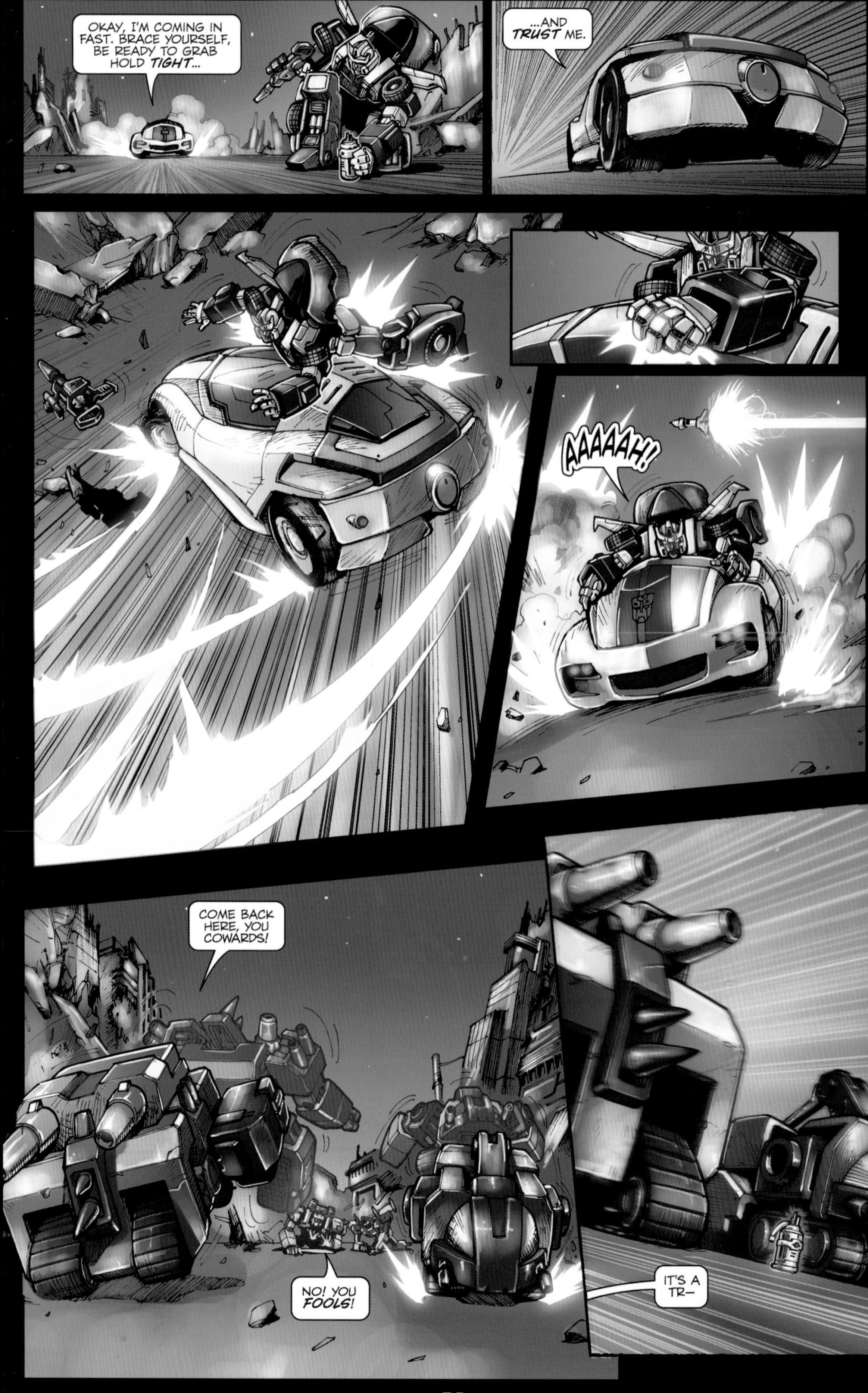
OKAY, I'M COMING IN FAST. BRACE YOURSELF, BE READY TO GRAB HOLD *TIGHT*...
...AND *TRUST* ME.
AAAAAH!
COME BACK HERE, YOU COWARDS!
NO! YOU *FOOLS*!
IT'S A TR—

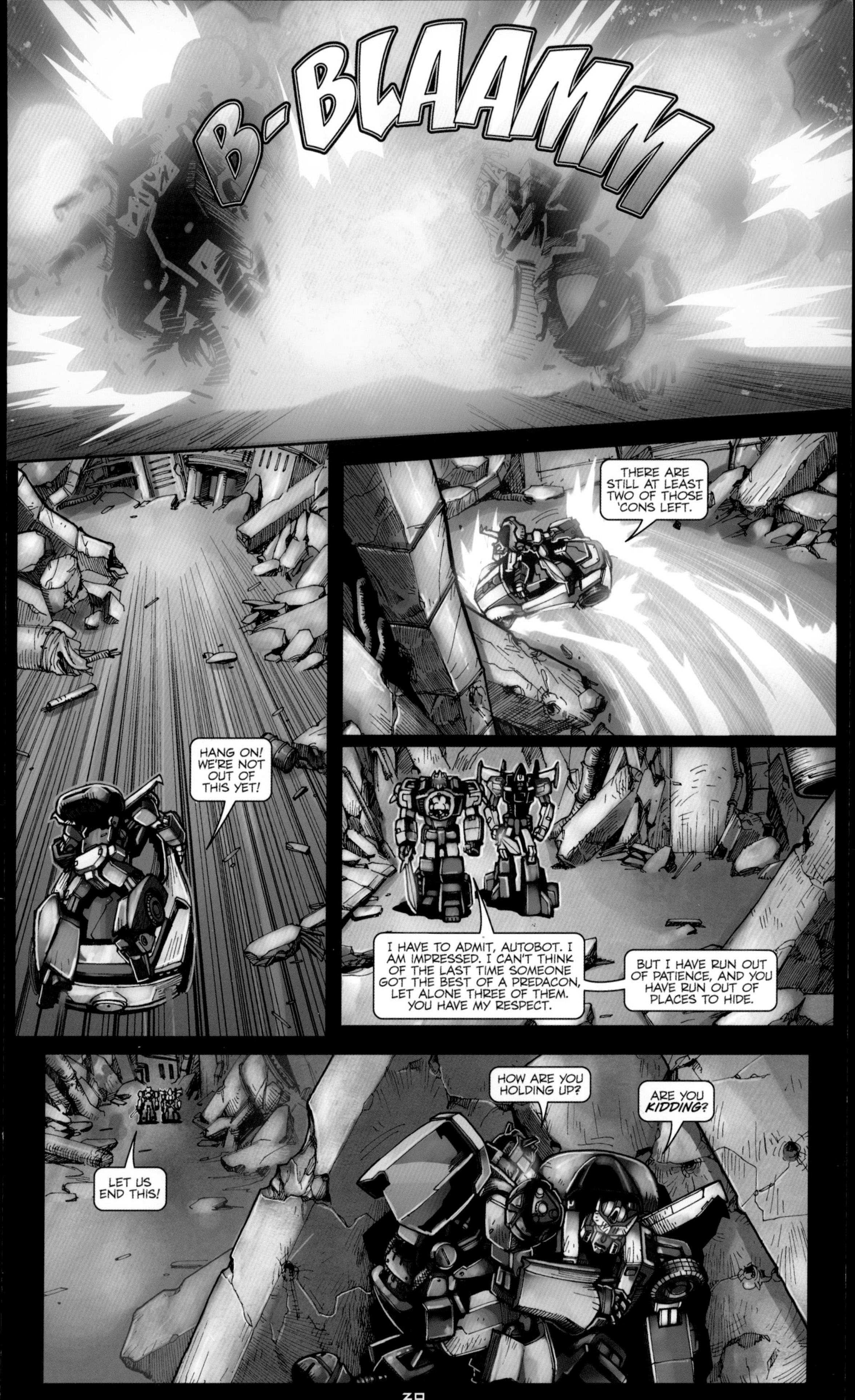
B-BLAAMM
HANG ON! WE'RE NOT OUT OF THIS YET!
THERE ARE STILL AT LEAST TWO OF THOSE 'CONS LEFT.
I HAVE TO ADMIT, AUTOBOT. I AM IMPRESSED. I CAN'T THINK OF THE LAST TIME SOMEONE GOT THE BEST OF A PREDACON, LET ALONE THREE OF THEM. YOU HAVE MY RESPECT.
BUT I HAVE RUN OUT OF PATIENCE, AND YOU HAVE RUN OUT OF PLACES TO HIDE.
LET US END THIS!
HOW ARE YOU HOLDING UP?
ARE YOU *KIDDING*?

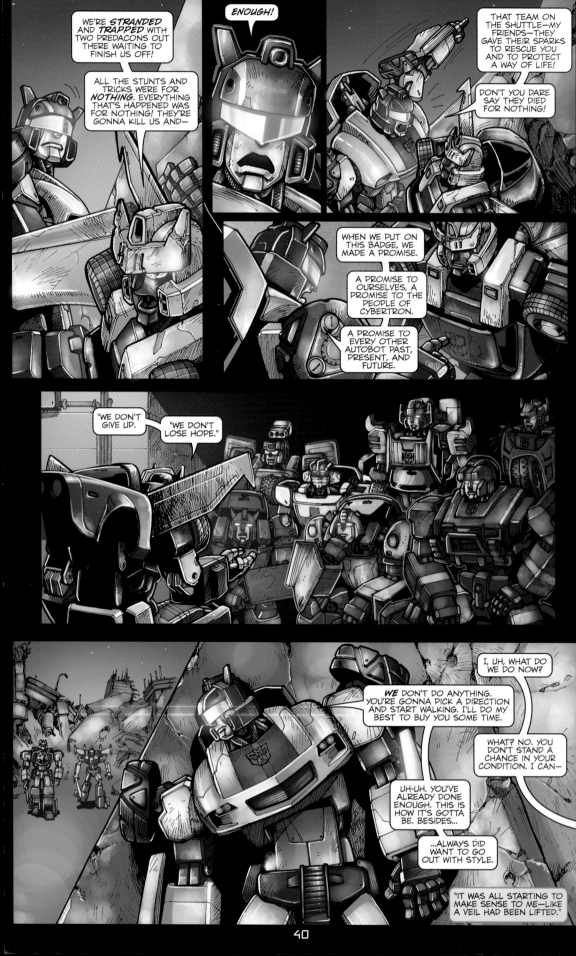

WE'RE **STRANDED** AND **TRAPPED** WITH TWO PREDACONS OUT THERE WAITING TO FINISH US OFF!

ALL THE STUNTS AND TRICKS WERE FOR **NOTHING**. EVERYTHING THAT'S HAPPENED WAS FOR NOTHING! THEY'RE GONNA KILL US AND—

ENOUGH!

THAT TEAM ON THE SHUTTLE—MY FRIENDS—THEY GAVE THEIR SPARKS TO RESCUE YOU AND TO PROTECT A WAY OF LIFE!

DON'T YOU DARE SAY THEY DIED FOR NOTHING!

WHEN WE PUT ON THIS BADGE, WE MADE A PROMISE.

A PROMISE TO OURSELVES, A PROMISE TO THE PEOPLE OF CYBERTRON.

A PROMISE TO EVERY OTHER AUTOBOT PAST, PRESENT, AND FUTURE.

"WE DON'T GIVE UP."

"WE DON'T LOSE HOPE."

I, UH, WHAT DO WE DO NOW?

WE DON'T DO ANYTHING. YOU'RE GONNA PICK A DIRECTION AND START WALKING. I'LL DO MY BEST TO BUY YOU SOME TIME.

WHAT? NO. YOU DON'T STAND A CHANCE IN YOUR CONDITION. I CAN—

UH-UH. YOU'VE ALREADY DONE ENOUGH. THIS IS HOW IT'S GOTTA BE. BESIDES...

...ALWAYS DID WANT TO GO OUT WITH STYLE.

"IT WAS ALL STARTING TO MAKE SENSE TO ME—LIKE A VEIL HAD BEEN LIFTED."

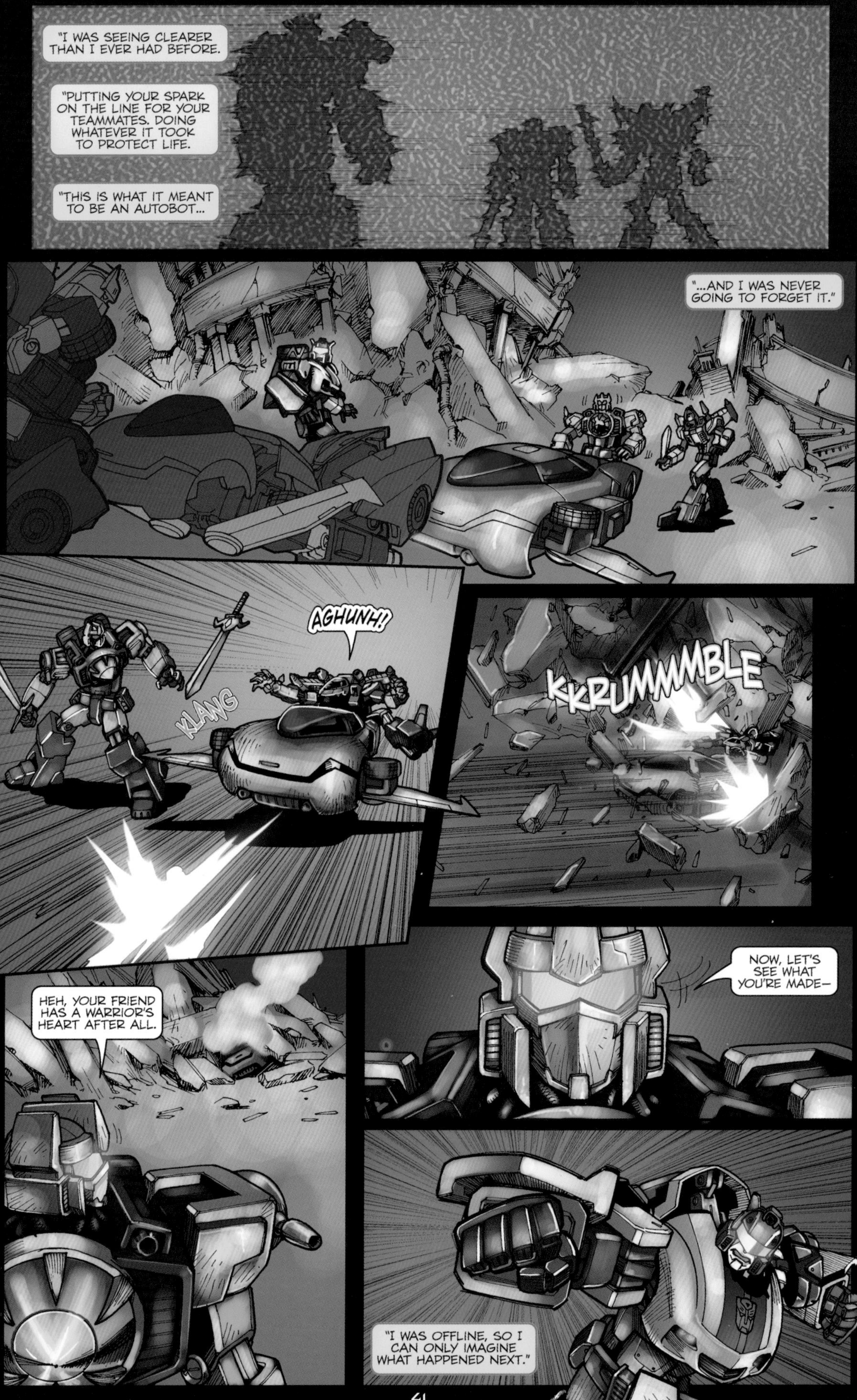
"I WAS SEEING CLEARER THAN I EVER HAD BEFORE.
"PUTTING YOUR SPARK ON THE LINE FOR YOUR TEAMMATES. DOING WHATEVER IT TOOK TO PROTECT LIFE.
"THIS IS WHAT IT MEANT TO BE AN AUTOBOT...
"...AND I WAS NEVER GOING TO FORGET IT."
KLANG
AGHUNH!
K-KRUMMMMBLE
HEH, YOUR FRIEND HAS A WARRIOR'S HEART AFTER ALL.
NOW, LET'S SEE WHAT YOU'RE MADE–
"I WAS OFFLINE, SO I CAN ONLY IMAGINE WHAT HAPPENED NEXT."

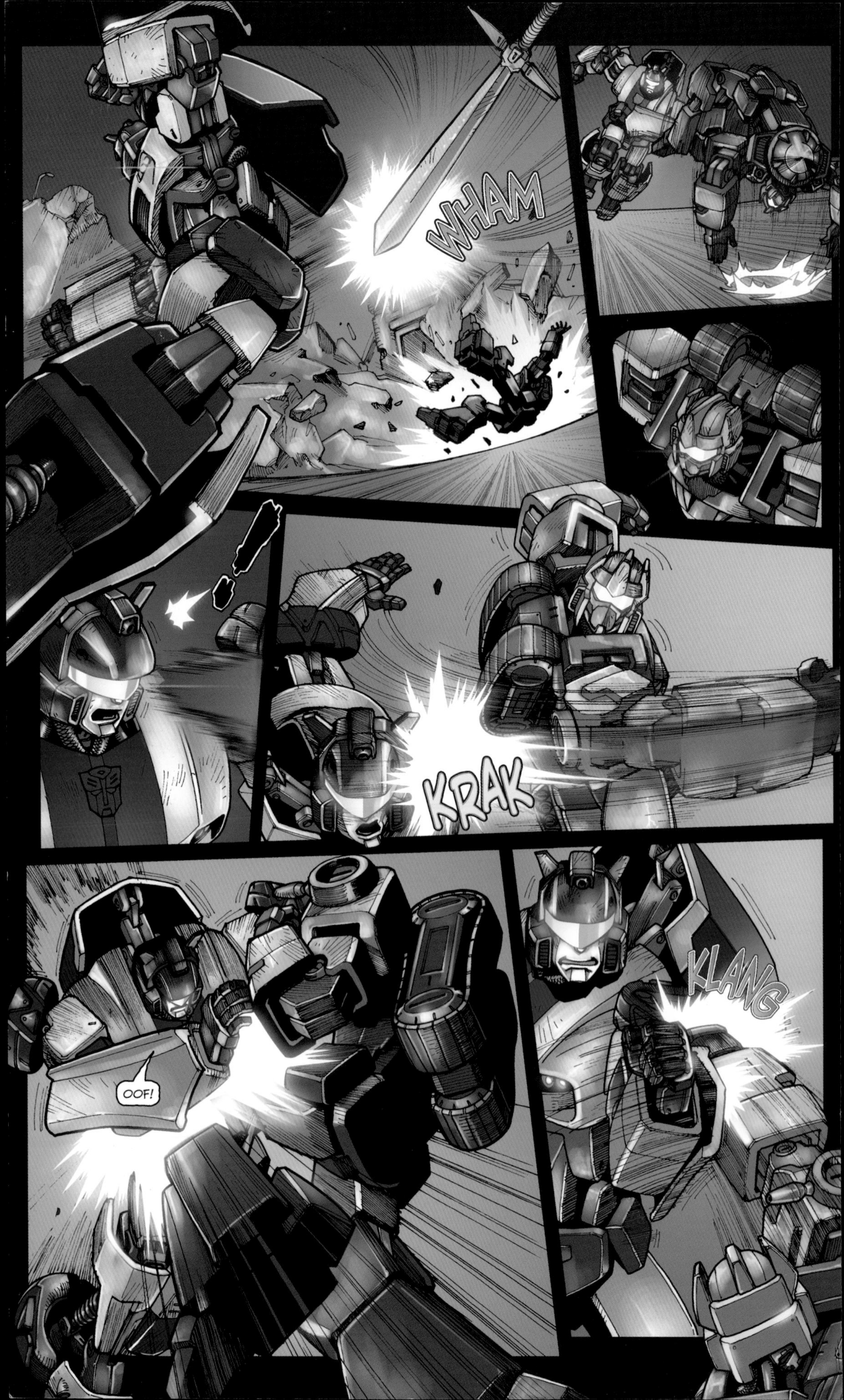
WHAM
KRAK
OOF!
KLANG

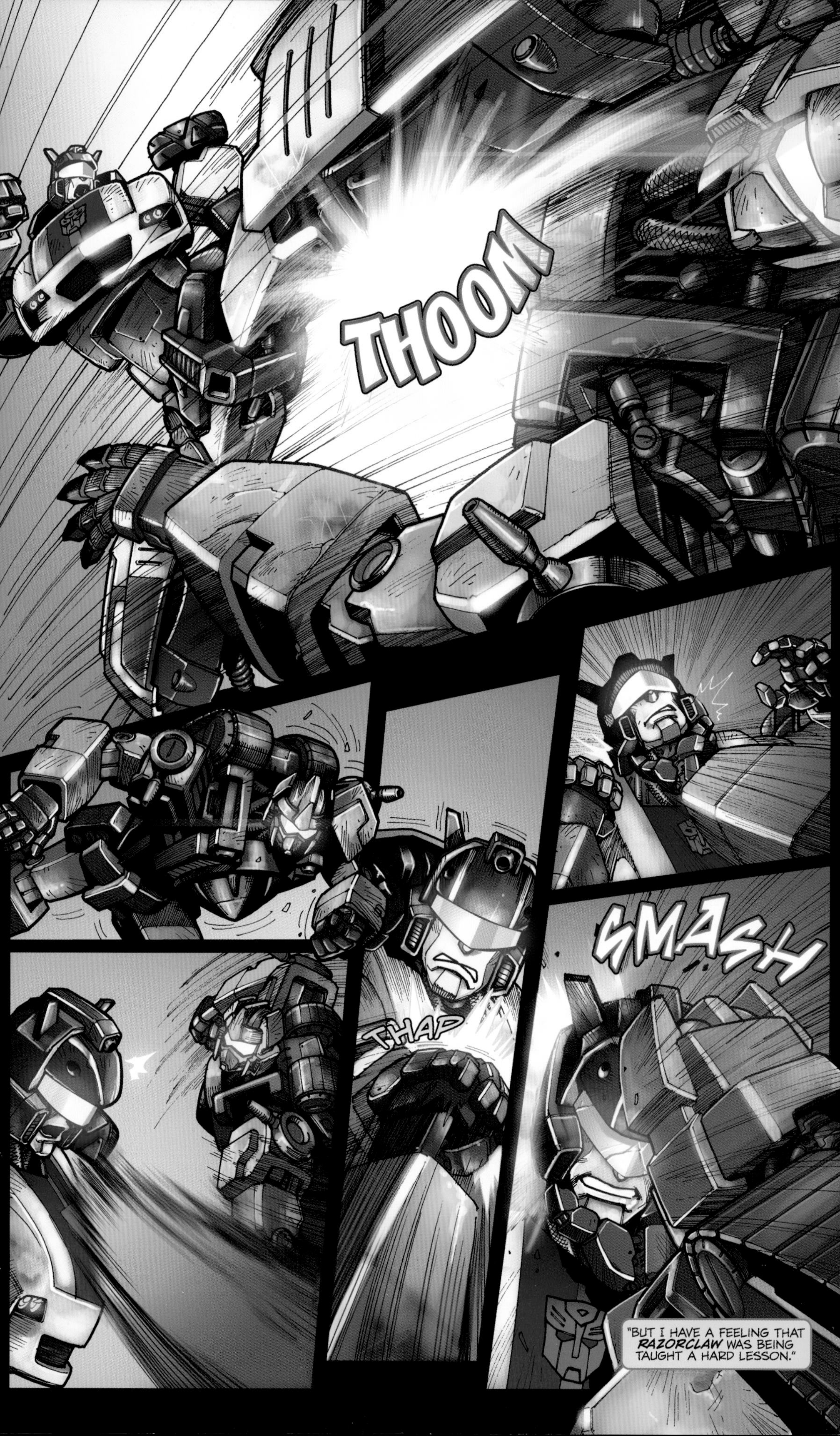
THOOM
SMASH
THAP
"BUT I HAVE A FEELING THAT RAZORCLAW WAS BEING TAUGHT A HARD LESSON."

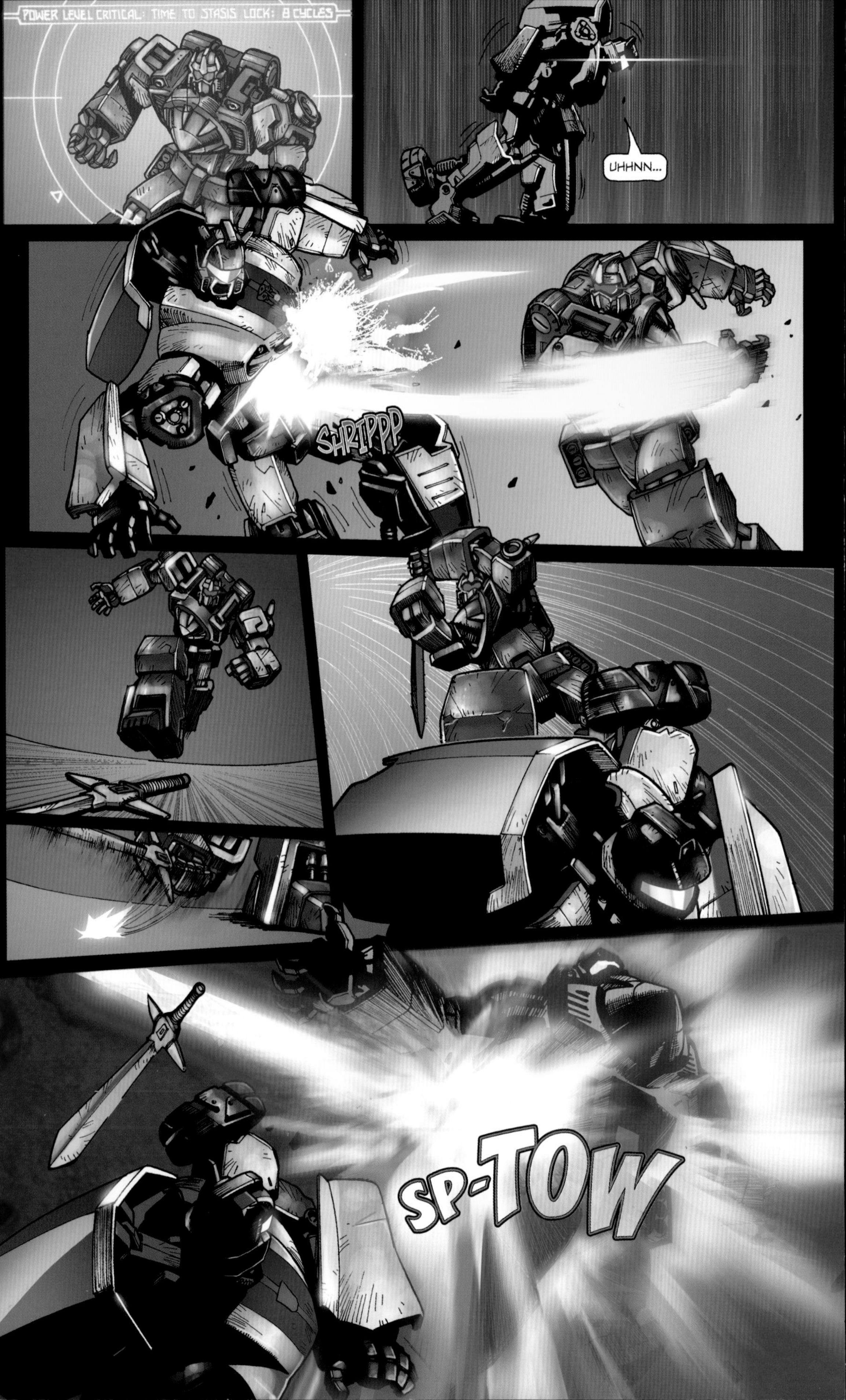
POWER LEVEL CRITICAL: TIME TO STASIS LOCK: 8 CYCLES
UHHNN...
SHRIPPP
SP-TOW

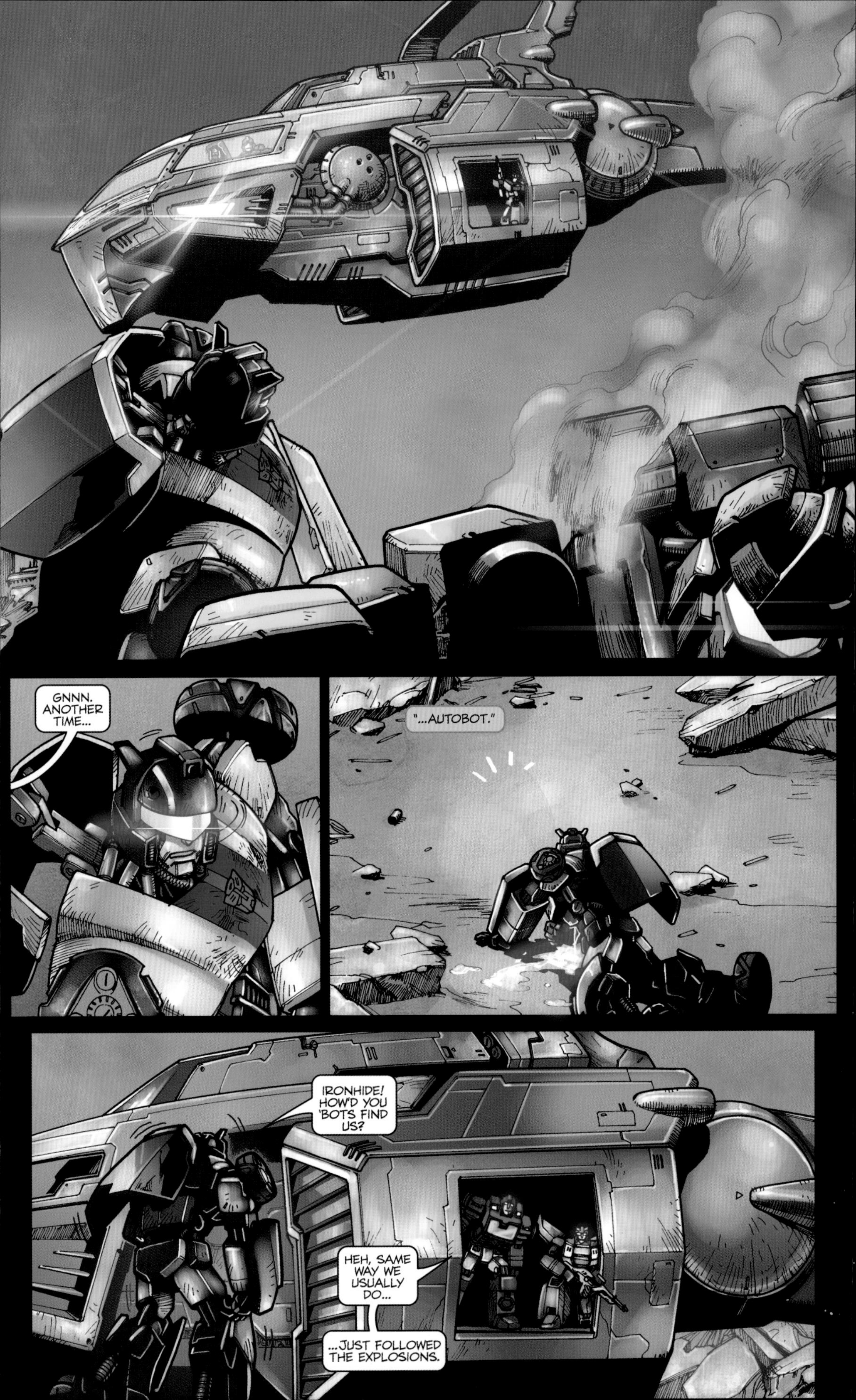
GNNN. ANOTHER TIME...
"...AUTOBOT."
IRONHIDE! HOW'D YOU 'BOTS FIND US?
HEH, SAME WAY WE USUALLY DO...
...JUST FOLLOWED THE EXPLOSIONS.

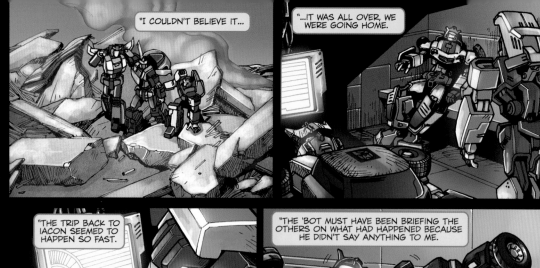

"I COULDN'T BELIEVE IT...

"...IT WAS ALL OVER, WE WERE GOING HOME.

"THE TRIP BACK TO IACON SEEMED TO HAPPEN SO FAST.

"THE 'BOT MUST HAVE BEEN BRIEFING THE OTHERS ON WHAT HAD HAPPENED BECAUSE HE DIDN'T SAY ANYTHING TO ME.

"I DIDN'T MIND, HE'D ALREADY TOLD ME MORE THAN ANYONE ELSE EVER HAD."

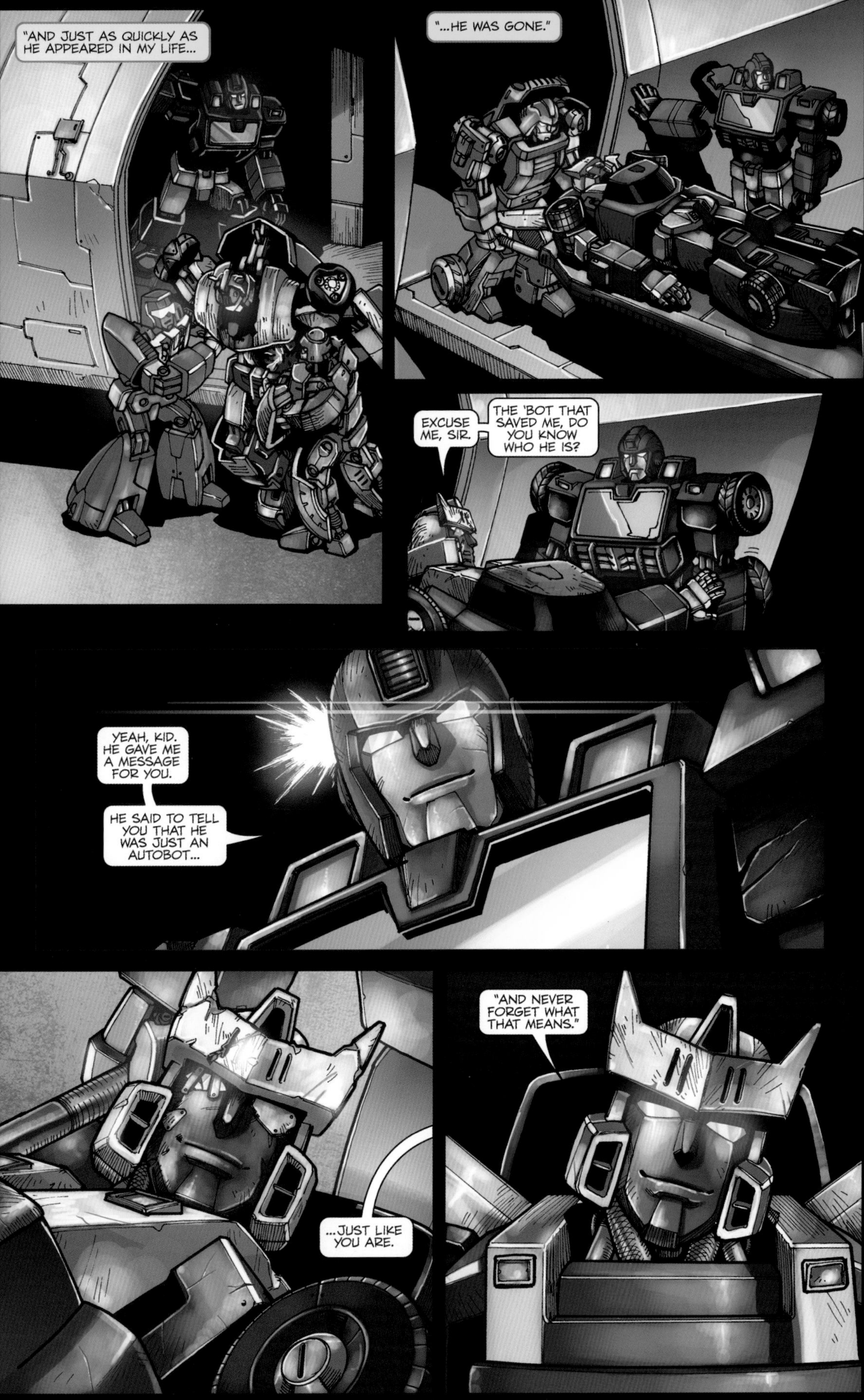
"AND JUST AS QUICKLY AS HE APPEARED IN MY LIFE...
"...HE WAS GONE."
EXCUSE ME, SIR.
THE 'BOT THAT SAVED ME, DO YOU KNOW WHO HE IS?
YEAH, KID. HE GAVE ME A MESSAGE FOR YOU.
HE SAID TO TELL YOU THAT HE WAS JUST AN AUTOBOT...
...JUST LIKE YOU ARE.
"AND NEVER FORGET WHAT THAT MEANS."

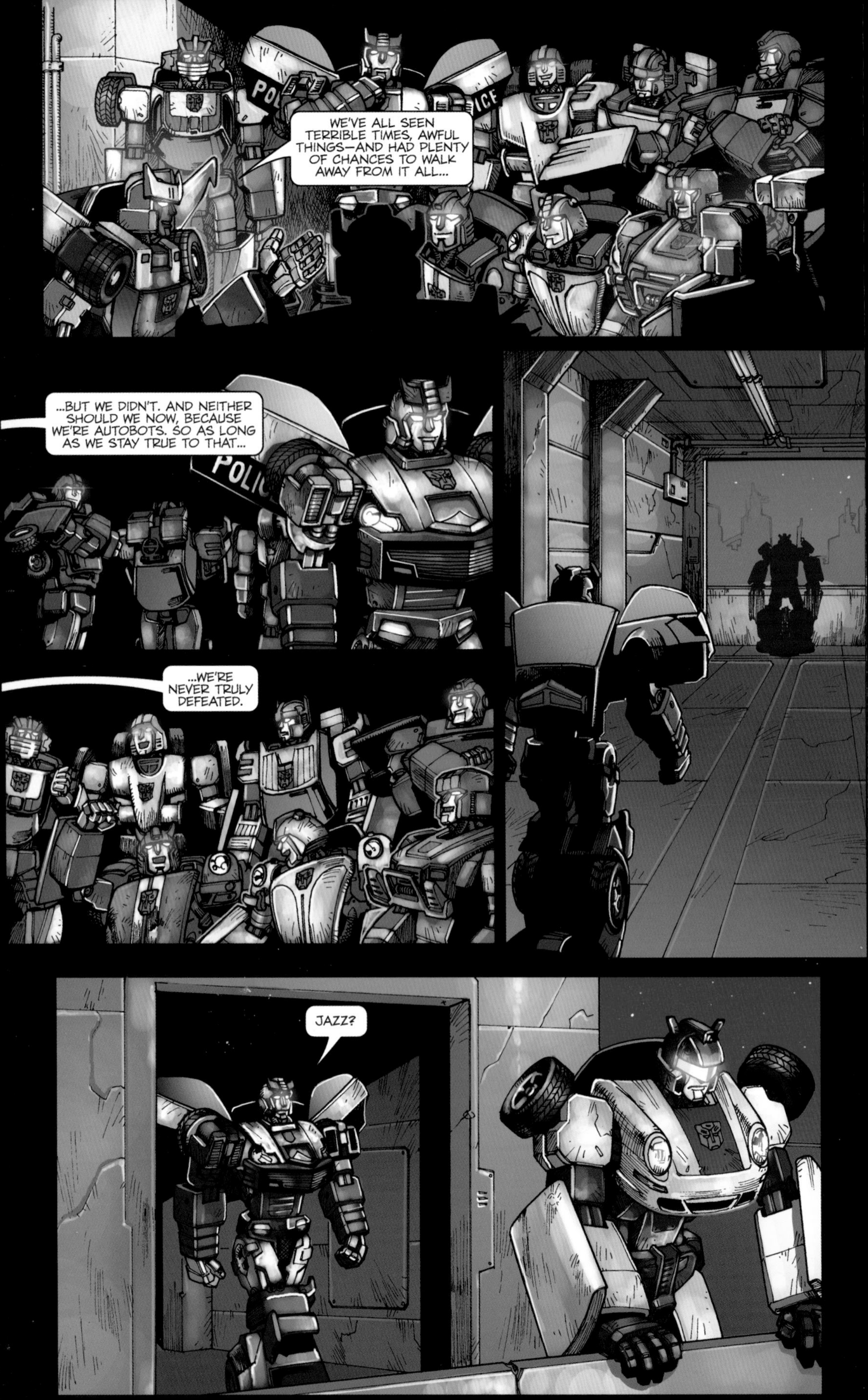
WE'VE ALL SEEN TERRIBLE TIMES, AWFUL THINGS—AND HAD PLENTY OF CHANCES TO WALK AWAY FROM IT ALL...
...BUT WE DIDN'T. AND NEITHER SHOULD WE NOW, BECAUSE WE'RE AUTOBOTS. SO AS LONG AS WE STAY TRUE TO THAT...
...WE'RE NEVER TRULY DEFEATED.
JAZZ?

AH, HEY, PROWL.

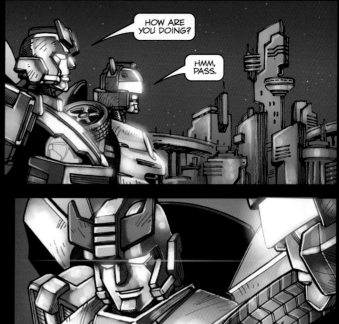

HOW ARE YOU DOING?

HMM, PASS.

WELL, I JUST HEARD SOMETHING THAT MIGHT CHEER YOU UP.

YEAH?

YEAH. TRACKS WAS JUST TELLING EVERYONE A VERY INTERESTING STORY.

AH, YES, THE ONE ABOUT THAT MYSTERIOUS SUPER AUTOBOT WHO TOOK ON ALL FIVE OF THE PREDACONS ALONE?

WELL, IT'S GOOD TO HEAR HE STILL TELLS THAT STORY.

BECAUSE IF THERE'S ONE THING WE ALL COULD USE RIGHT NOW...

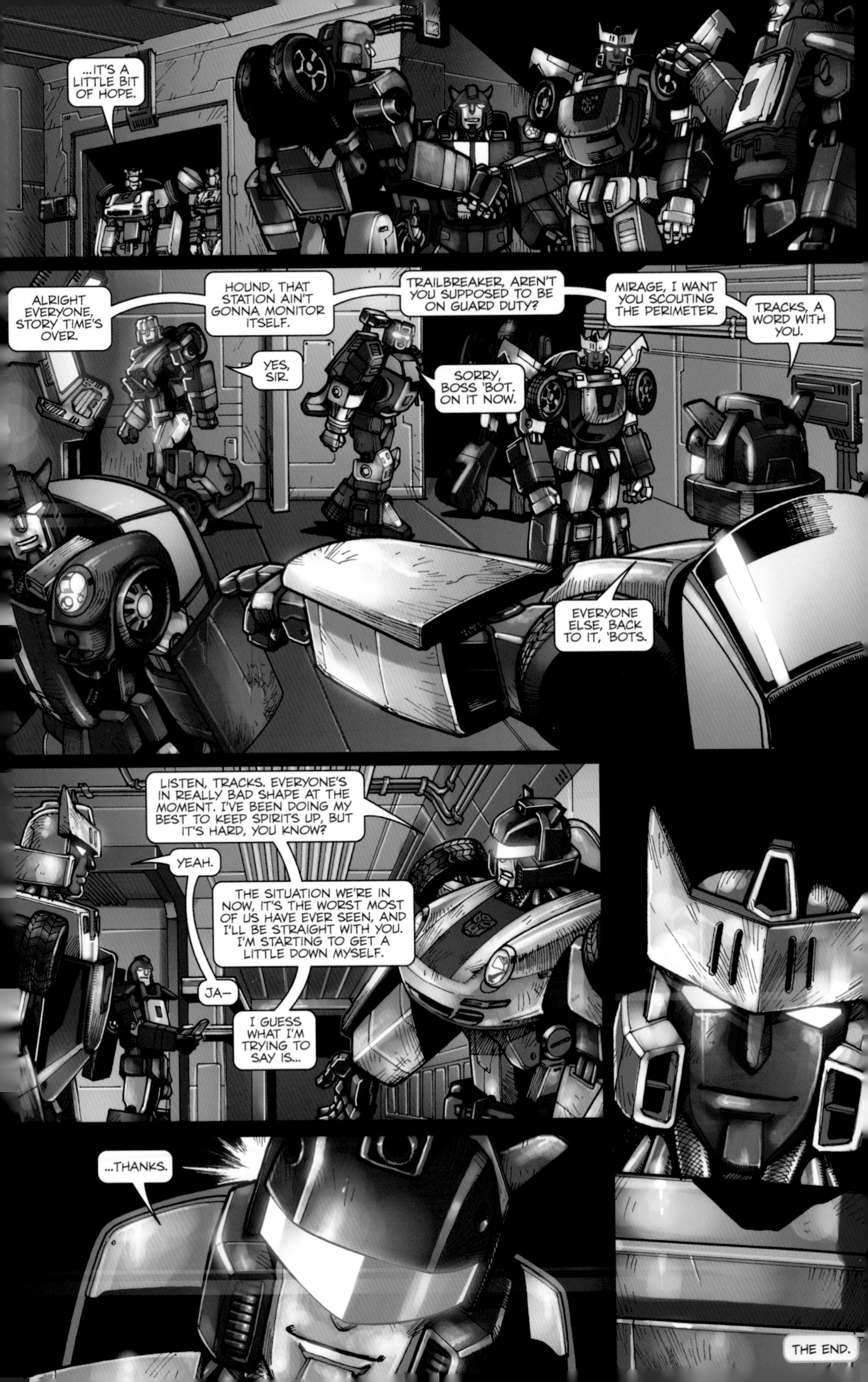
...IT'S A LITTLE BIT OF HOPE.
ALRIGHT EVERYONE, STORY TIME'S OVER.
HOUND, THAT STATION AIN'T GONNA MONITOR ITSELF.
YES, SIR.
TRAILBREAKER, AREN'T YOU SUPPOSED TO BE ON GUARD DUTY?
SORRY, BOSS 'BOT. ON IT NOW.
MIRAGE, I WANT YOU SCOUTING THE PERIMETER.
TRACKS, A WORD WITH YOU.
EVERYONE ELSE, BACK TO IT, 'BOTS.
LISTEN, TRACKS. EVERYONE'S IN REALLY BAD SHAPE AT THE MOMENT. I'VE BEEN DOING MY BEST TO KEEP SPIRITS UP, BUT IT'S HARD, YOU KNOW?
YEAH.
THE SITUATION WE'RE IN NOW, IT'S THE WORST MOST OF US HAVE EVER SEEN, AND I'LL BE STRAIGHT WITH YOU. I'M STARTING TO GET A LITTLE DOWN MYSELF.
JA—
I GUESS WHAT I'M TRYING TO SAY IS...
...THANKS.
THE END.

Art by E.J. Su

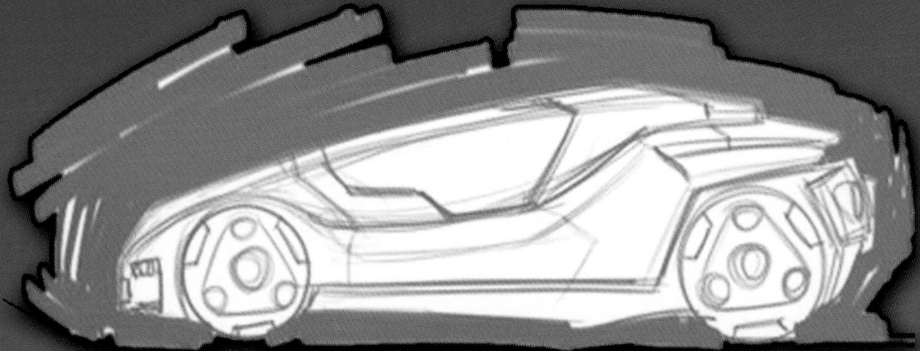

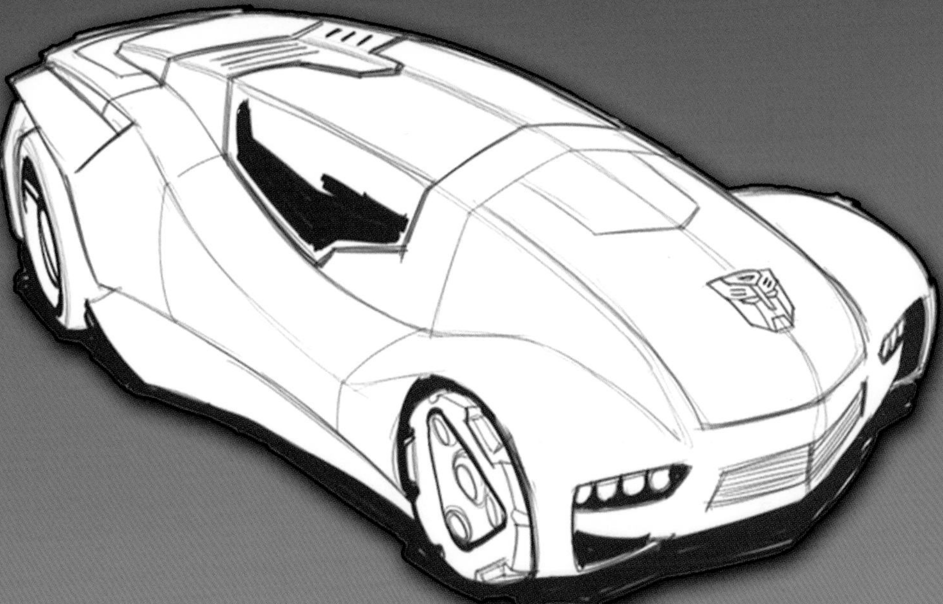

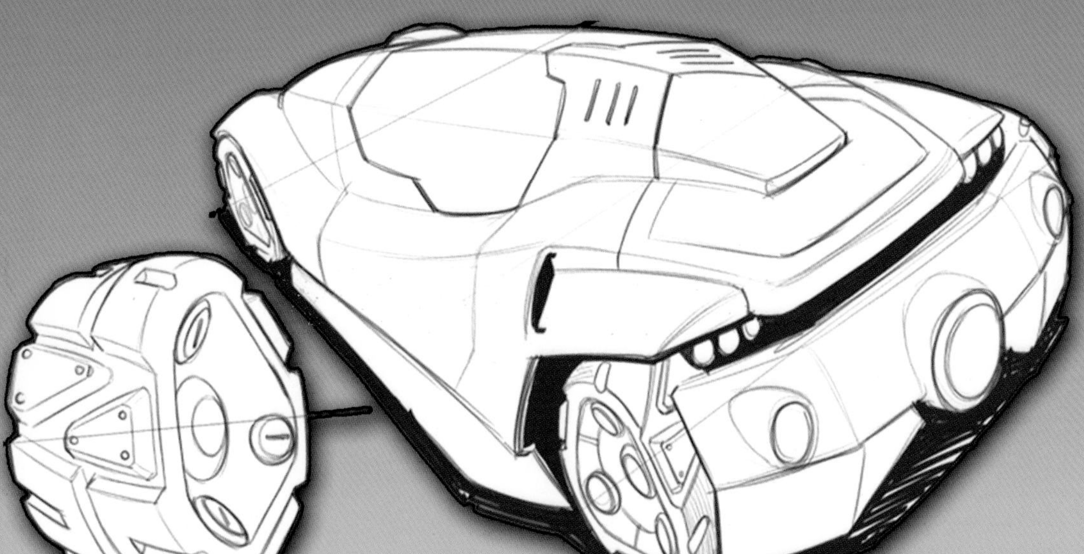

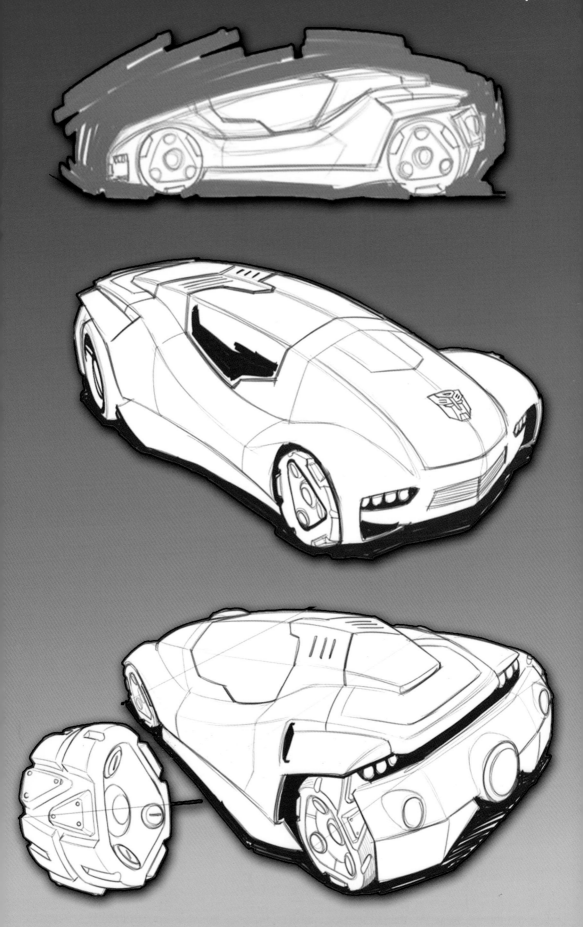

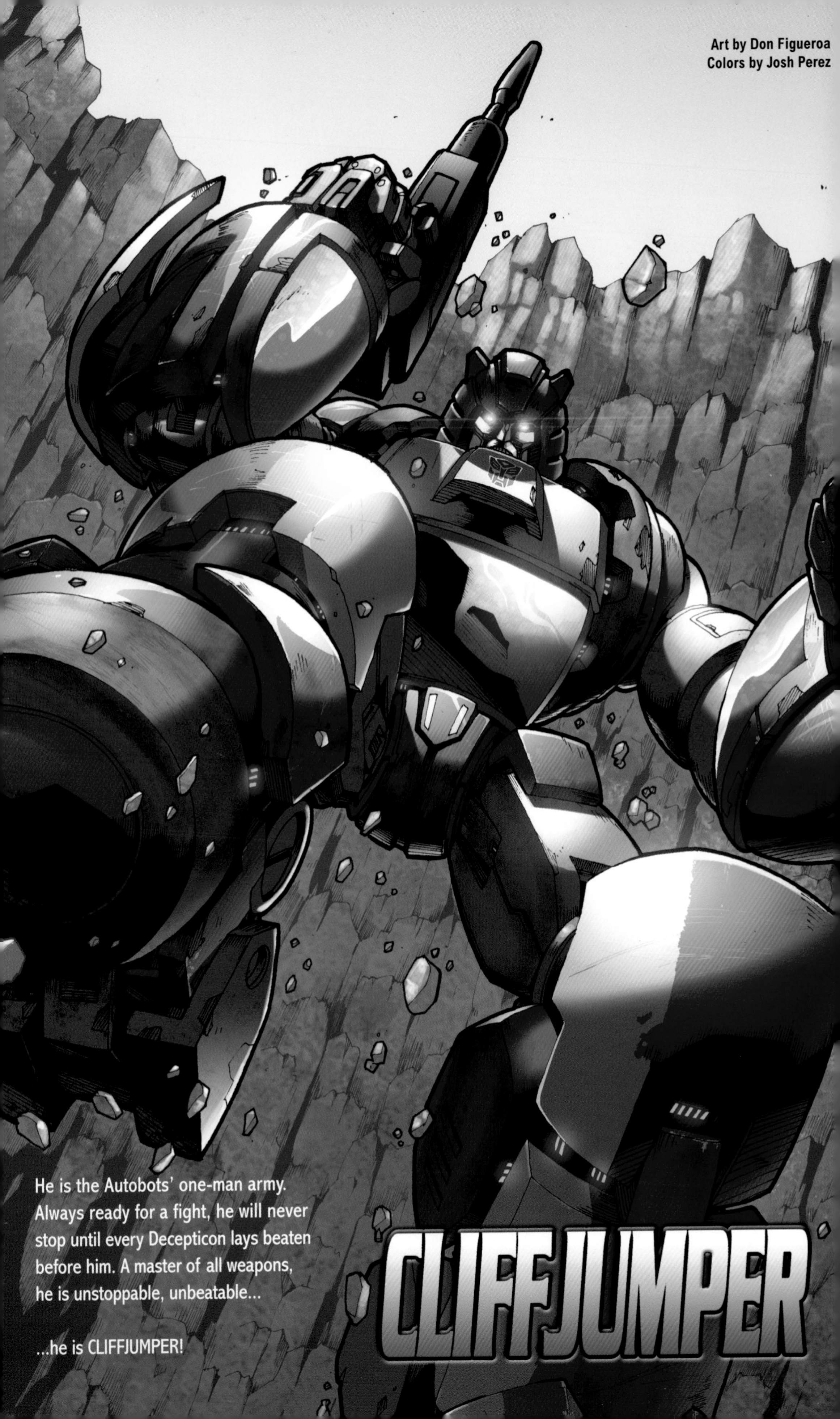

Art by Don Figueroa
Colors by Josh Perez
He is the Autobots' one-man army. Always ready for a fight, he will never stop until every Decepticon lays beaten before him. A master of all weapons, he is unstoppable, unbeatable...
...he is CLIFFJUMPER!
CLIFFJUMPER

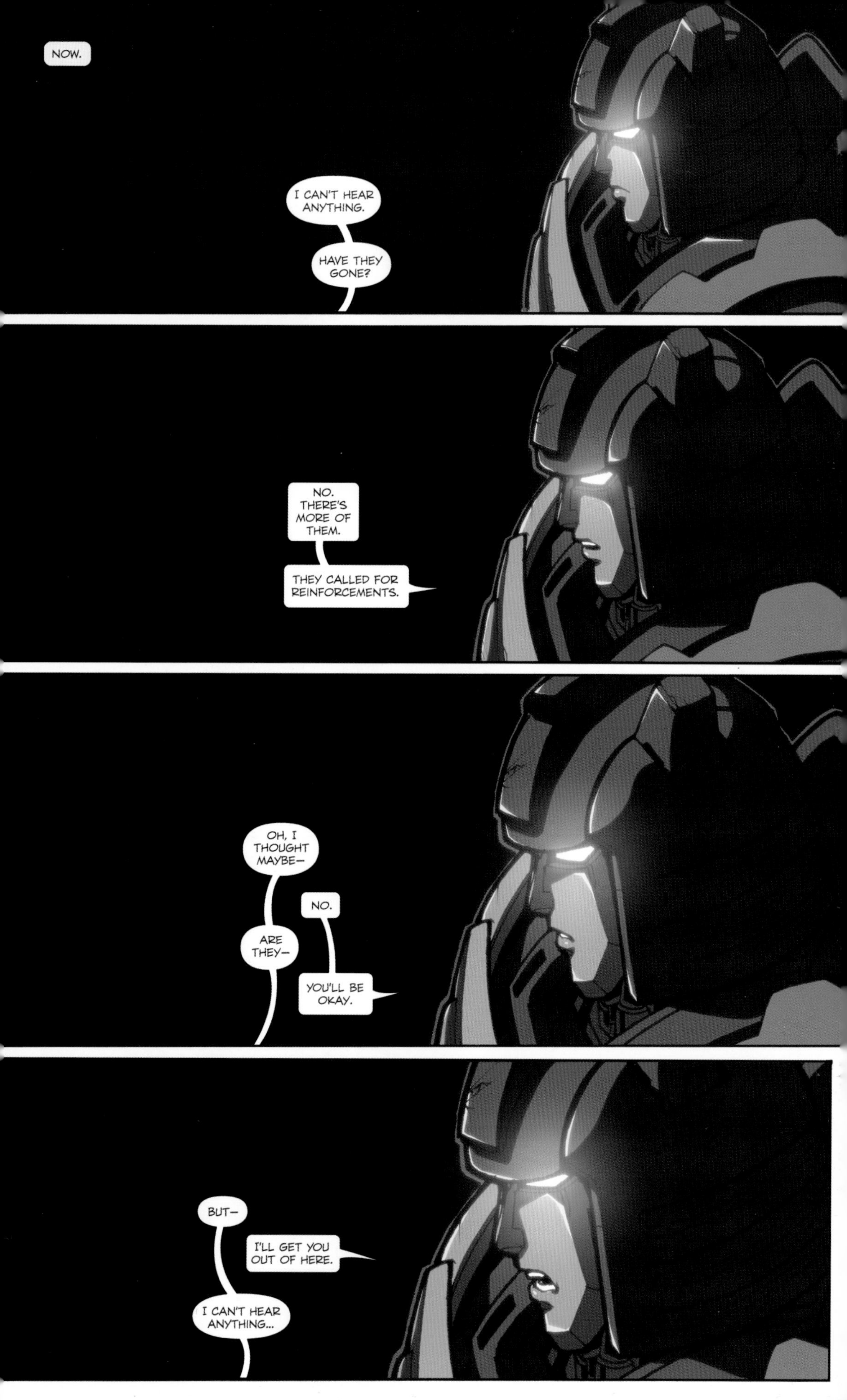
NOW.
I CAN'T HEAR ANYTHING.
HAVE THEY GONE?
NO. THERE'S MORE OF THEM.
THEY CALLED FOR REINFORCEMENTS.
OH, I THOUGHT MAYBE—
NO.
ARE THEY—
YOU'LL BE OKAY.
BUT—
I'LL GET YOU OUT OF HERE.
I CAN'T HEAR ANYTHING...

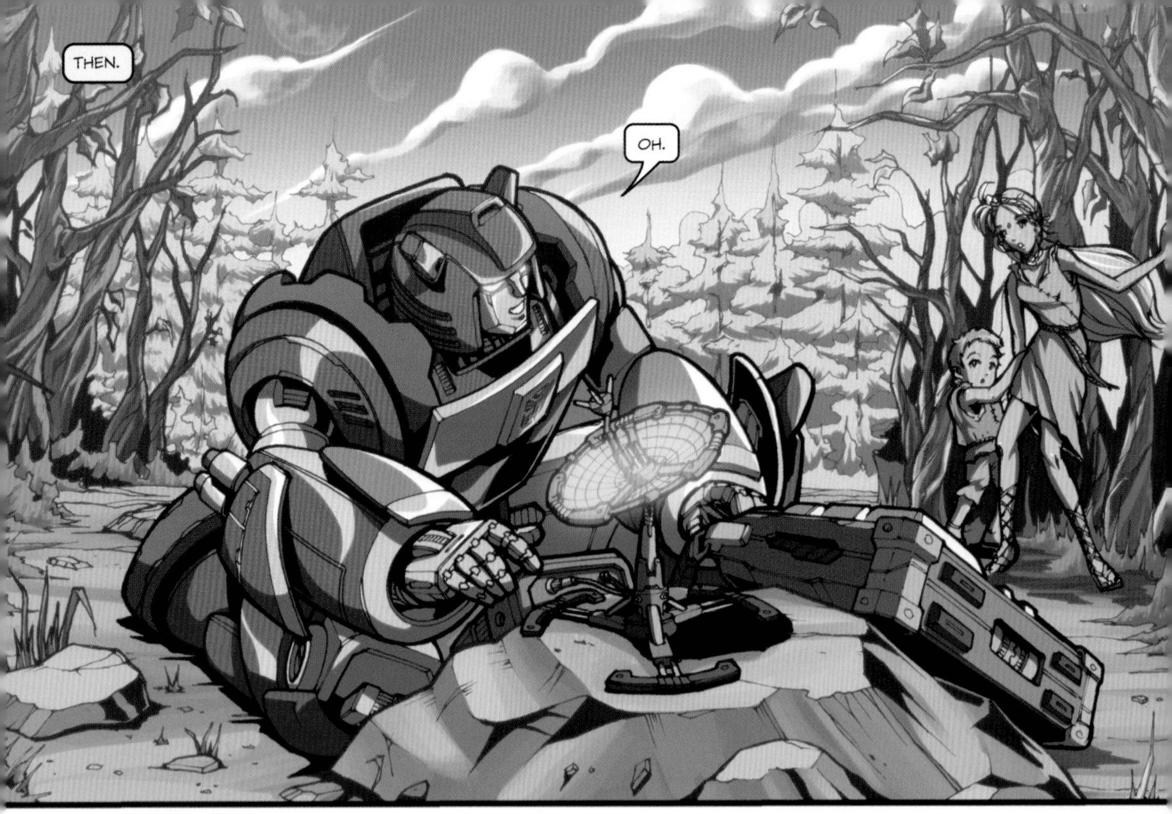
THEN.
OH.

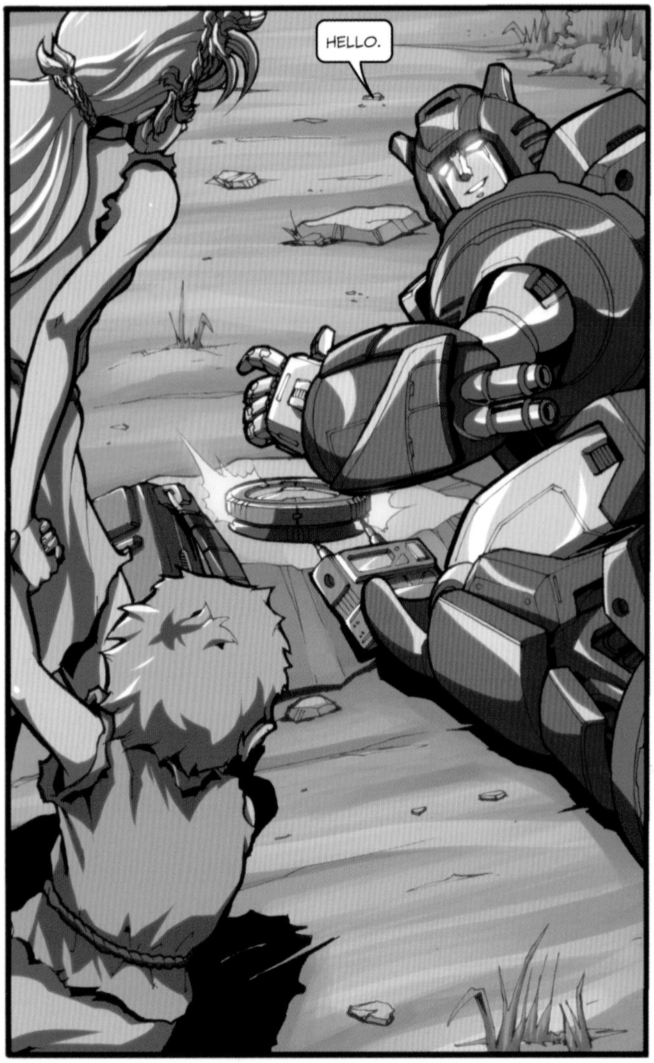
HELLO.

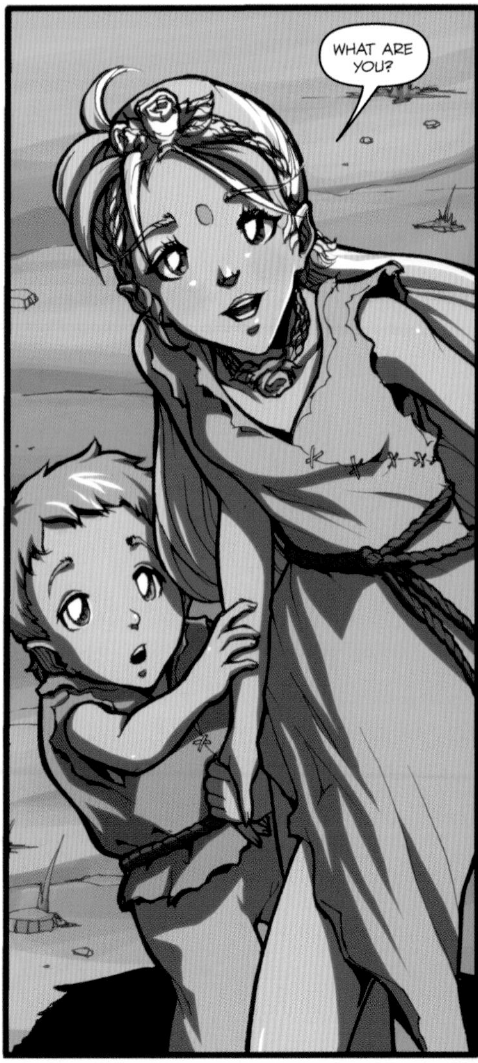
WHAT ARE YOU?

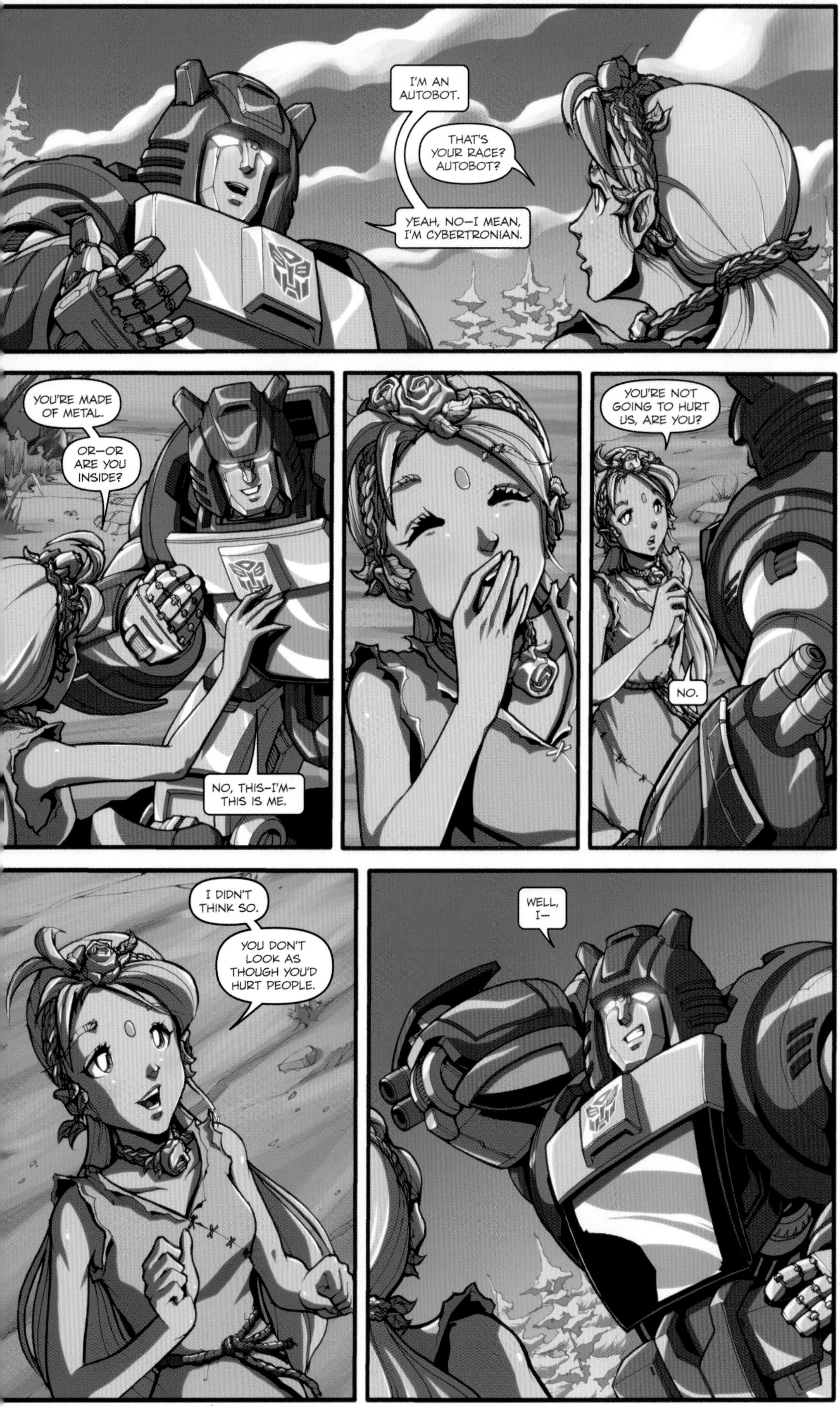
I'M AN AUTOBOT.
THAT'S YOUR RACE? AUTOBOT?
YEAH, NO—I MEAN, I'M CYBERTRONIAN.
YOU'RE MADE OF METAL.
OR—OR ARE YOU INSIDE?
NO, THIS—I'M—THIS IS ME.
YOU'RE NOT GOING TO HURT US, ARE YOU?
NO.
I DIDN'T THINK SO.
YOU DON'T LOOK AS THOUGH YOU'D HURT PEOPLE.
WELL, I—

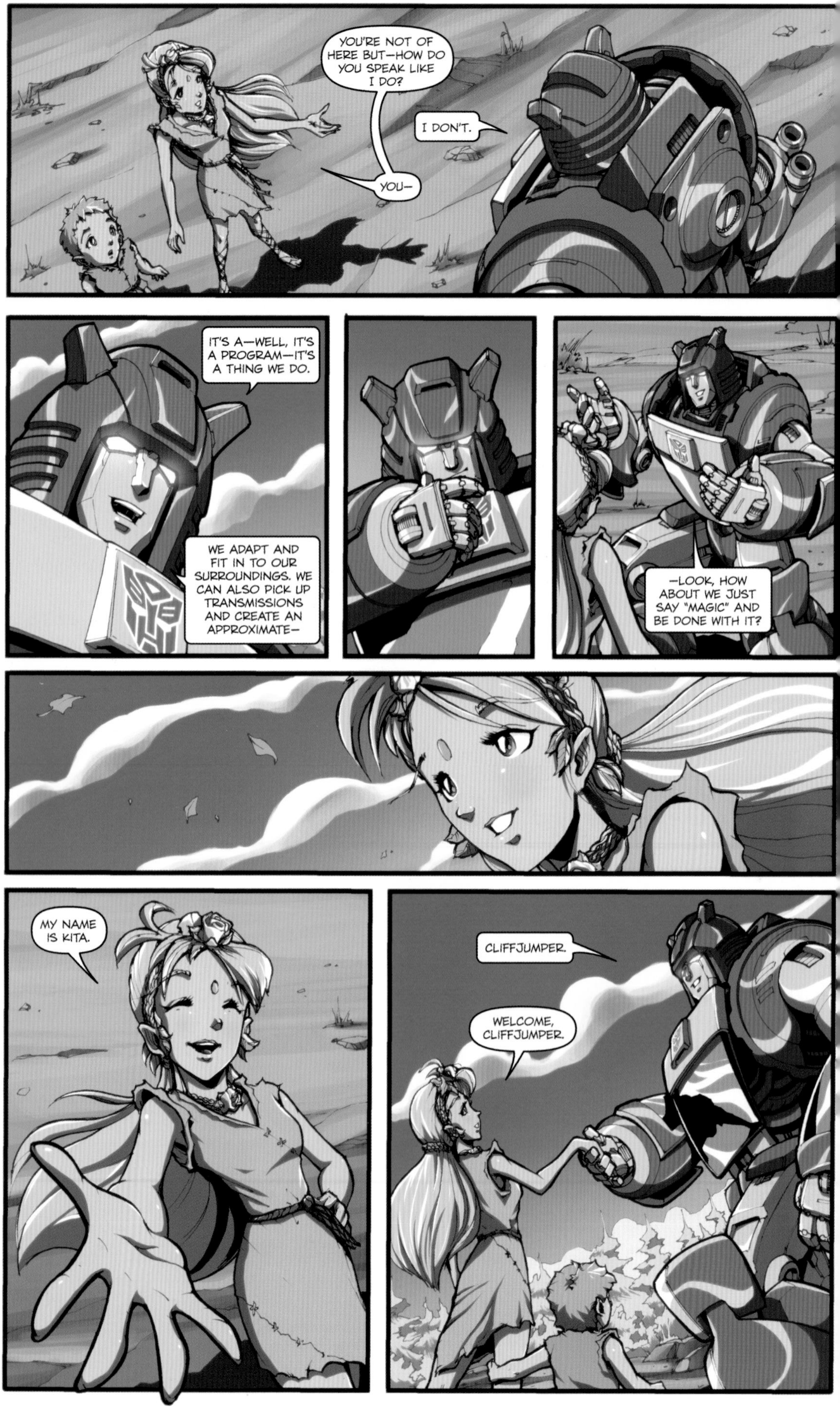
YOU'RE NOT OF HERE BUT—HOW DO YOU SPEAK LIKE I DO?
YOU—
I DON'T.
IT'S A—WELL, IT'S A PROGRAM—IT'S A THING WE DO.
WE ADAPT AND FIT IN TO OUR SURROUNDINGS. WE CAN ALSO PICK UP TRANSMISSIONS AND CREATE AN APPROXIMATE—
—LOOK, HOW ABOUT WE JUST SAY "MAGIC" AND BE DONE WITH IT?
MY NAME IS KITA.
CLIFFJUMPER.
WELCOME, CLIFFJUMPER.

"YOU'RE ALONE HERE?"

JUST MYSELF AND MY BROTHER, COLL.

WE WERE ONCE A FAMILY...

"...BUT NO LONGER."

"THE SICKNESS TOOK THEM FROM US."

NOW WE DO OUR BEST TO STAY ALIVE. IT CAN BE HARD, BUT WE MAKE DO.

WE ARE NOT ALONE ALL THE TIME. OUR PEOPLE NEARBY, THEY HELP WHEN ABLE.

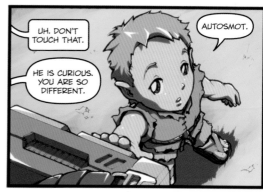

UH. DON'T TOUCH THAT.

HE IS CURIOUS. YOU ARE SO DIFFERENT.

AUTOSMOT.

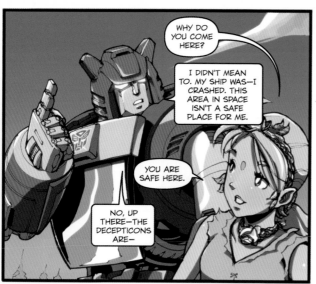

WHY DO YOU COME HERE?

I DIDN'T MEAN TO. MY SHIP WAS—I CRASHED. THIS AREA IN SPACE ISN'T A SAFE PLACE FOR ME.

YOU ARE SAFE HERE.

NO, UP THERE—THE DECEPTICONS ARE—

YOU ARE *SAFE* HERE.

57

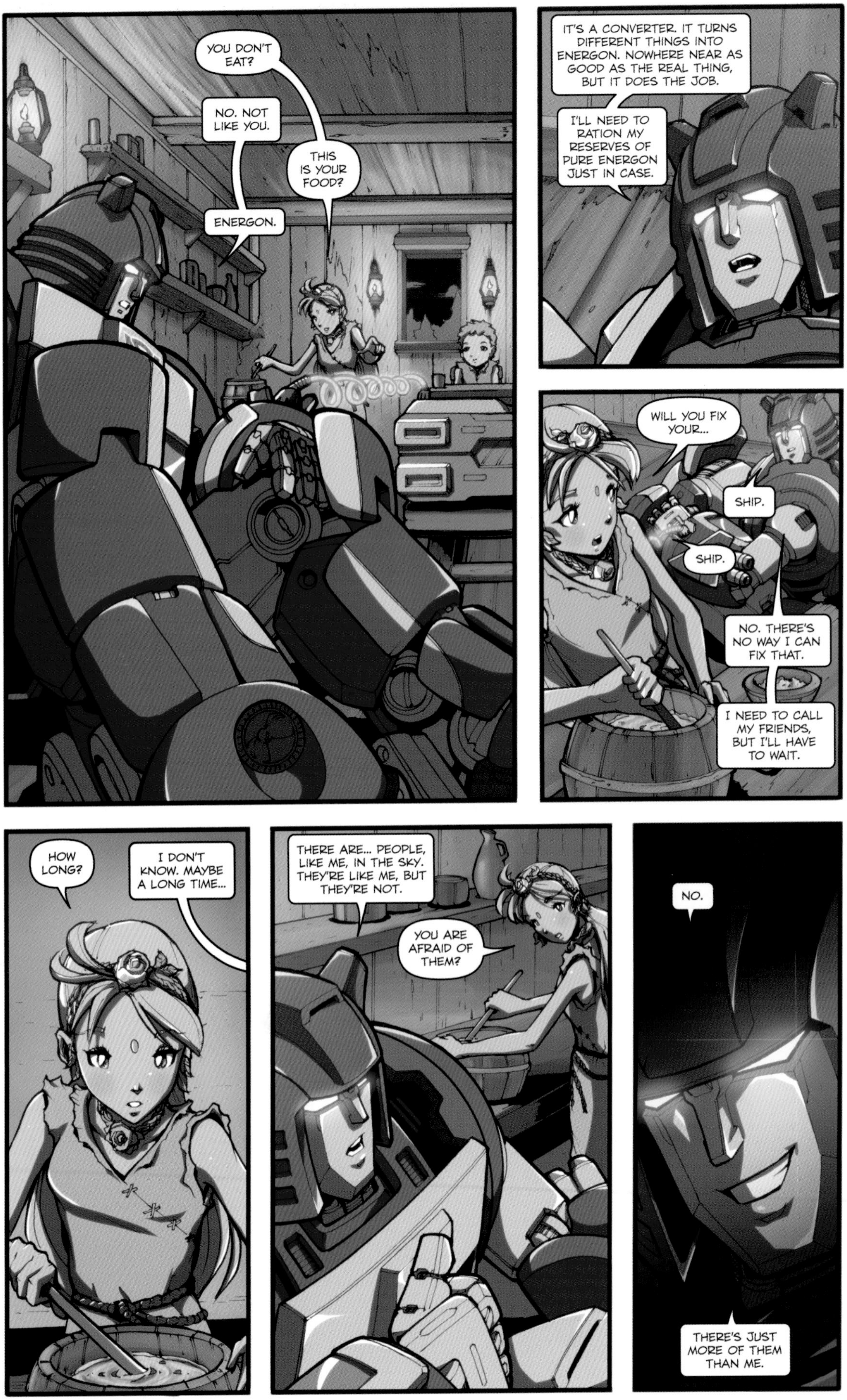
YOU DON'T EAT?
NO. NOT LIKE YOU.
THIS IS YOUR FOOD?
ENERGON.
IT'S A CONVERTER. IT TURNS DIFFERENT THINGS INTO ENERGON. NOWHERE NEAR AS GOOD AS THE REAL THING, BUT IT DOES THE JOB.
I'LL NEED TO RATION MY RESERVES OF PURE ENERGON JUST IN CASE.
WILL YOU FIX YOUR...
SHIP.
SHIP.
NO. THERE'S NO WAY I CAN FIX THAT.
I NEED TO CALL MY FRIENDS, BUT I'LL HAVE TO WAIT.
HOW LONG?
I DON'T KNOW. MAYBE A LONG TIME...
THERE ARE... PEOPLE, LIKE ME, IN THE SKY. THEY'RE LIKE ME, BUT THEY'RE NOT.
YOU ARE AFRAID OF THEM?
NO.
THERE'S JUST MORE OF THEM THAN ME.

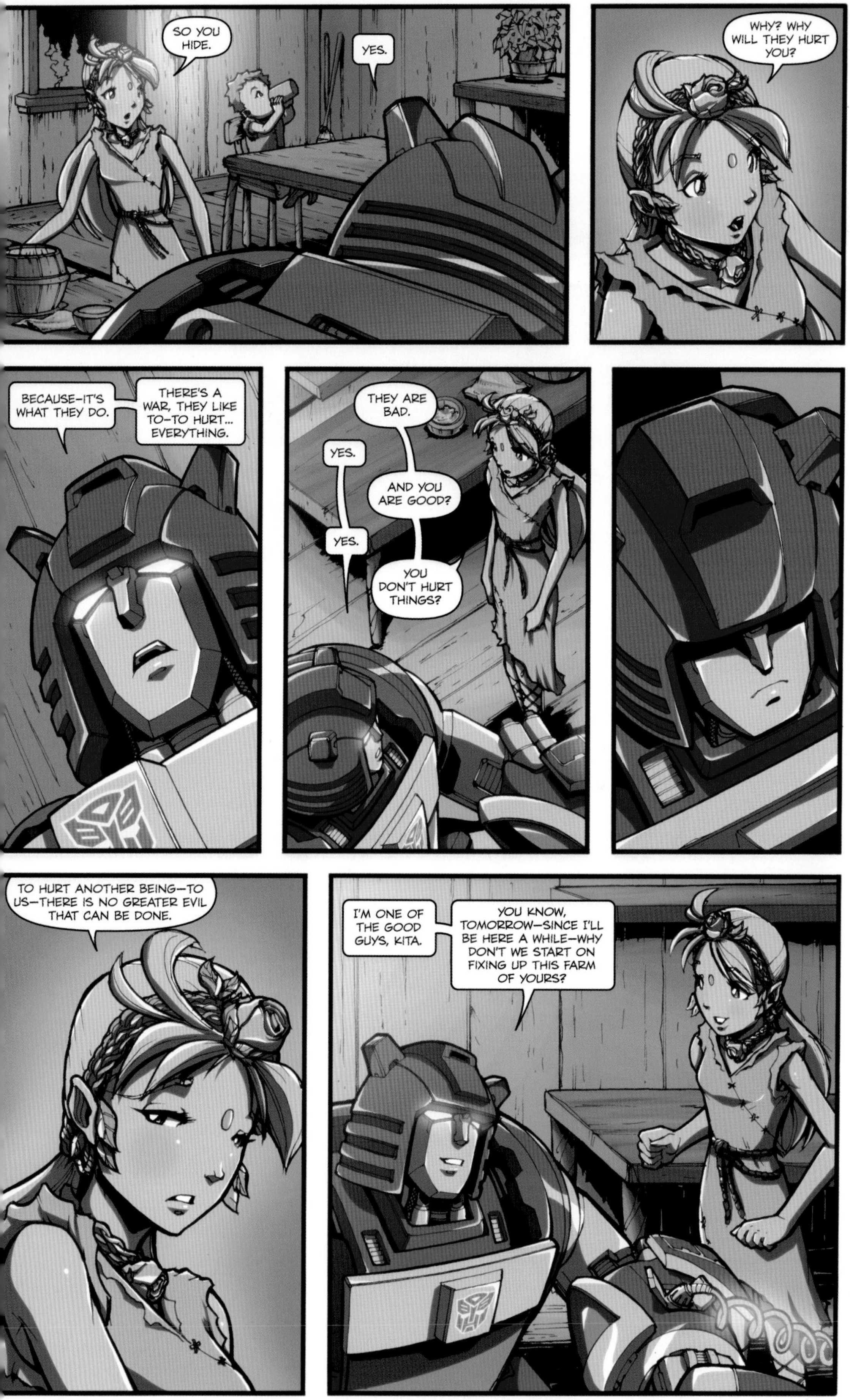
SO YOU HIDE.
YES.
WHY? WHY WILL THEY HURT YOU?
BECAUSE—IT'S WHAT THEY DO.
THERE'S A WAR, THEY LIKE TO—TO HURT... EVERYTHING.
THEY ARE BAD.
YES.
AND YOU ARE GOOD?
YES.
YOU DON'T HURT THINGS?
TO HURT ANOTHER BEING—TO US—THERE IS NO GREATER EVIL THAT CAN BE DONE.
I'M ONE OF THE GOOD GUYS, KITA.
YOU KNOW, TOMORROW—SINCE I'LL BE HERE A WHILE—WHY DON'T WE START ON FIXING UP THIS FARM OF YOURS?

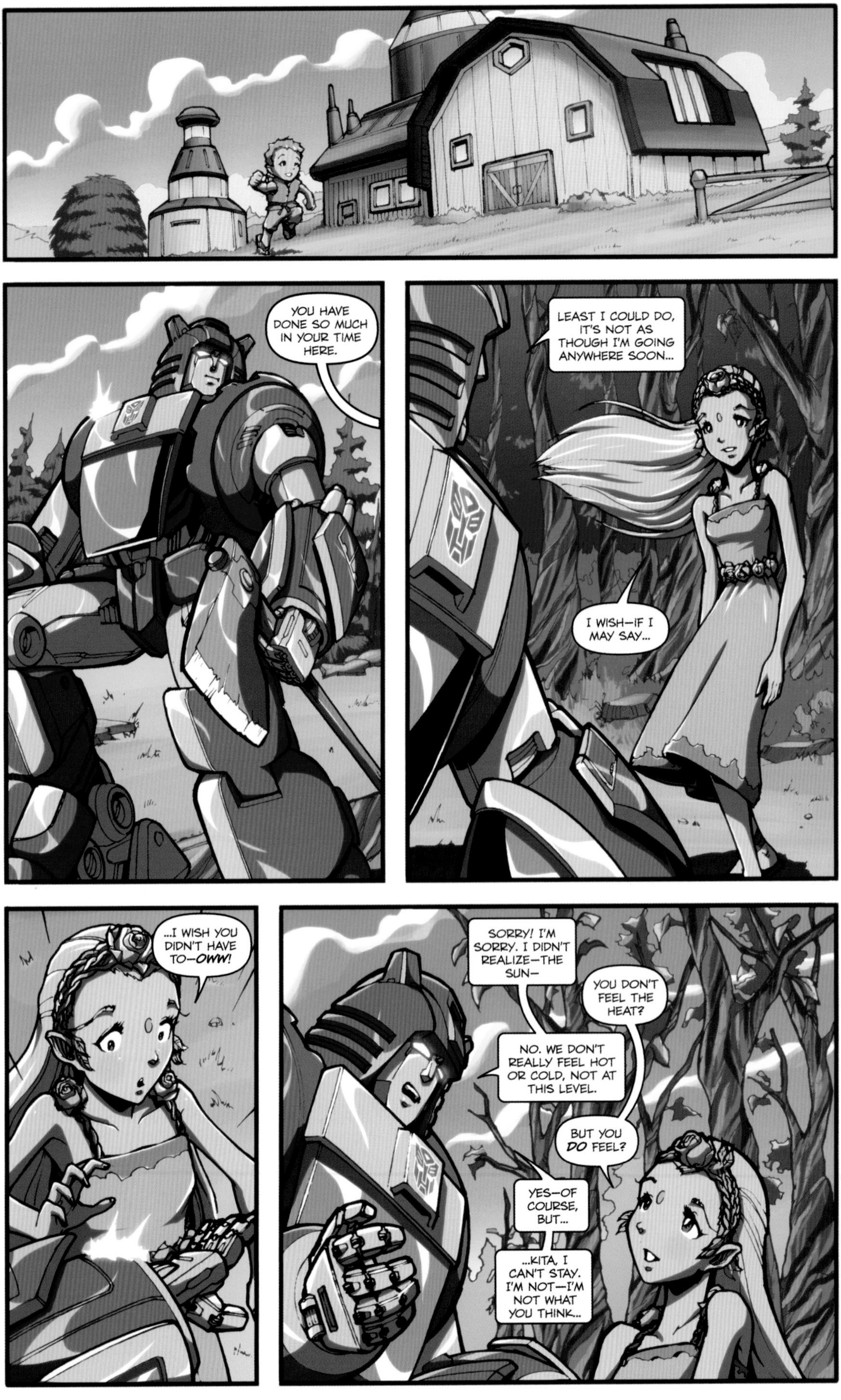

YOU HAVE DONE SO MUCH IN YOUR TIME HERE.
LEAST I COULD DO, IT'S NOT AS THOUGH I'M GOING ANYWHERE SOON...
I WISH—IF I MAY SAY...
...I WISH YOU DIDN'T HAVE TO—*OWW*!
SORRY! I'M SORRY. I DIDN'T REALIZE—THE SUN—
YOU DON'T FEEL THE HEAT?
NO. WE DON'T REALLY FEEL HOT OR COLD, NOT AT THIS LEVEL.
BUT YOU *DO* FEEL?
YES—OF COURSE, BUT...
...KITA, I CAN'T STAY. I'M NOT—I'M NOT WHAT YOU THINK...

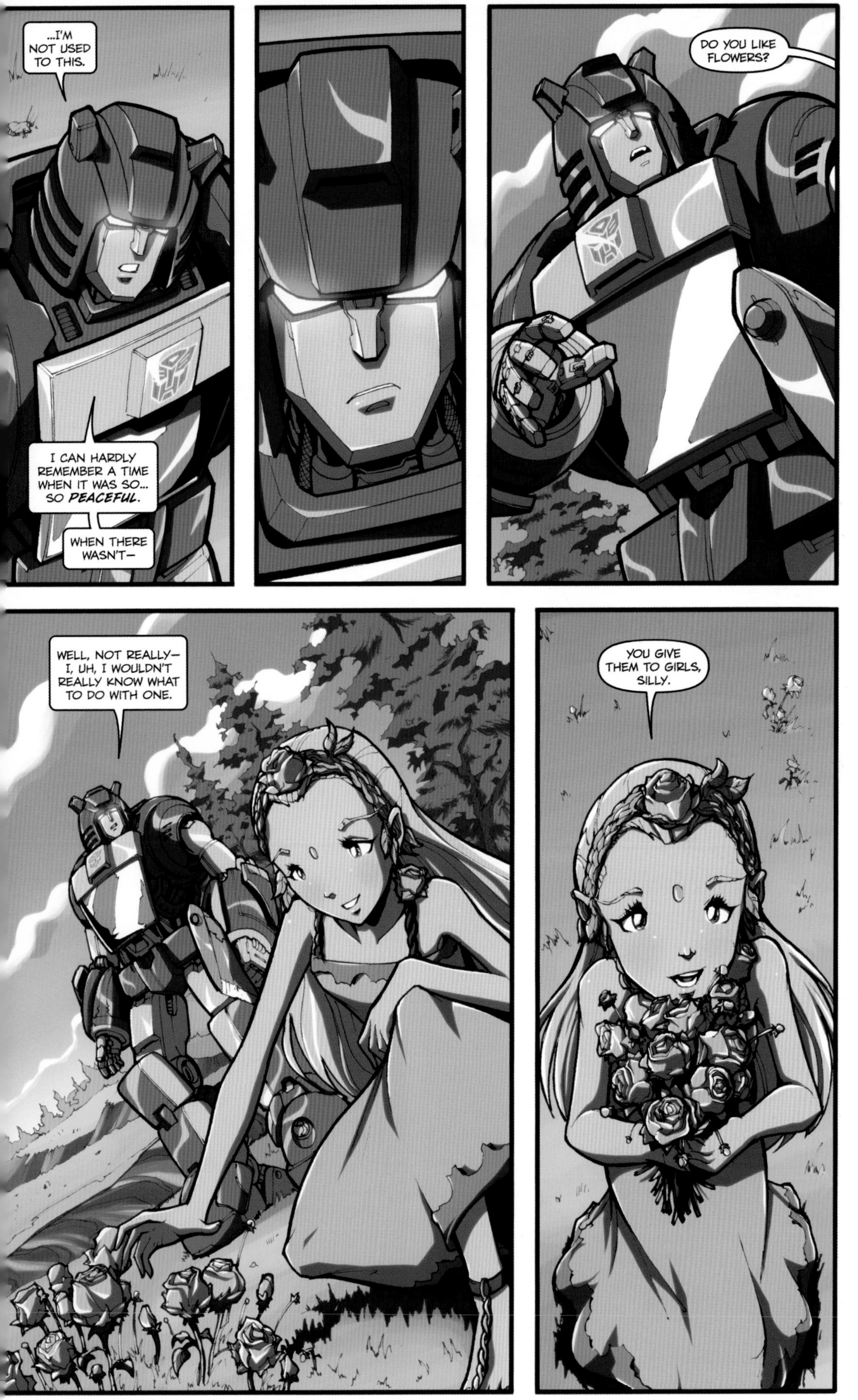
...I'M NOT USED TO THIS.
I CAN HARDLY REMEMBER A TIME WHEN IT WAS SO... SO *PEACEFUL*.
WHEN THERE WASN'T—
DO YOU LIKE FLOWERS?
WELL, NOT REALLY— I, UH, I WOULDN'T REALLY KNOW WHAT TO DO WITH ONE.
YOU GIVE THEM TO GIRLS, SILLY.

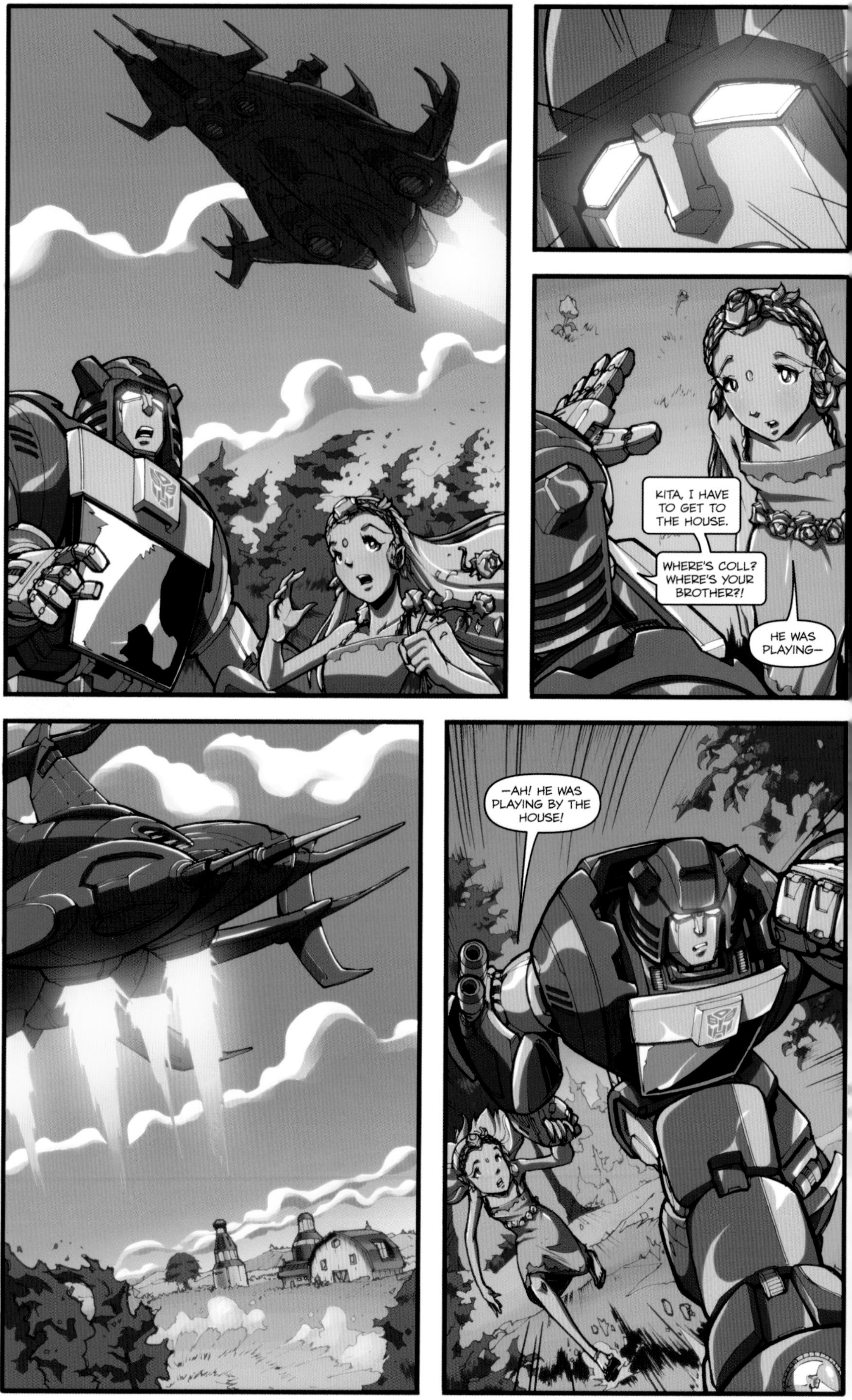
KITA, I HAVE TO GET TO THE HOUSE.
WHERE'S COLL? WHERE'S YOUR BROTHER?!
HE WAS PLAYING—
—AH! HE WAS PLAYING BY THE HOUSE!

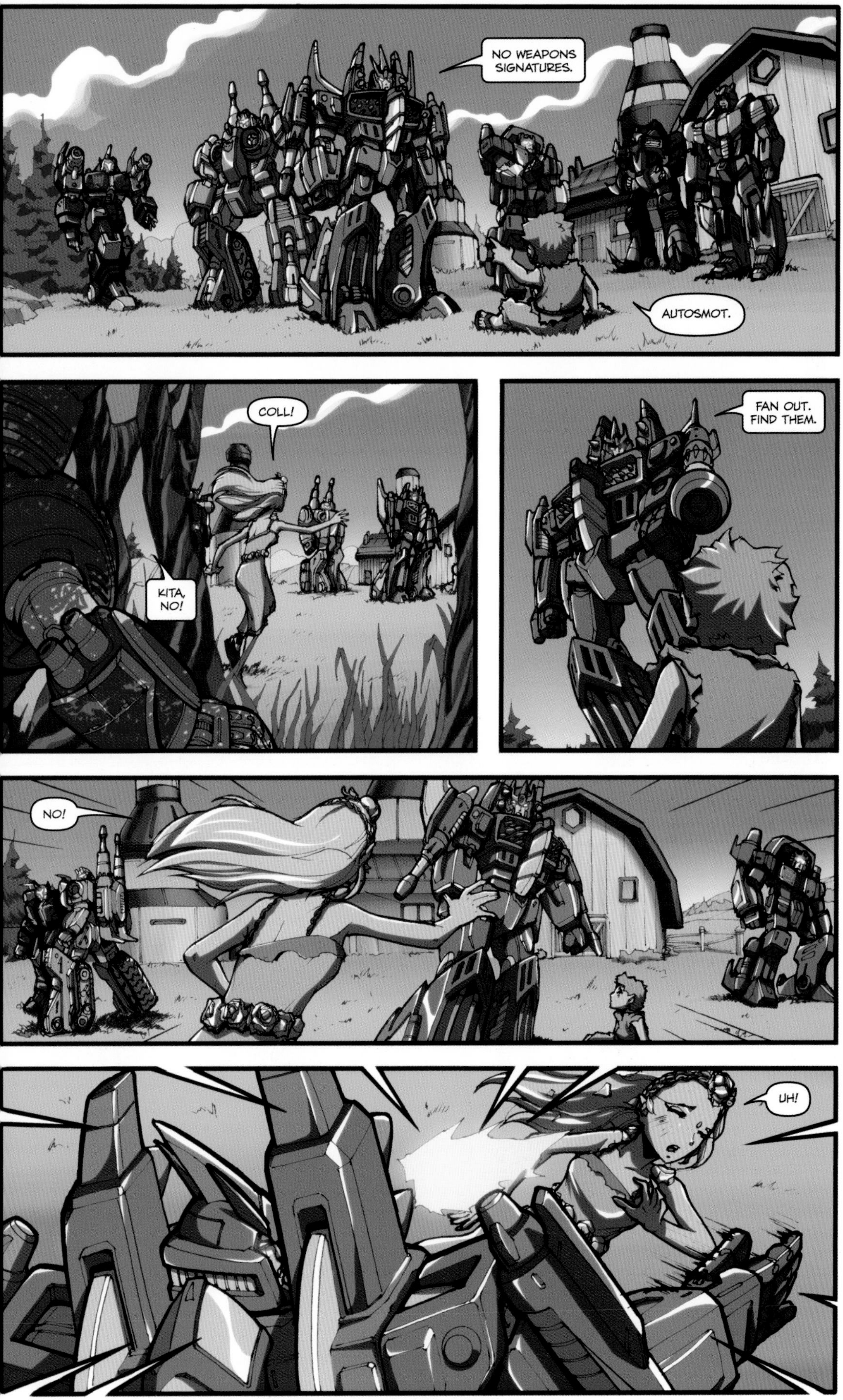
NO WEAPONS SIGNATURES.
AUTOSMOT.
COLL!
KITA, NO!
FAN OUT. FIND THEM.
NO!
UH!

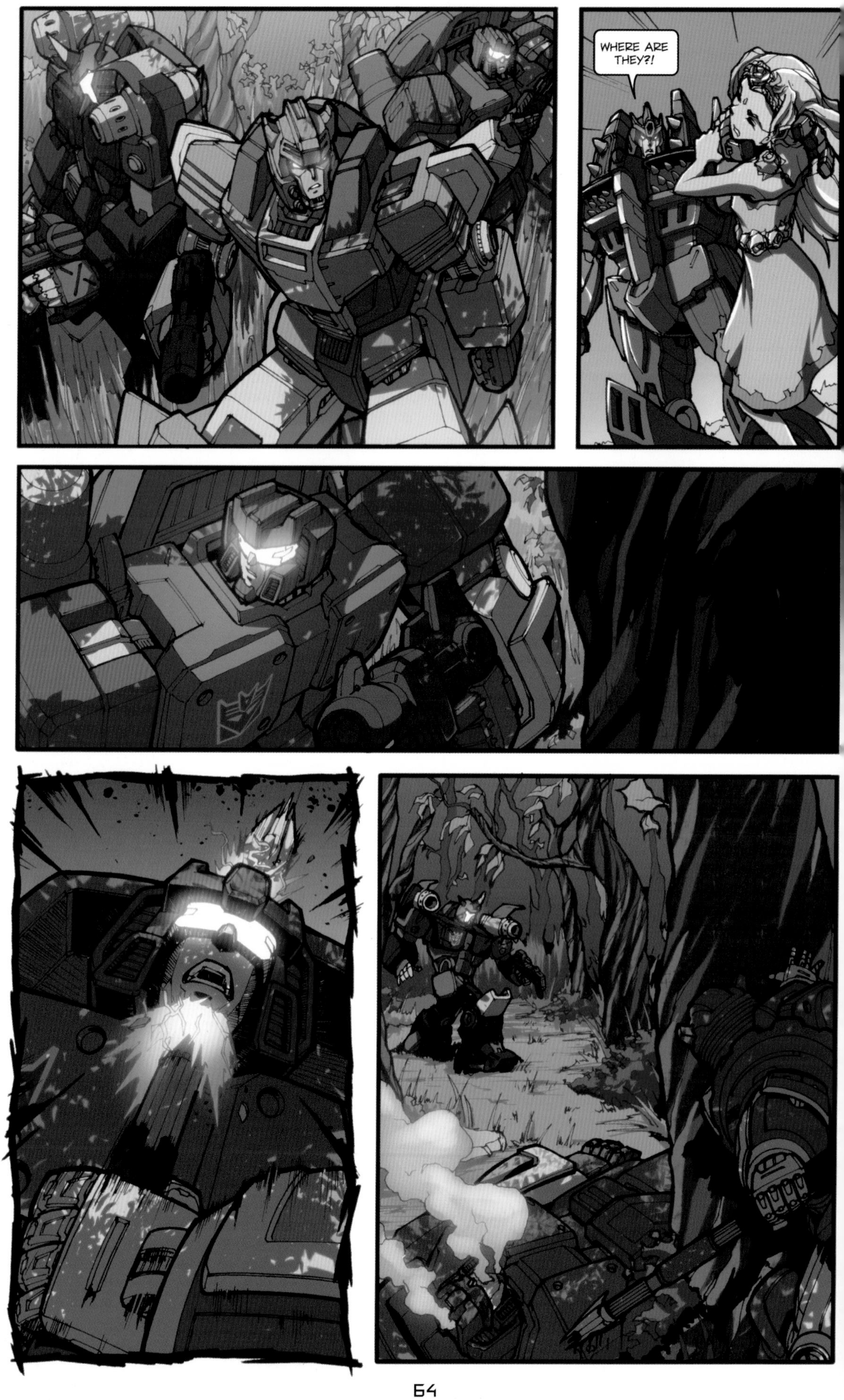
WHERE ARE THEY?!

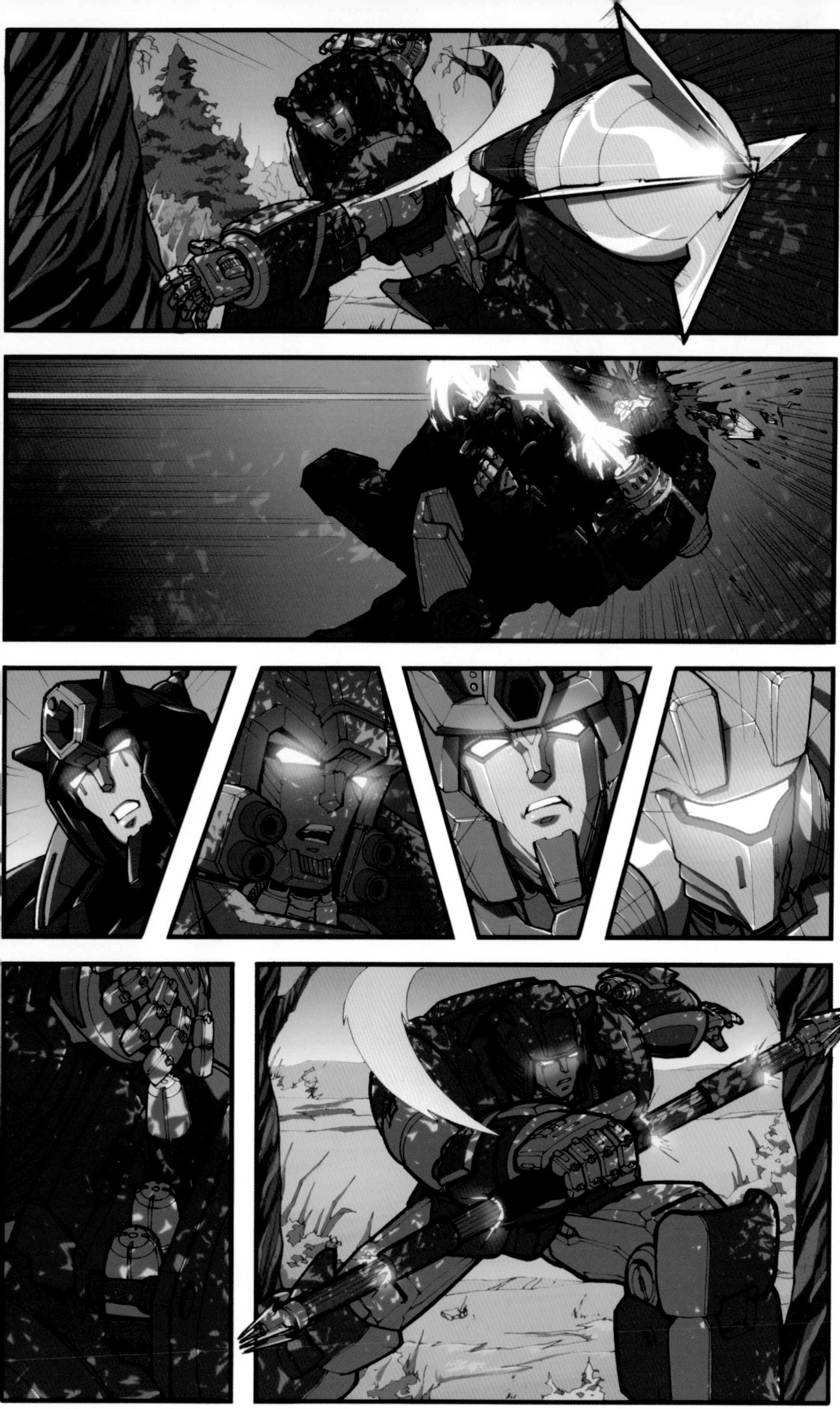

FOUND 'EM?

CALL FOR REINFORCEMENTS.

WE COULD—

DO IT!

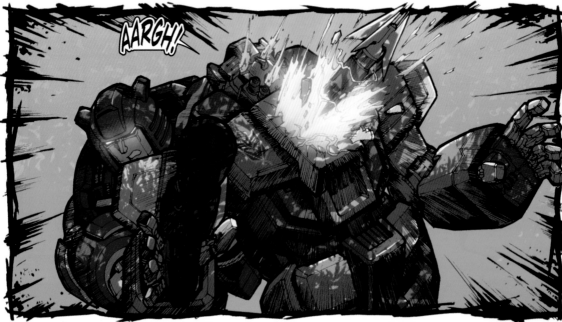

AARGH!

HOW MANY YOU THINK THERE ARE?

NOT SURE. AT LEAST FIVE.

PLEASE—DON'T. DON'T HURT HIM. PLEASE—

WHAT?

HE WILL NOT HURT YOU. PLEASE—HE IS PEACEFUL.

"HE"?

HE ONLY WISHES TO FIND HIS FRIENDS AND—

TOLD YOU THEY WERE THE HEROES, DID THEY?

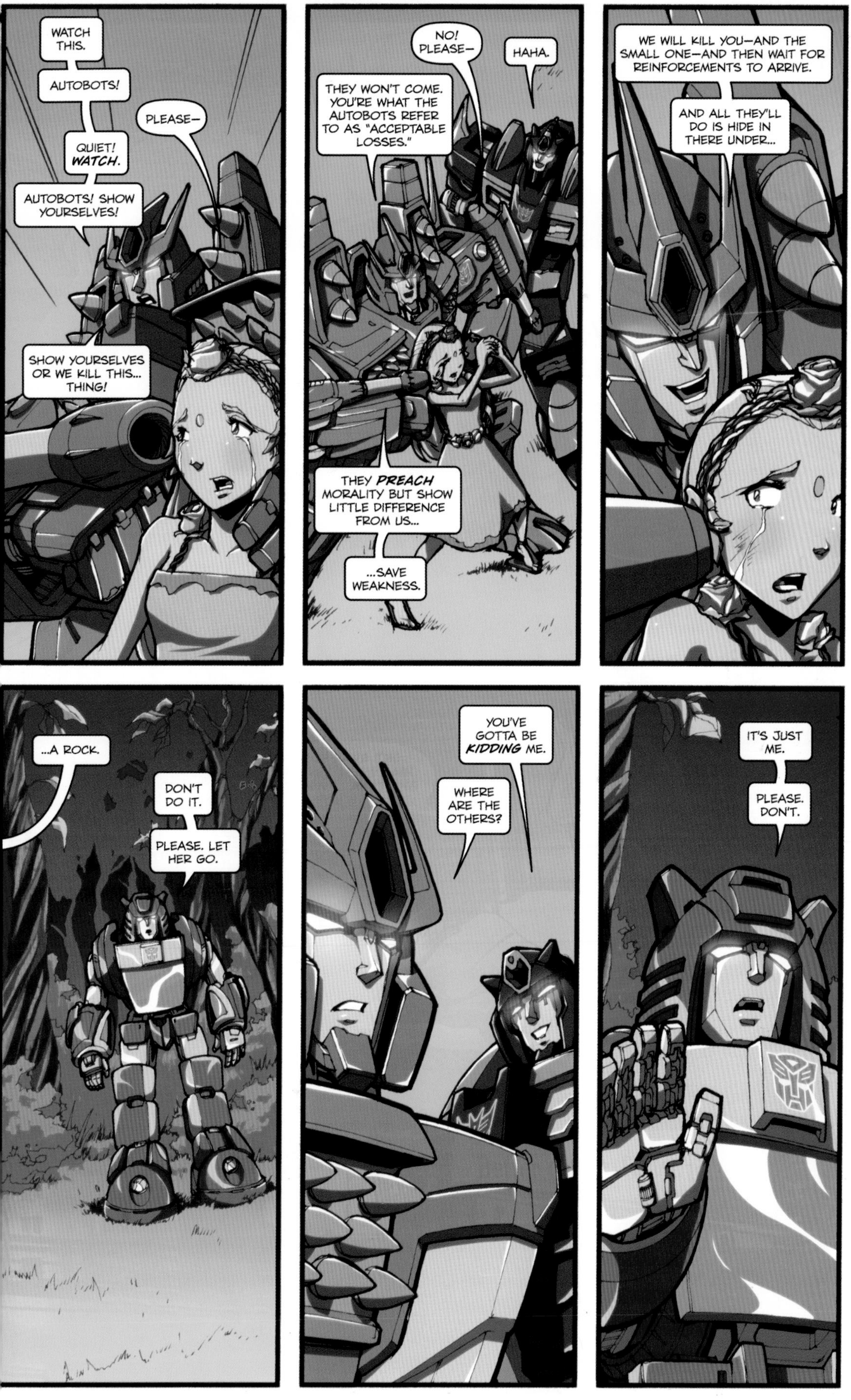
WATCH THIS.
AUTOBOTS!
PLEASE—
QUIET! *WATCH*.
AUTOBOTS! SHOW YOURSELVES!
SHOW YOURSELVES OR WE KILL THIS... THING!
NO! PLEASE—
HAHA.
THEY WON'T COME. YOU'RE WHAT THE AUTOBOTS REFER TO AS "ACCEPTABLE LOSSES."
THEY *PREACH* MORALITY BUT SHOW LITTLE DIFFERENCE FROM US...
...SAVE WEAKNESS.
WE WILL KILL YOU—AND THE SMALL ONE—AND THEN WAIT FOR REINFORCEMENTS TO ARRIVE.
AND ALL THEY'LL DO IS HIDE IN THERE UNDER...
...A ROCK.
DON'T DO IT.
PLEASE. LET HER GO.
YOU'VE GOTTA BE *KIDDING* ME.
WHERE ARE THE OTHERS?
IT'S JUST ME.
PLEASE. DON'T.

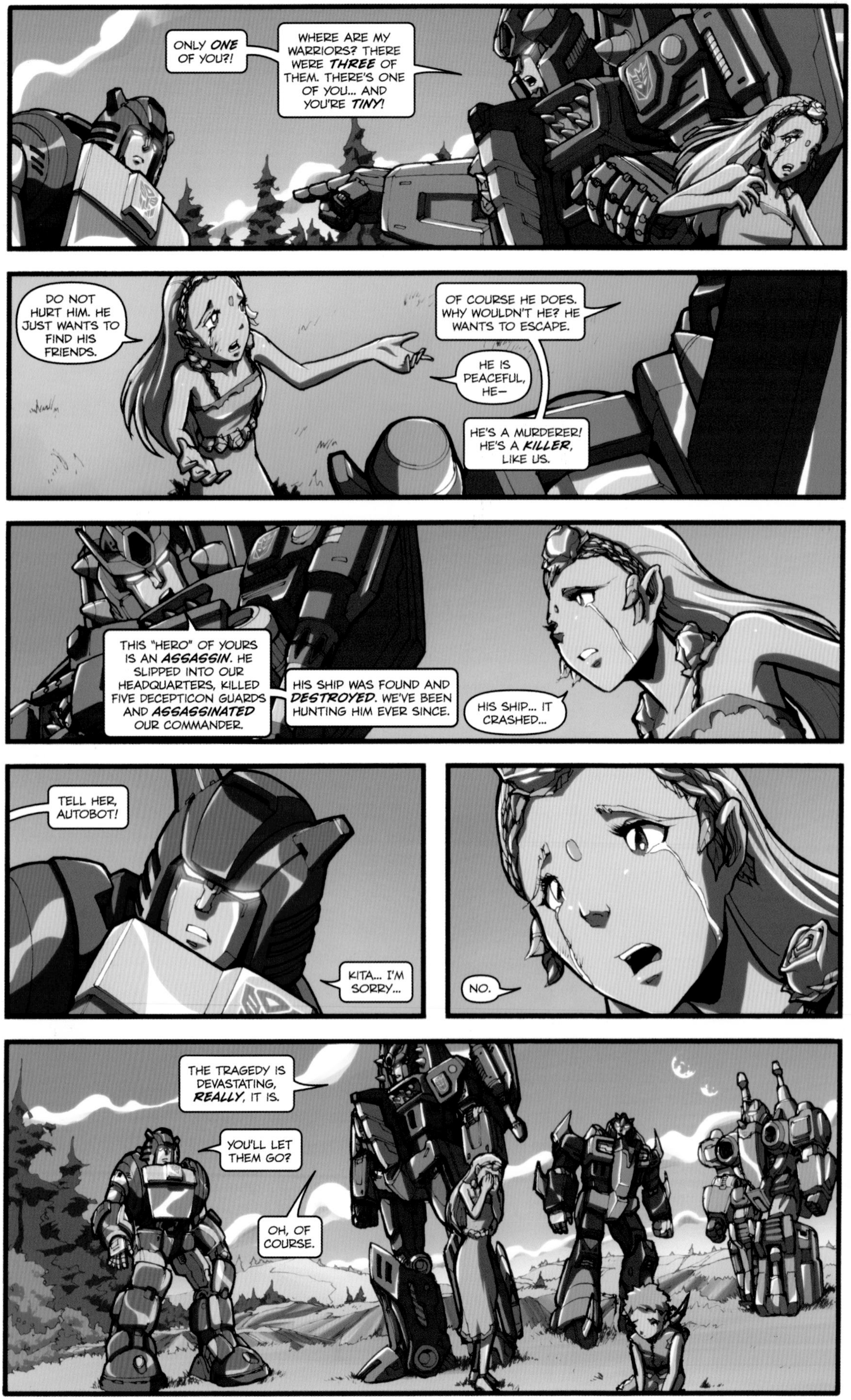
ONLY *ONE* OF YOU?!
WHERE ARE MY WARRIORS? THERE WERE *THREE* OF THEM. THERE'S ONE OF YOU... AND YOU'RE *TINY*!
DO NOT HURT HIM. HE JUST WANTS TO FIND HIS FRIENDS.
OF COURSE HE DOES. WHY WOULDN'T HE? HE WANTS TO ESCAPE.
HE IS PEACEFUL, HE—
HE'S A MURDERER! HE'S A *KILLER*, LIKE US.
THIS "HERO" OF YOURS IS AN *ASSASSIN*. HE SLIPPED INTO OUR HEADQUARTERS, KILLED FIVE DECEPTICON GUARDS AND *ASSASSINATED* OUR COMMANDER.
HIS SHIP WAS FOUND AND *DESTROYED*. WE'VE BEEN HUNTING HIM EVER SINCE.
HIS SHIP... IT CRASHED...
TELL HER, AUTOBOT!
KITA... I'M SORRY...
NO.
THE TRAGEDY IS DEVASTATING, *REALLY*, IT IS.
YOU'LL LET THEM GO?
OH, OF COURSE.

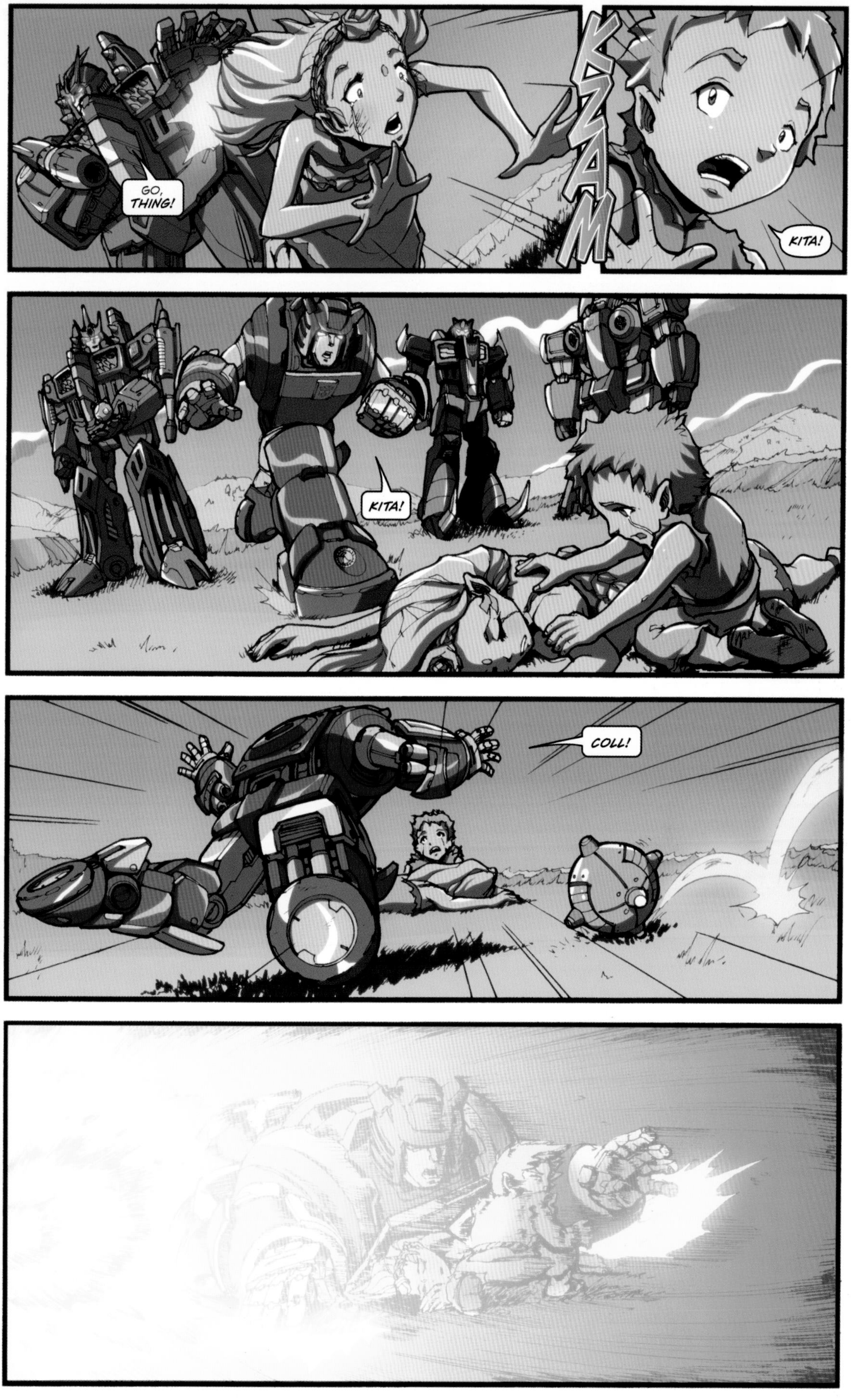
GO, THING!
KZZAM
KITA!
KITA!
COLL!

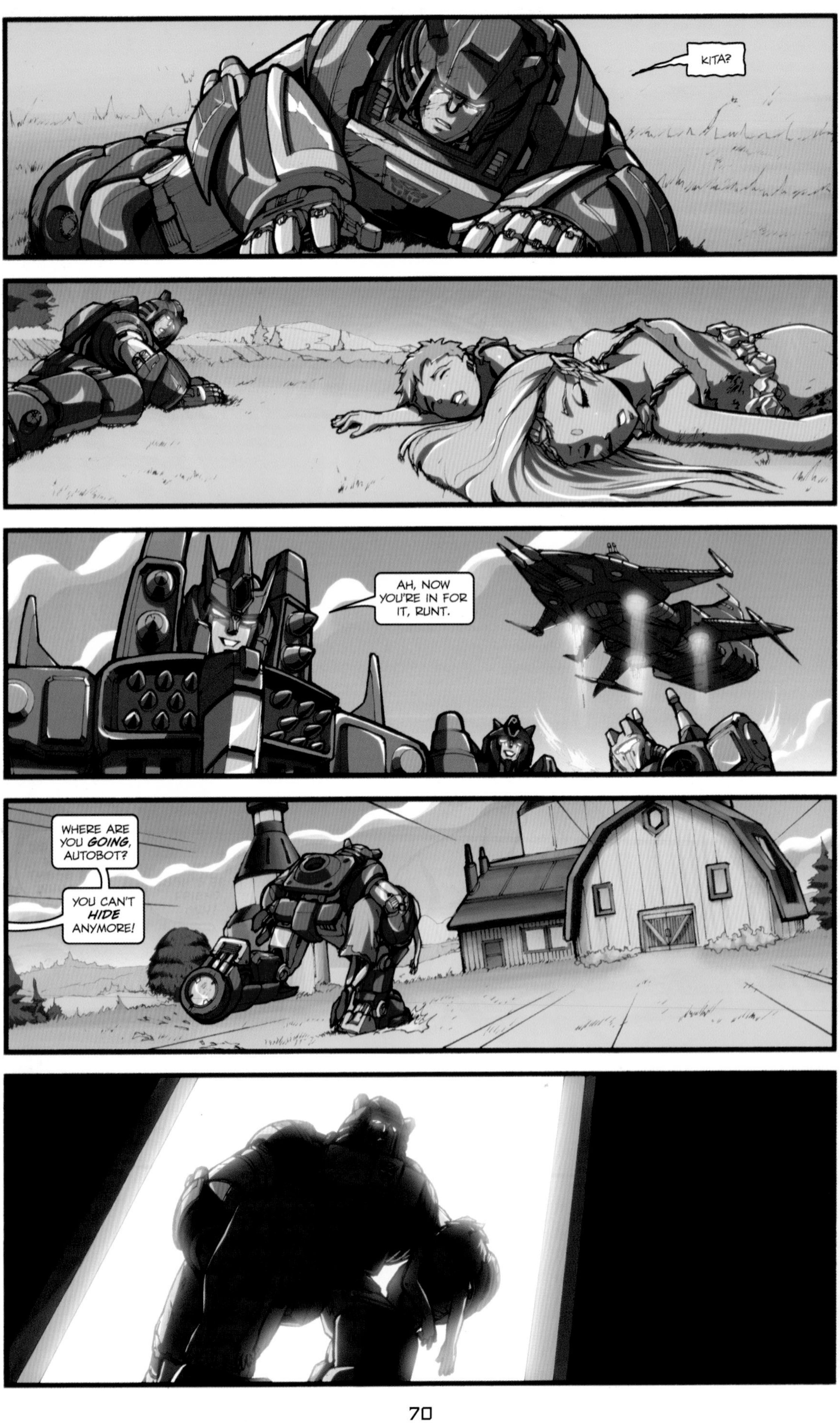
KITA?
AH, NOW YOU'RE IN FOR IT, RUNT.
WHERE ARE YOU *GOING*, AUTOBOT?
YOU CAN'T *HIDE* ANYMORE!

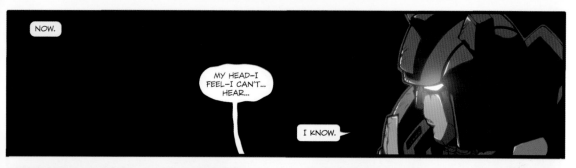

NOW.

MY HEAD—I FEEL—I CAN'T... HEAR...

I KNOW.

I'M—COLL IS HE—WHERE'S—

KITA?

IT'S COLD. I FEEL—IS IT COLD?

I TOLD YOU... I CAN'T FEEL THE COLD.

I...

COLL, STAY WITH KITA.

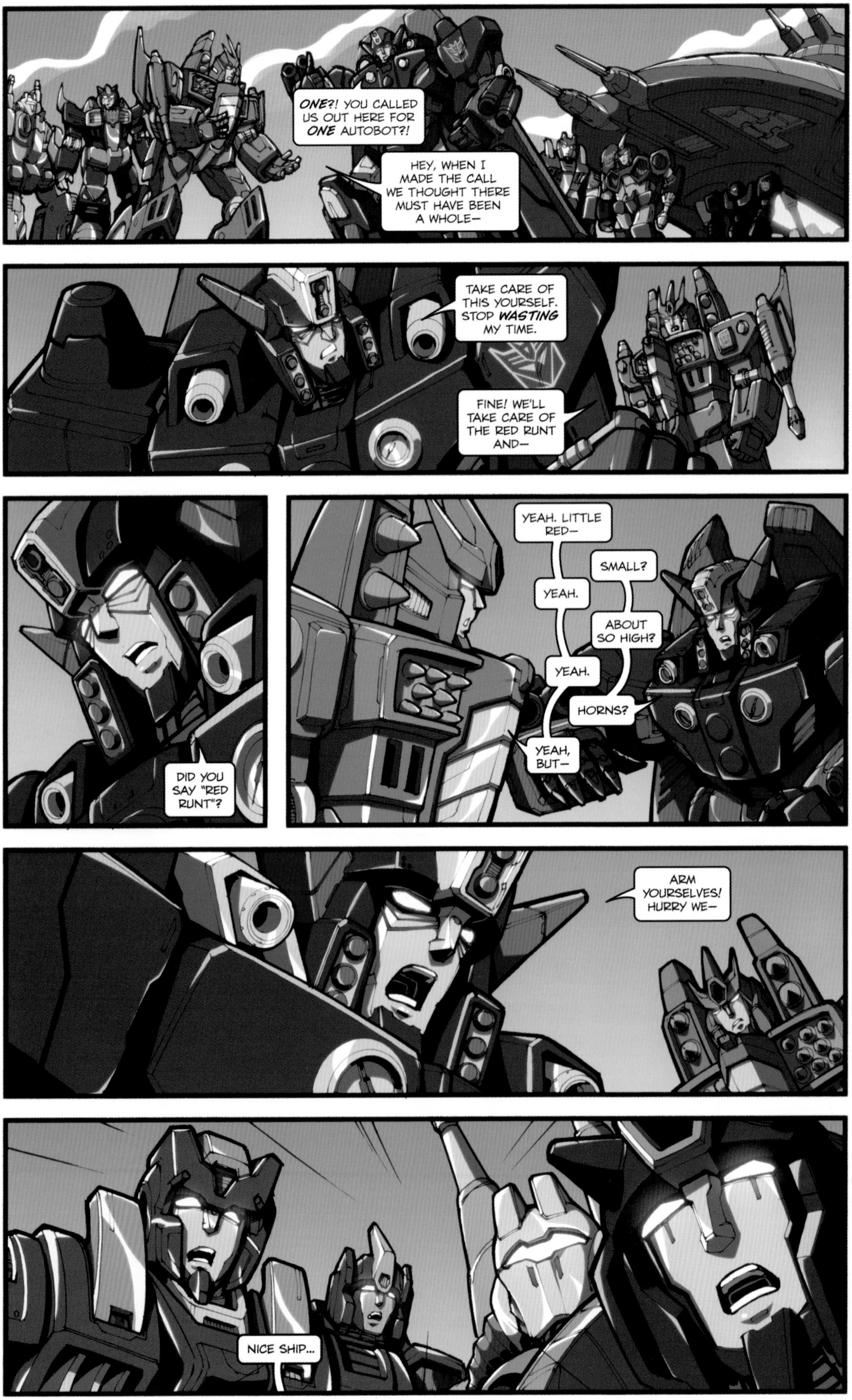
ONE?! YOU CALLED US OUT HERE FOR ONE AUTOBOT?!
HEY, WHEN I MADE THE CALL WE THOUGHT THERE MUST HAVE BEEN A WHOLE—
TAKE CARE OF THIS YOURSELF. STOP WASTING MY TIME.
FINE! WE'LL TAKE CARE OF THE RED RUNT AND—
DID YOU SAY "RED RUNT"?
YEAH. LITTLE RED—
SMALL?
YEAH.
ABOUT SO HIGH?
YEAH.
HORNS?
YEAH, BUT—
ARM YOURSELVES! HURRY WE—
NICE SHIP...

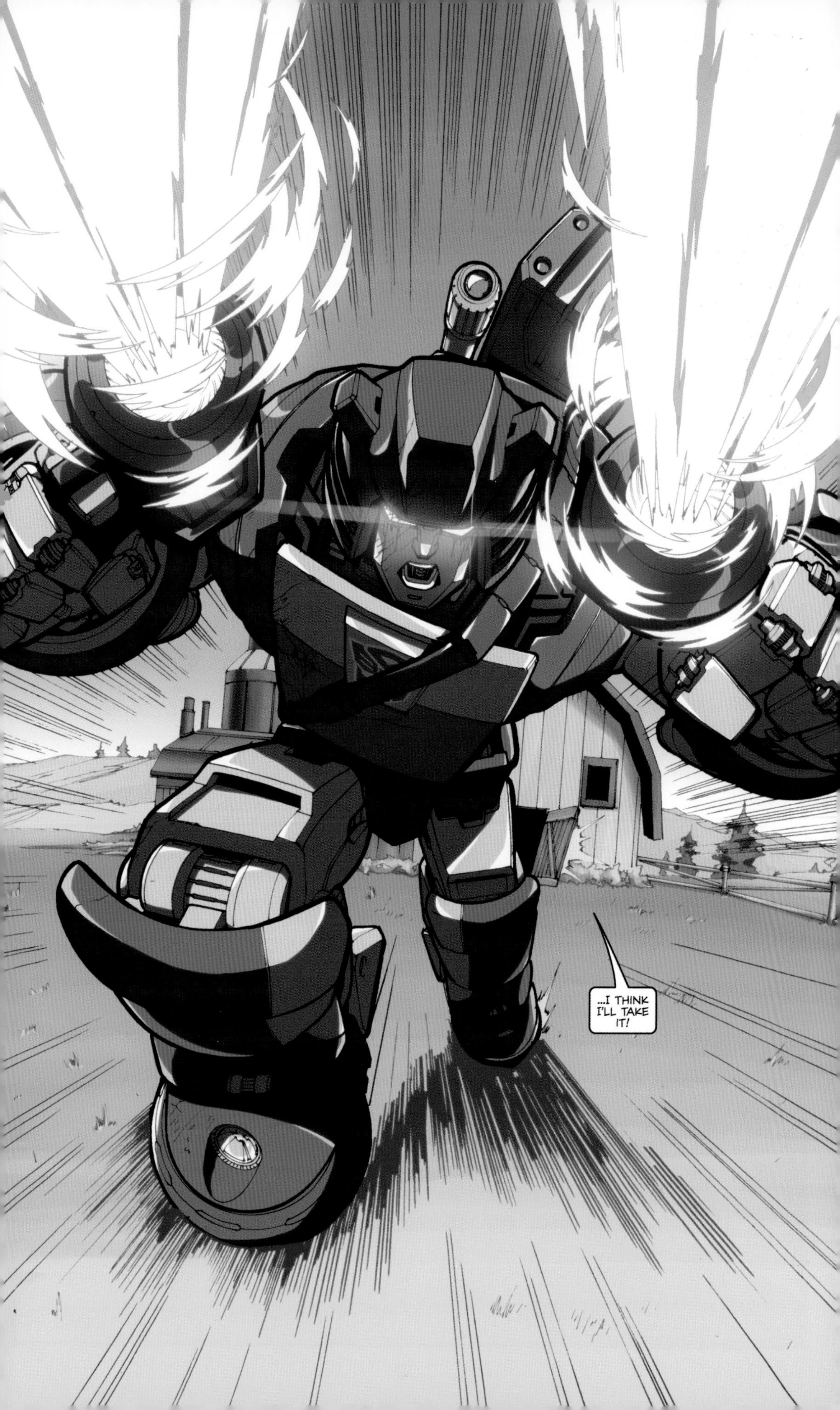
...I THINK I'LL TAKE IT!

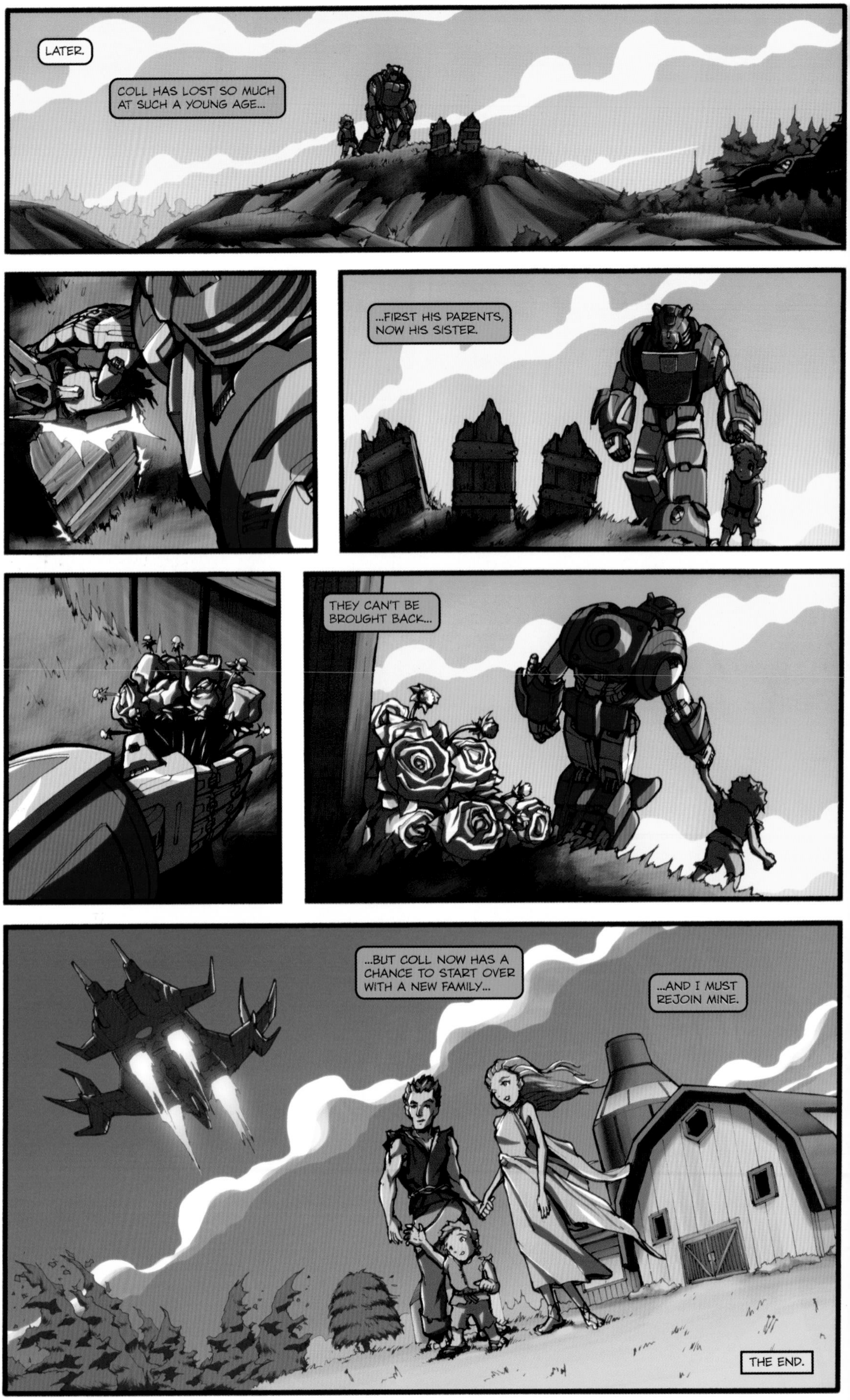
LATER.
COLL HAS LOST SO MUCH AT SUCH A YOUNG AGE...
...FIRST HIS PARENTS, NOW HIS SISTER.
THEY CAN'T BE BROUGHT BACK...
...BUT COLL NOW HAS A CHANCE TO START OVER WITH A NEW FAMILY...
...AND I MUST REJOIN MINE.
THE END.

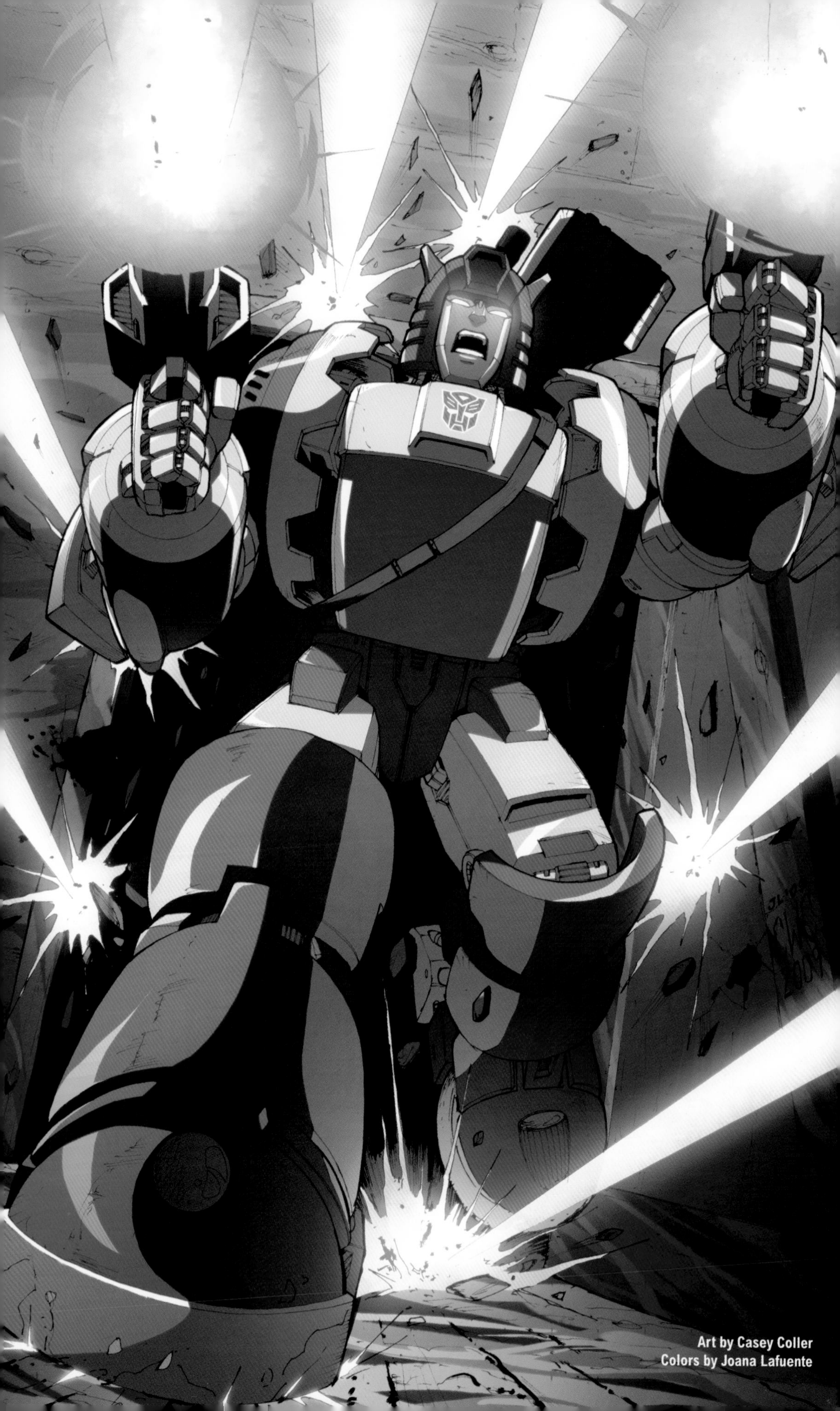

Art by Casey Coller
Colors by Joana Lafuente

DRIFT

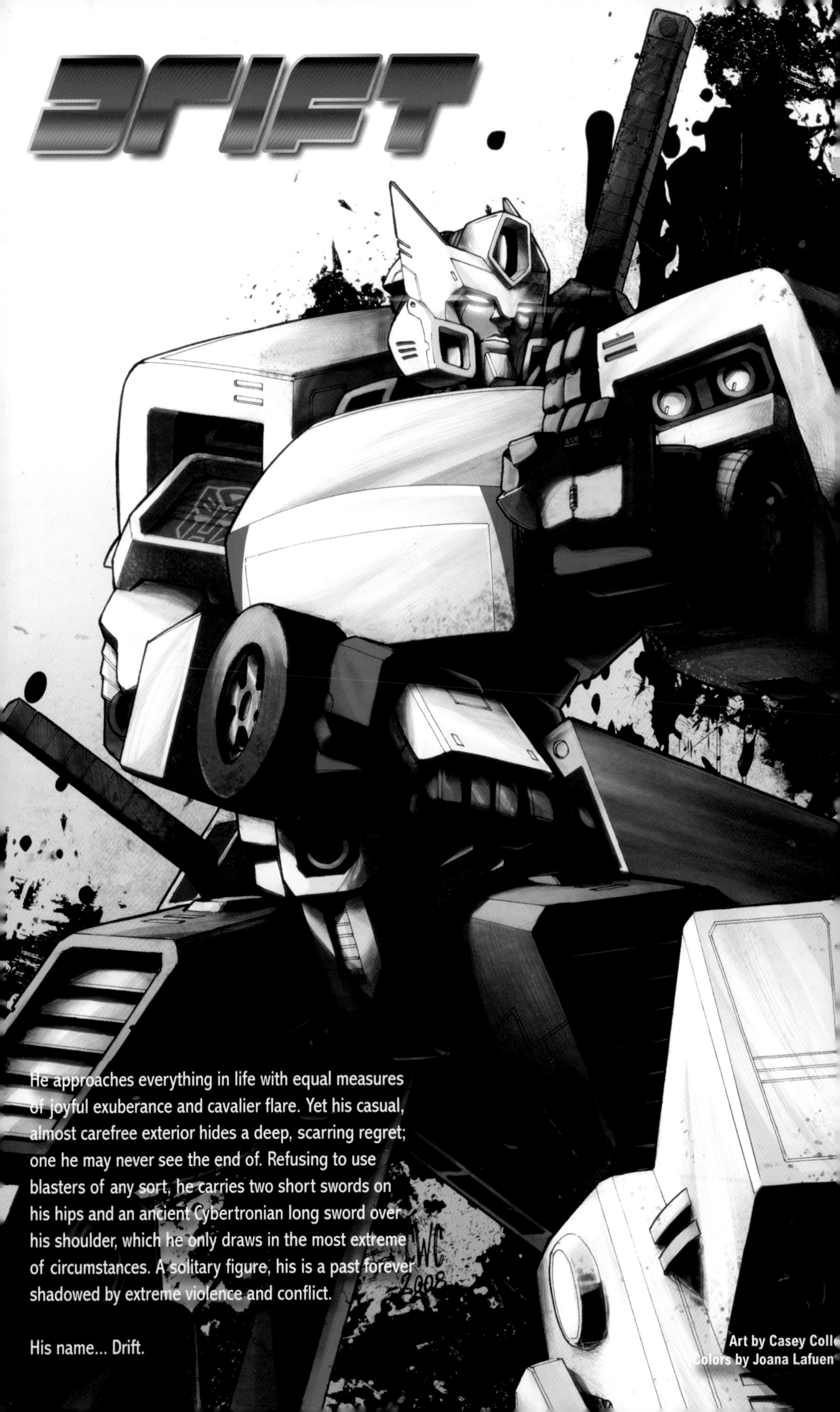

He approaches everything in life with equal measures of joyful exuberance and cavalier flare. Yet his casual, almost carefree exterior hides a deep, scarring regret; one he may never see the end of. Refusing to use blasters of any sort, he carries two short swords on his hips and an ancient Cybertronian long sword over his shoulder, which he only draws in the most extreme of circumstances. A solitary figure, his is a past forever shadowed by extreme violence and conflict.

His name... Drift.

Art by Casey Coll
Colors by Joana Lafuen

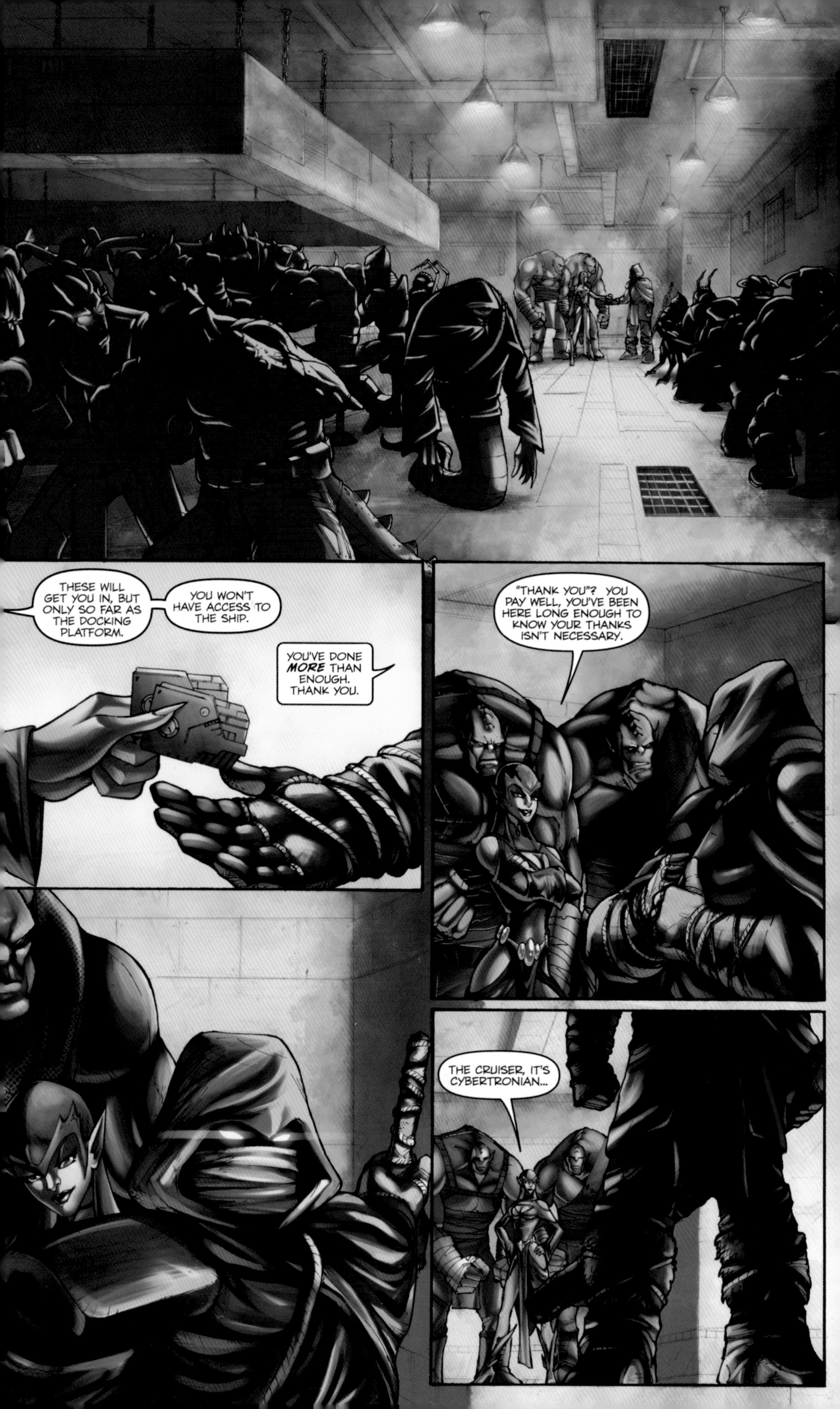
THESE WILL GET YOU IN, BUT ONLY SO FAR AS THE DOCKING PLATFORM.
YOU WON'T HAVE ACCESS TO THE SHIP.
YOU'VE DONE *MORE* THAN ENOUGH. THANK YOU.
"THANK YOU"? YOU PAY WELL, YOU'VE BEEN HERE LONG ENOUGH TO KNOW YOUR THANKS ISN'T NECESSARY.
THE CRUISER, IT'S CYBERTRONIAN...

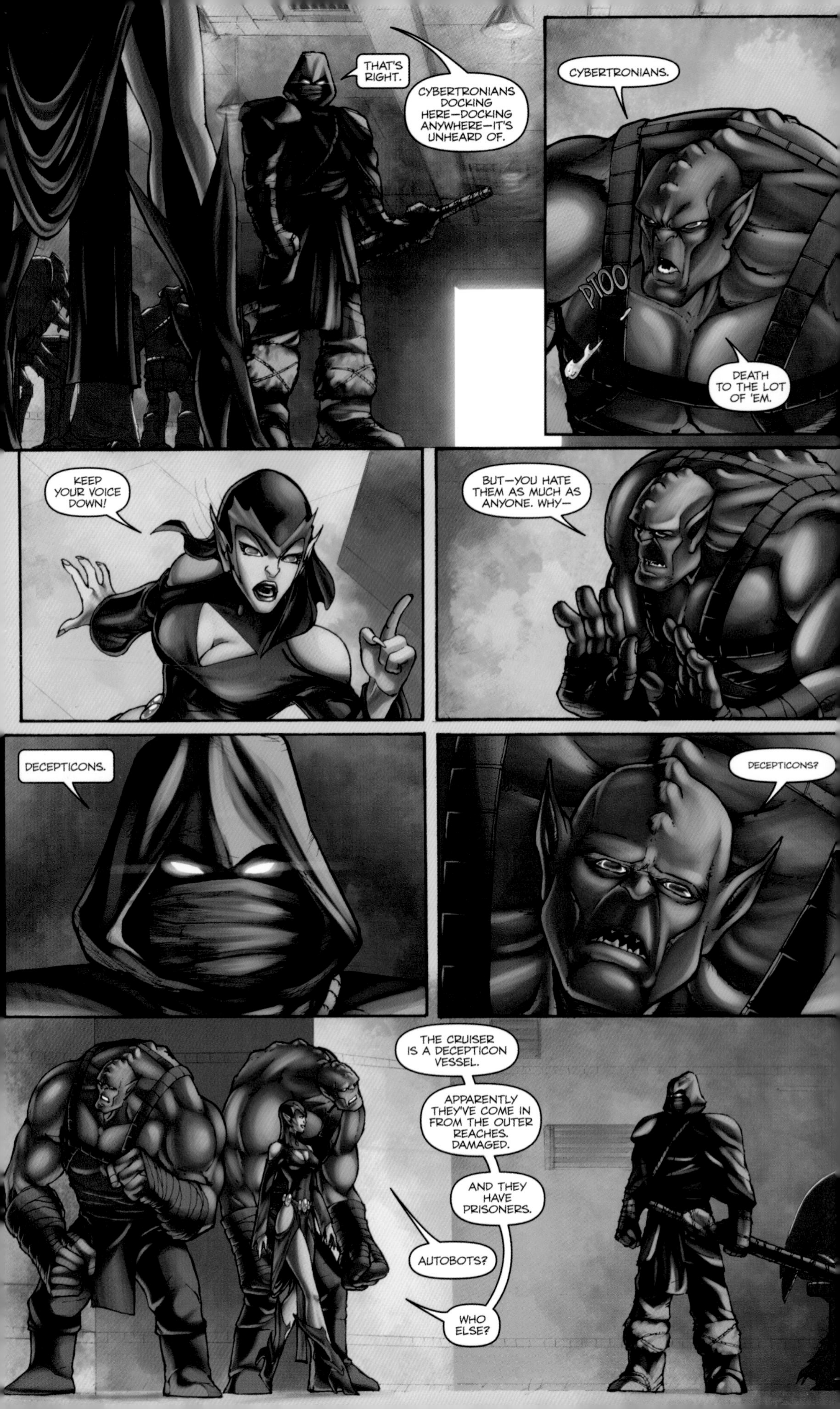
THAT'S RIGHT.
CYBERTRONIANS DOCKING HERE—DOCKING ANYWHERE—IT'S UNHEARD OF.
CYBERTRONIANS.
PTOO
DEATH TO THE LOT OF 'EM.
KEEP YOUR VOICE DOWN!
BUT—YOU HATE THEM AS MUCH AS ANYONE. WHY—
DECEPTICONS.
DECEPTICONS?
THE CRUISER IS A DECEPTICON VESSEL.
APPARENTLY THEY'VE COME IN FROM THE OUTER REACHES. DAMAGED.
AND THEY HAVE PRISONERS.
AUTOBOTS?
WHO ELSE?

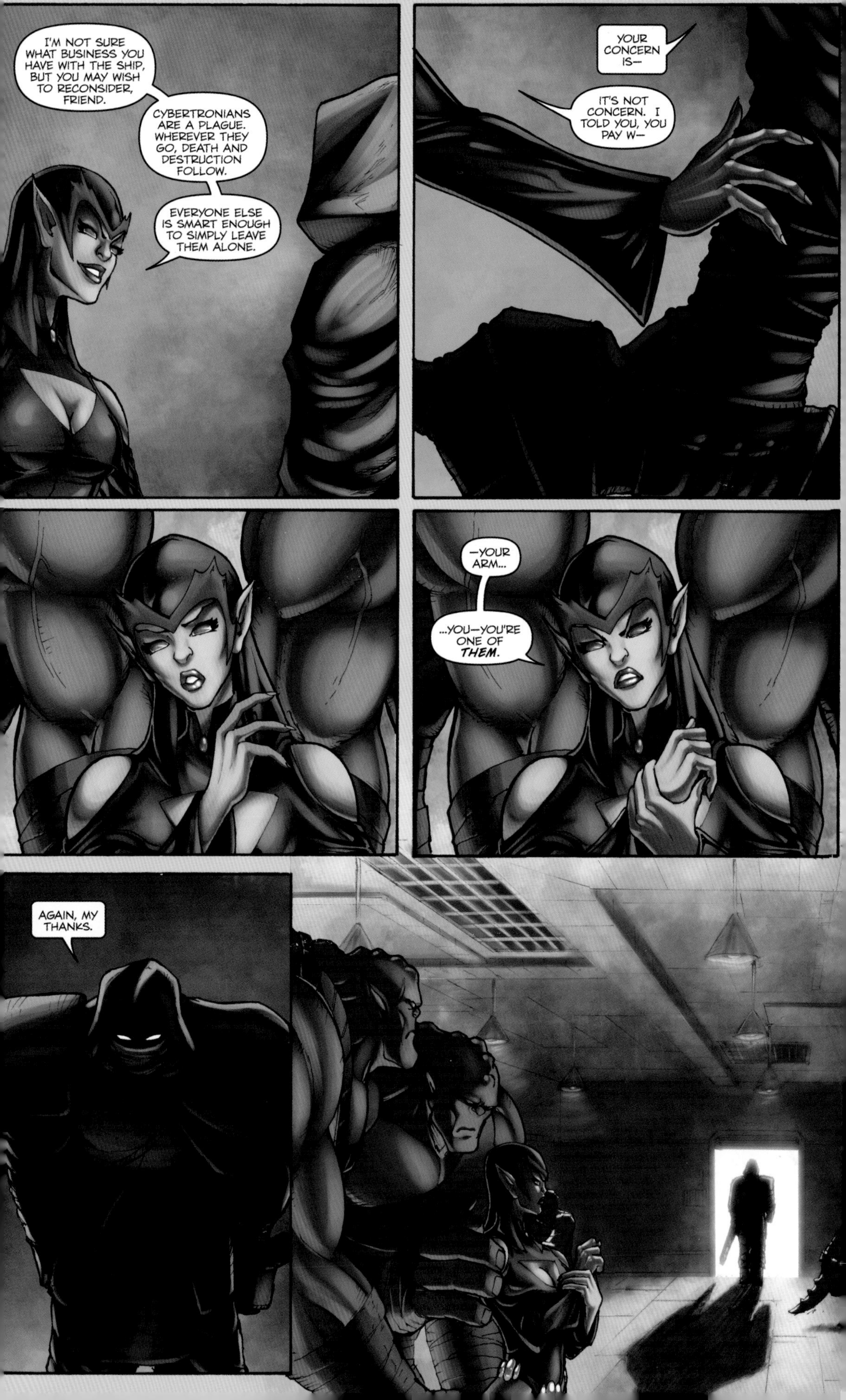
I'M NOT SURE WHAT BUSINESS YOU HAVE WITH THE SHIP, BUT YOU MAY WISH TO RECONSIDER, FRIEND.
CYBERTRONIANS ARE A PLAGUE. WHEREVER THEY GO, DEATH AND DESTRUCTION FOLLOW.
EVERYONE ELSE IS SMART ENOUGH TO SIMPLY LEAVE THEM ALONE.
YOUR CONCERN IS—
IT'S NOT CONCERN. I TOLD YOU, YOU PAY W—
—YOUR ARM...
...YOU—YOU'RE ONE OF *THEM*.
AGAIN, MY THANKS.

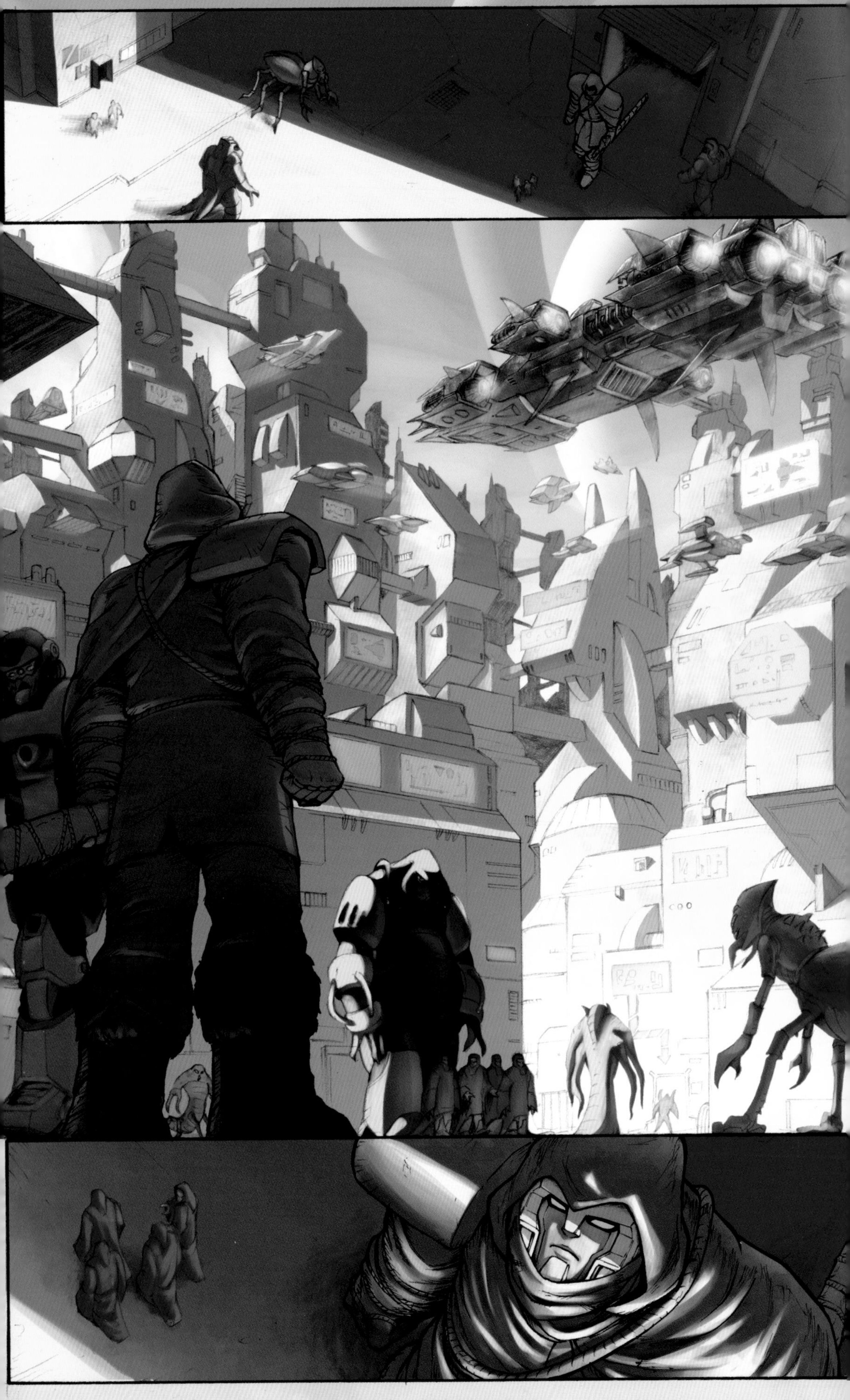

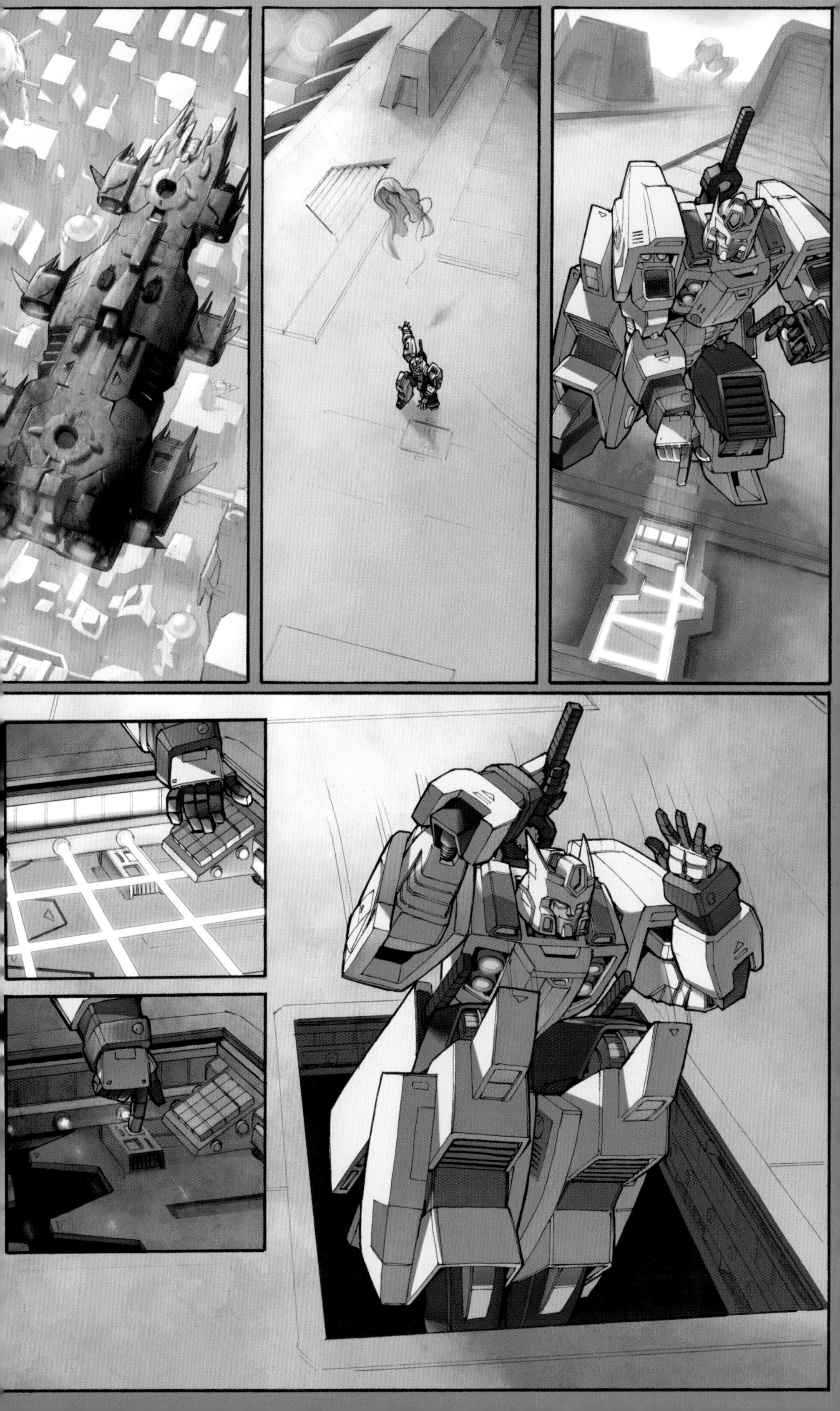

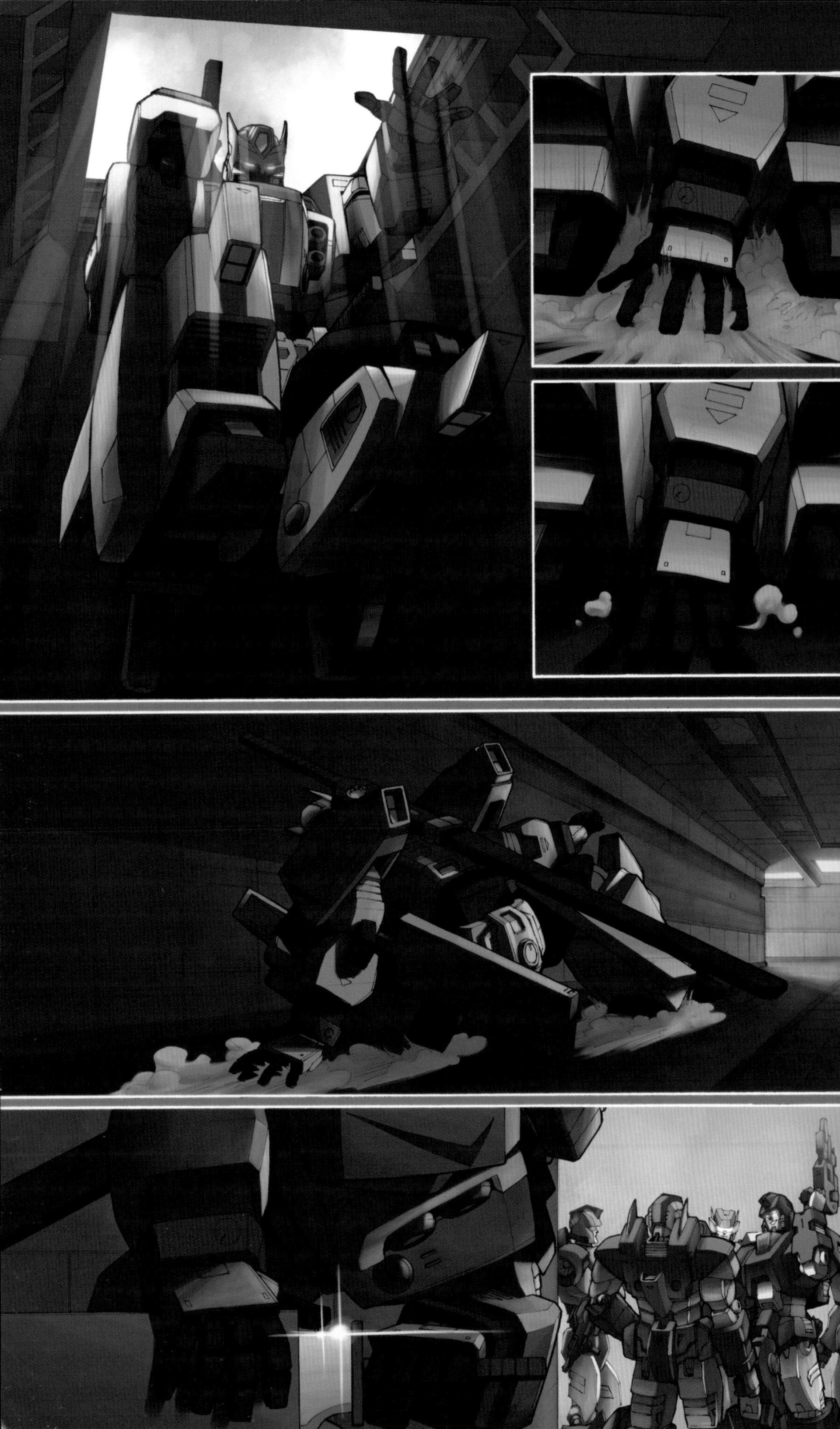

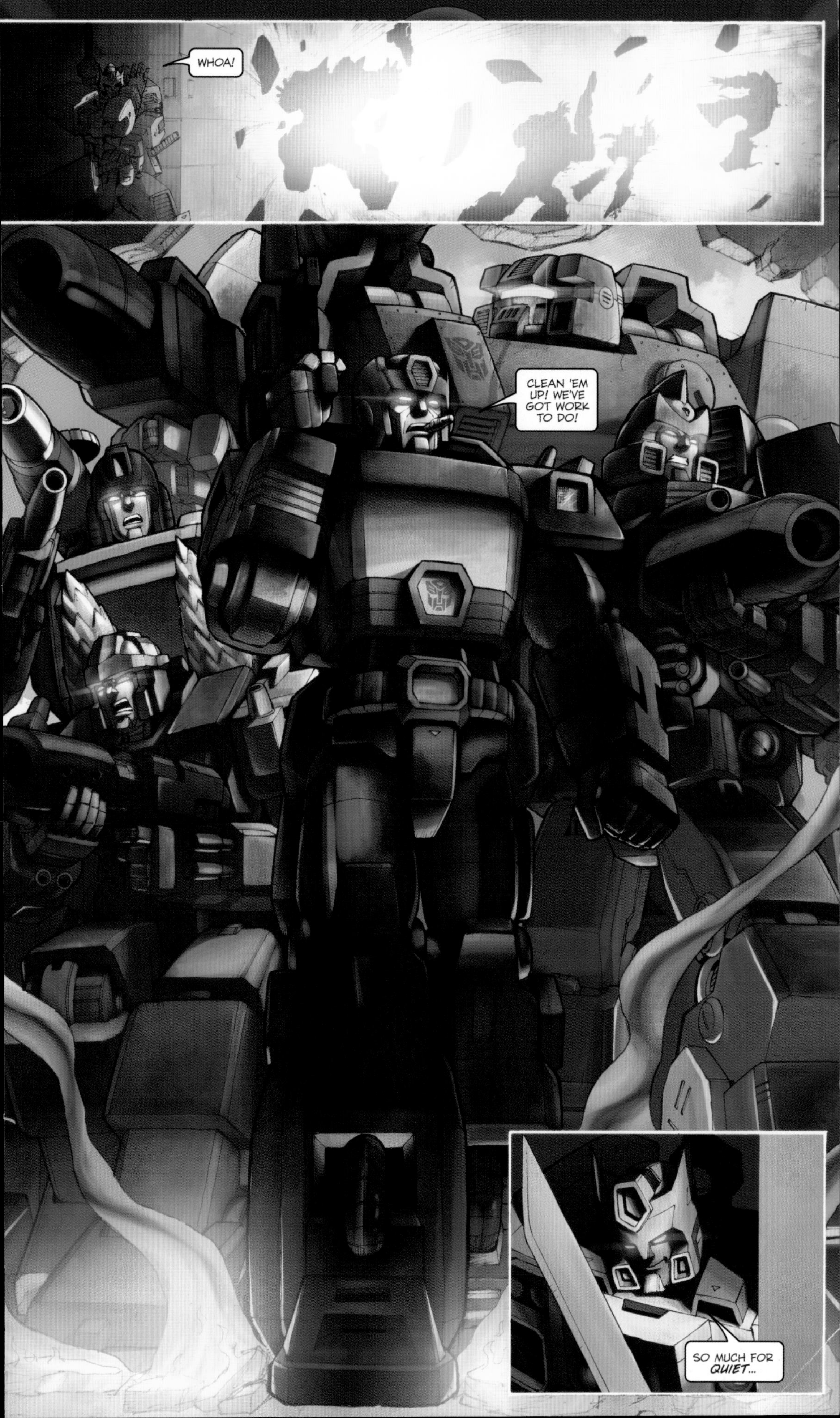
WHOA!
CLEAN 'EM UP! WE'VE GOT WORK TO DO!
SO MUCH FOR *QUIET*...

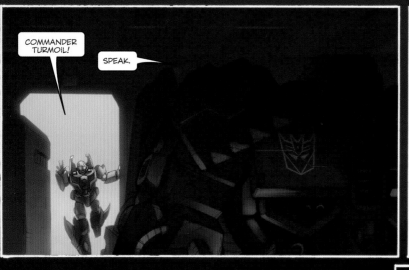

COMMANDER TURMOIL!

SPEAK.

COMMANDER, THE SHIP HAS BEEN *BREACHED!*

BREACHED?! WHO *DARES*?!

A SMALL ASSAULT FORCE.

OUR SENSORS PICKED THEM UP?

NOT EXACTLY.

THE GROUP JUST—WELL—THEY JUST BLEW A HOLE IN THE SIDE OF THE SHIP.

KUP.

"WHO'S *THAT* GUY?

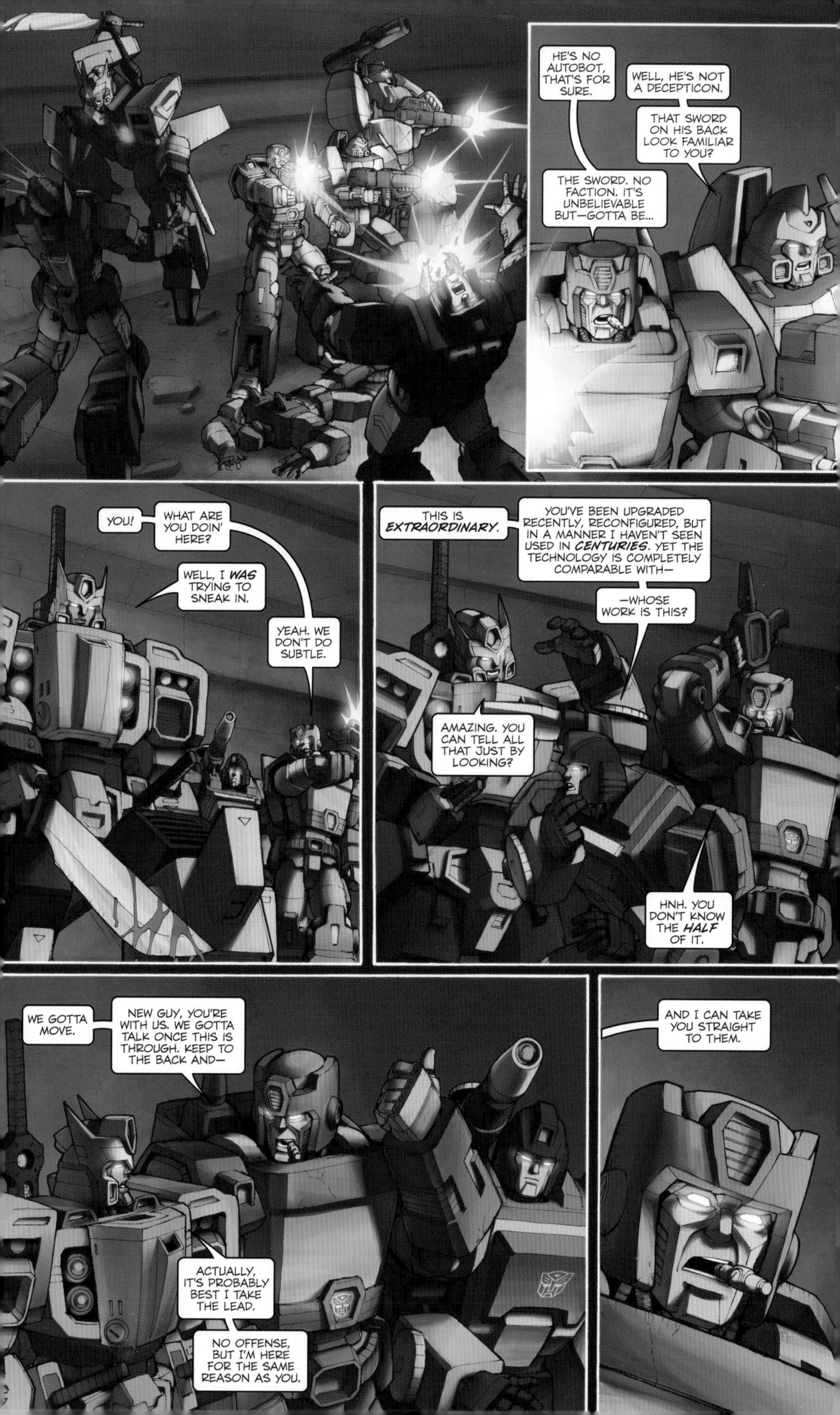
HE'S NO AUTOBOT, THAT'S FOR SURE.
WELL, HE'S NOT A DECEPTICON.
THAT SWORD ON HIS BACK LOOK FAMILIAR TO YOU?
THE SWORD. NO FACTION. IT'S UNBELIEVABLE BUT—GOTTA BE...
YOU!
WHAT ARE YOU DOIN' HERE?
WELL, I *WAS* TRYING TO SNEAK IN.
YEAH. WE DON'T DO SUBTLE.
THIS IS *EXTRAORDINARY*.
YOU'VE BEEN UPGRADED RECENTLY, RECONFIGURED, BUT IN A MANNER I HAVEN'T SEEN USED IN *CENTURIES*. YET THE TECHNOLOGY IS COMPLETELY COMPARABLE WITH—
—WHOSE WORK IS THIS?
AMAZING. YOU CAN TELL ALL THAT JUST BY LOOKING?
HNH. YOU DON'T KNOW THE *HALF* OF IT.
WE GOTTA MOVE.
NEW GUY, YOU'RE WITH US. WE GOTTA TALK ONCE THIS IS THROUGH. KEEP TO THE BACK AND—
ACTUALLY, IT'S PROBABLY BEST I TAKE THE LEAD.
NO OFFENSE, BUT I'M HERE FOR THE SAME REASON AS YOU.
AND I CAN TAKE YOU STRAIGHT TO THEM.

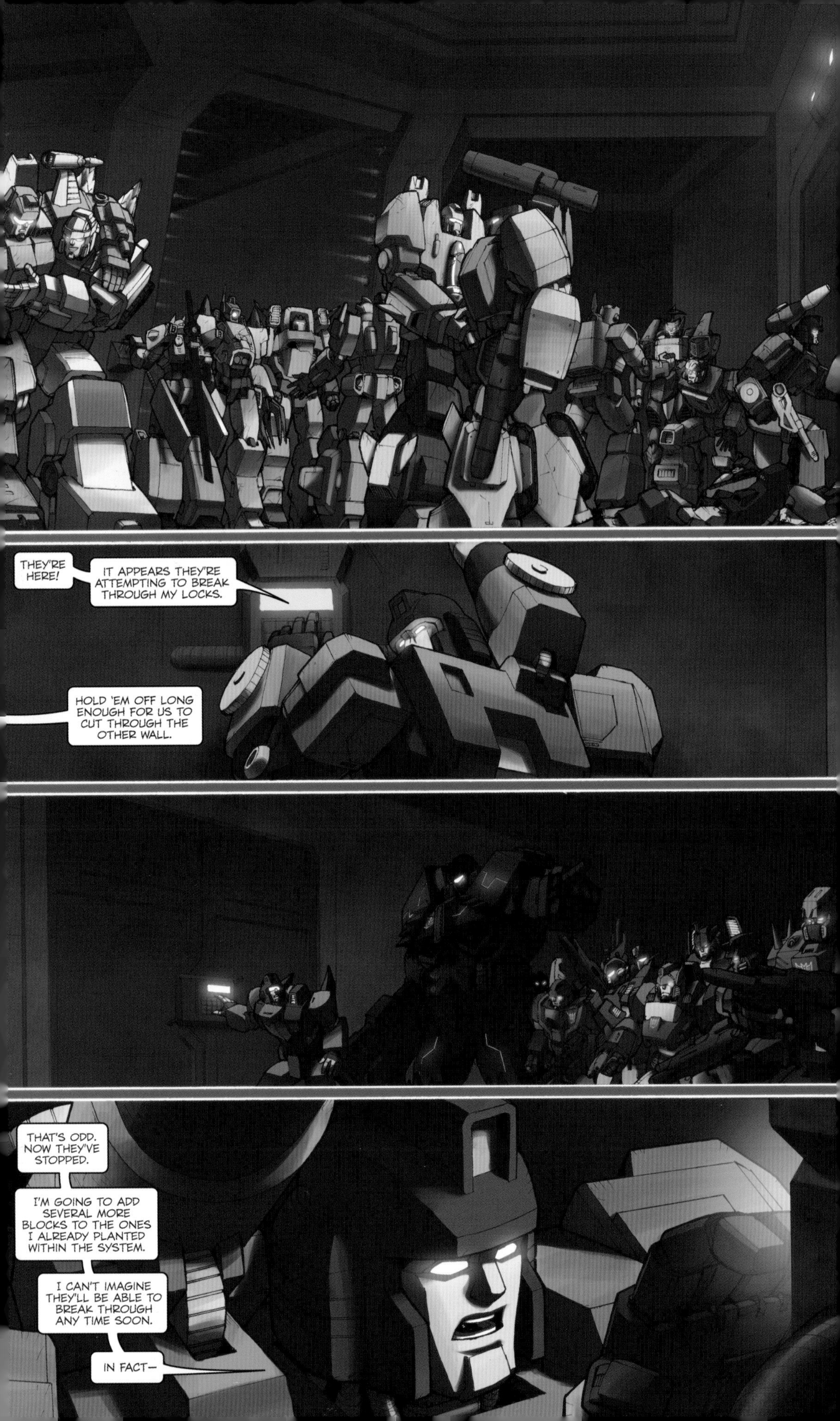
THEY'RE HERE!
IT APPEARS THEY'RE ATTEMPTING TO BREAK THROUGH MY LOCKS.
HOLD 'EM OFF LONG ENOUGH FOR US TO CUT THROUGH THE OTHER WALL.
THAT'S ODD. NOW THEY'VE STOPPED.
I'M GOING TO ADD SEVERAL MORE BLOCKS TO THE ONES I ALREADY PLANTED WITHIN THE SYSTEM.
I CAN'T IMAGINE THEY'LL BE ABLE TO BREAK THROUGH ANY TIME SOON.
IN FACT—

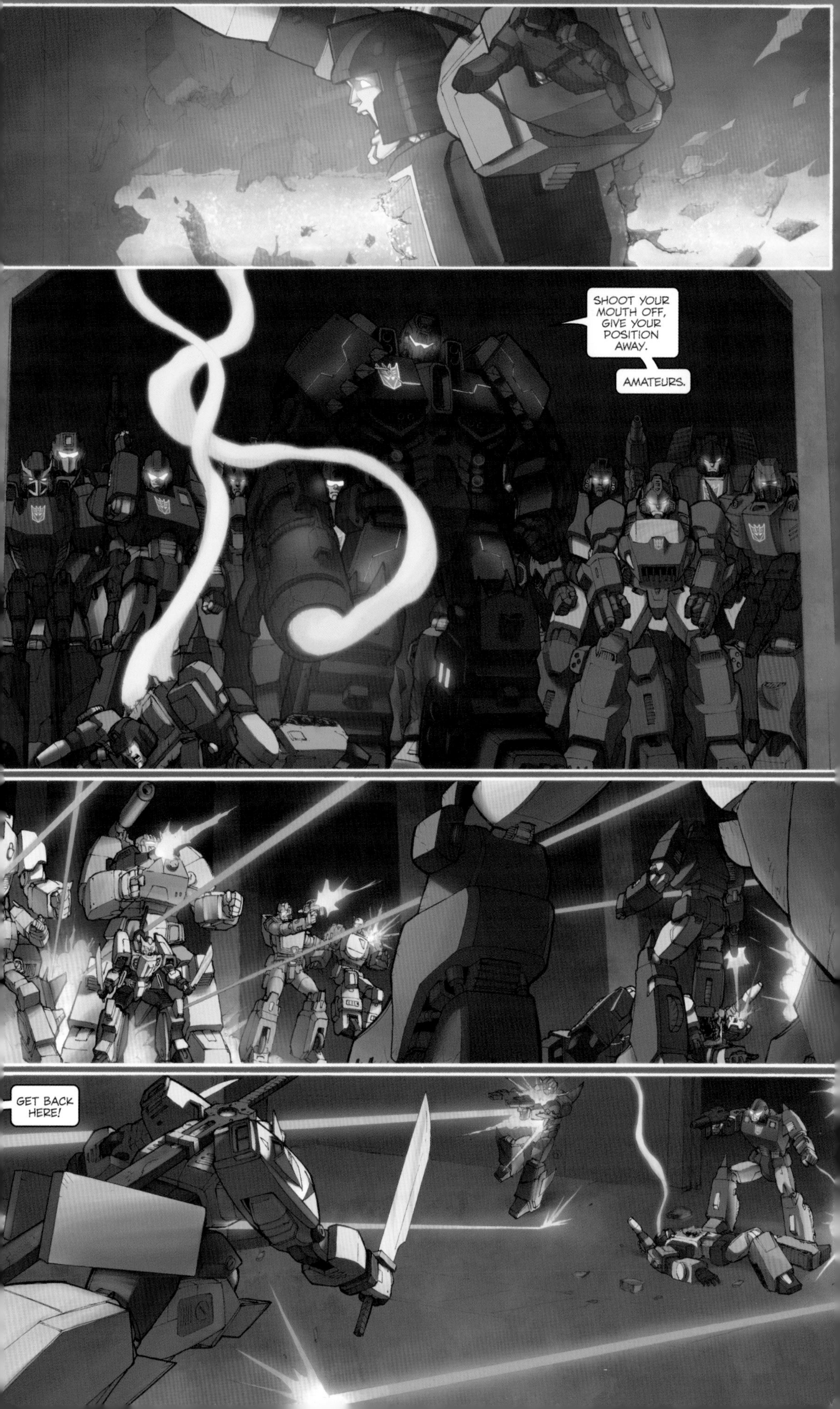
SHOOT YOUR MOUTH OFF, GIVE YOUR POSITION AWAY.
AMATEURS.
GET BACK HERE!

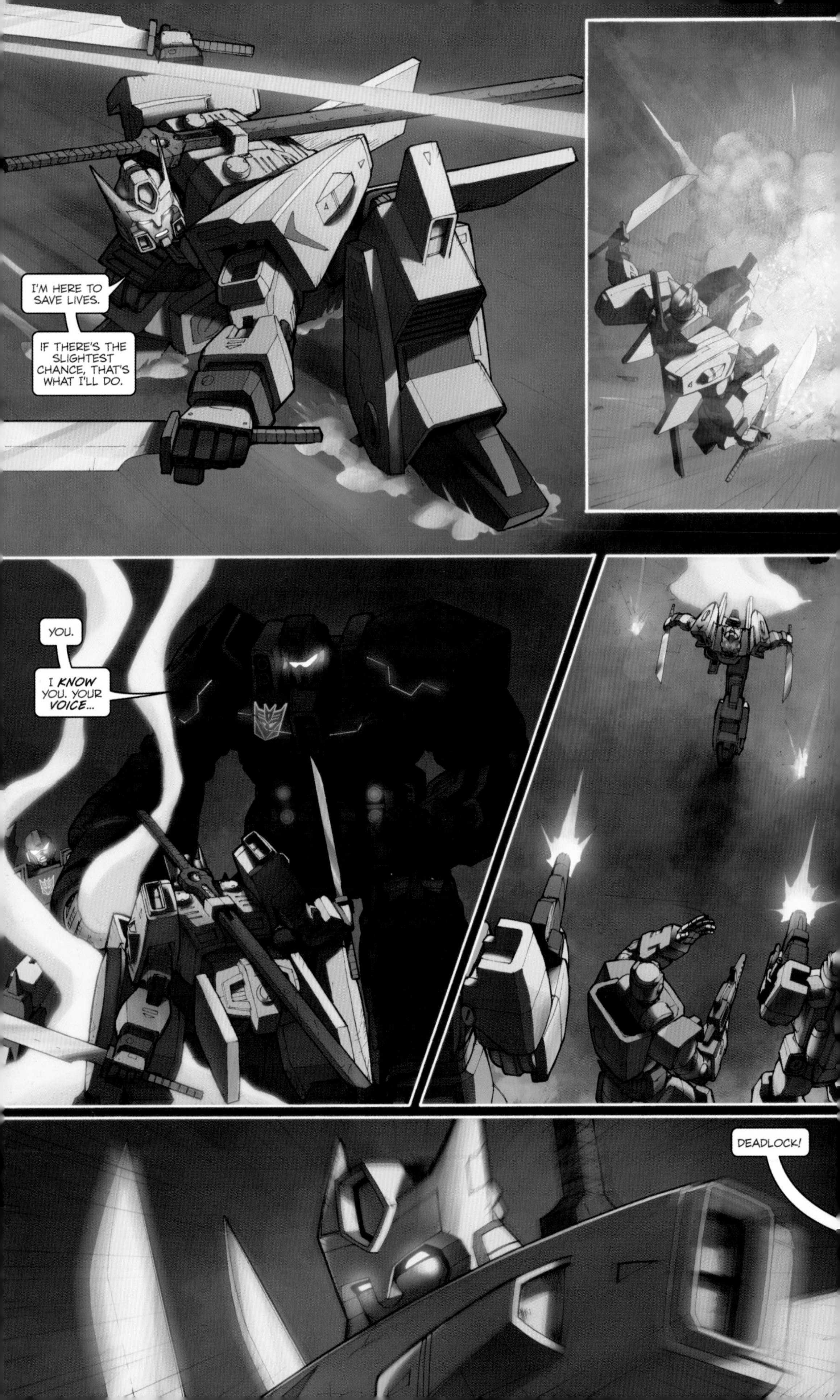
I'M HERE TO SAVE LIVES.
IF THERE'S THE SLIGHTEST CHANCE, THAT'S WHAT I'LL DO.
YOU.
I *KNOW* YOU. YOUR *VOICE*...
DEADLOCK!

DECEPTICON TRAITOR!
TZAKK

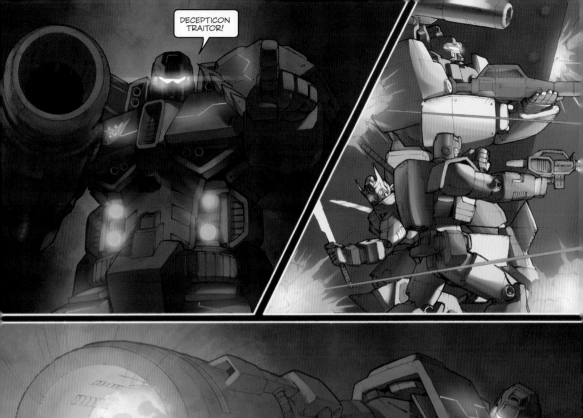

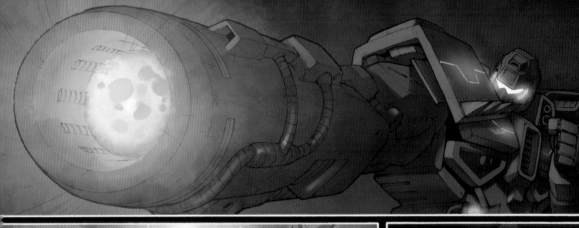

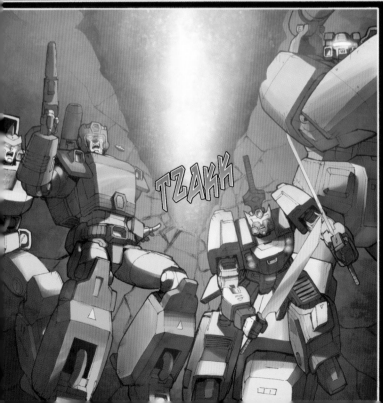

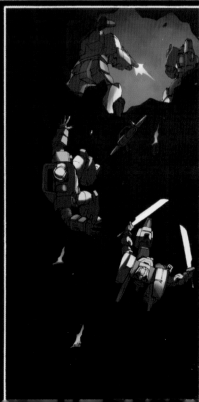

SO YOU **ARE** A DECEPTICON.

DEADLOCK.

NO.

I DON'T GO BY THAT NAME ANYMORE.

THAT'S HELPFUL, CONSIDERING DEADLOCK HAPPENED TO HAVE SLAUGHTERED QUITE A FEW AUTOBOTS.

LONG TIME AGO—SO LONG AGO IT'S BECOME MUDDLED AS TO THE OUTCOME—THERE WAS A THIRD FACTION.

WELL, MORE OF A FACTION **AGAINST** FACTIONS.

A GROUP FORMED ON CYBERTRON, A BIG ONE, A GROUP THAT REFUSED TO HAVE ANY PART OF THE GREAT WAR.

REFUSED TO TAKE SIDES. UP AND LEFT.

NO ONE'S SURE WHAT HAPPENED TO 'EM.

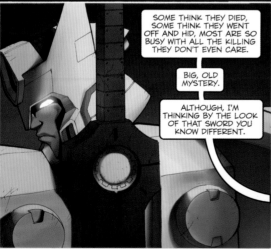

SOME THINK THEY DIED, SOME THINK THEY WENT OFF AND HID, MOST ARE SO BUSY WITH ALL THE KILLING THEY DON'T EVEN CARE.

BIG, OLD MYSTERY.

ALTHOUGH, I'M THINKING BY THE LOOK OF THAT SWORD YOU KNOW DIFFERENT.

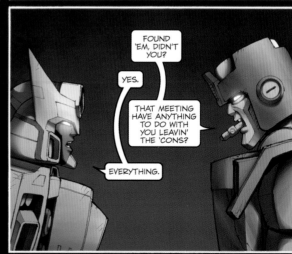

FOUND 'EM, DIDN'T YOU?

YES.

THAT MEETING HAVE ANYTHING TO DO WITH YOU LEAVIN' THE 'CONS?

EVERYTHING.

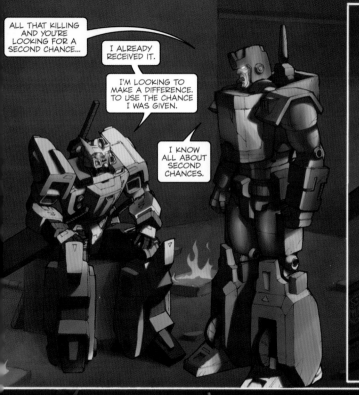

ALL THAT KILLING AND YOU'RE LOOKING FOR A SECOND CHANCE...

I ALREADY RECEIVED IT.

I'M LOOKING TO MAKE A DIFFERENCE. TO USE THE CHANCE I WAS GIVEN.

I KNOW ALL ABOUT SECOND CHANCES.

THAT 'BOT YOU TRIED TO SAVE IN THERE—PERCEPTOR—HE WOULDN'T NORMALLY BE ALONG. NOT THE TYPE.

HE WAS KEEPIN' AN EYE OUT, FOR ME. DESIGNED THIS NEW BODY, FIXED IT SO I WAS MY OLD SELF AGAIN—*BETTER* EVEN.

ANYWAY, IT—LOOK, YOU DIDN'T OWE HIM ANYTHING, BUT YOU TRIED.

I KNOW ALL ABOUT SECOND CHANCES.

WE BETTER GET A MOVE ON.

WAIT.

I KNOW I'M NO AUTOBOT.

I'M NOT SURE WHAT I AM, BUT...

...HOW WOULD YOU FEEL ABOUT BRINGING THIS WHOLE PLACE DOWN?

I'M LISTENIN'.

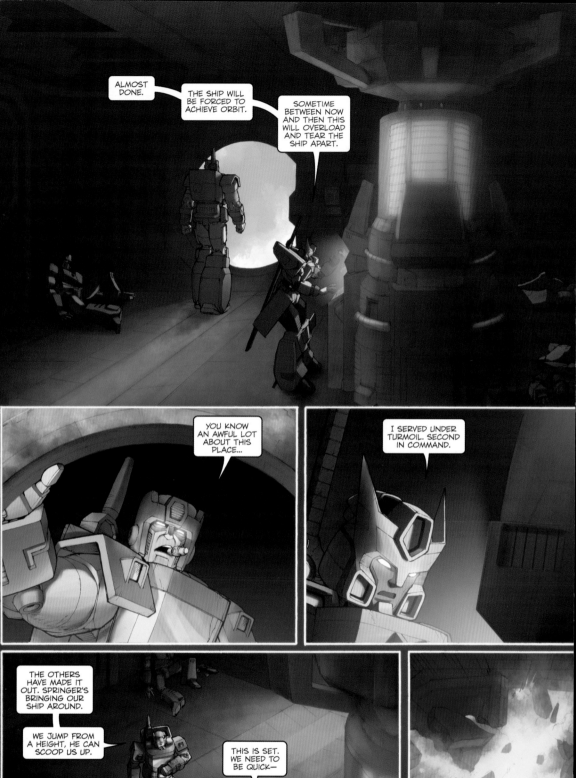

ALMOST DONE.

THE SHIP WILL BE FORCED TO ACHIEVE ORBIT.

SOMETIME BETWEEN NOW AND THEN THIS WILL OVERLOAD AND TEAR THE SHIP APART.

YOU KNOW AN AWFUL LOT ABOUT THIS PLACE...

I SERVED UNDER TURMOIL. SECOND IN COMMAND.

THE OTHERS HAVE MADE IT OUT. SPRINGER'S BRINGING OUR SHIP AROUND.

WE JUMP FROM A HEIGHT, HE CAN SCOOP US UP.

THIS IS SET. WE NEED TO BE QUICK—

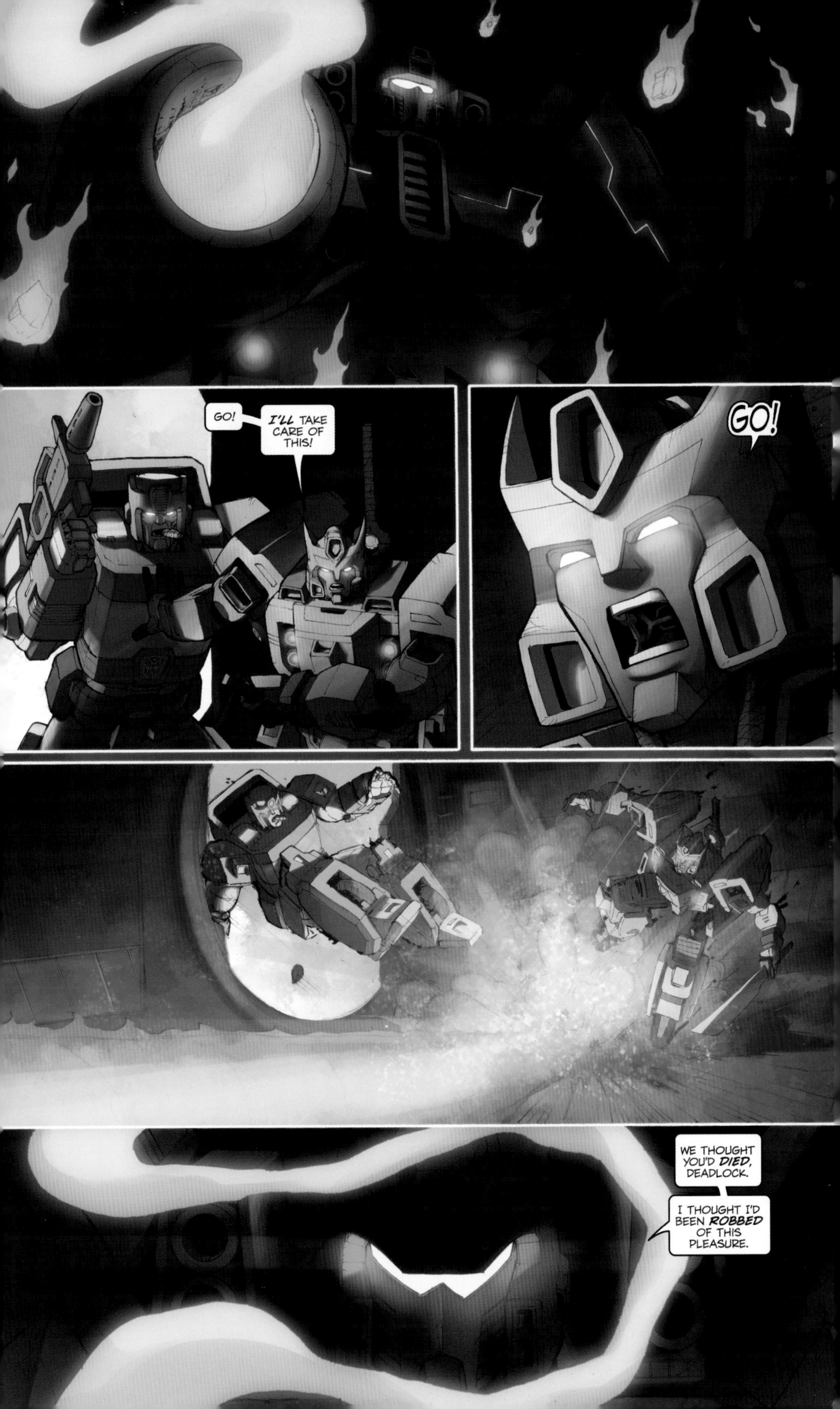
GO!
I'LL TAKE CARE OF THIS!
GO!
WE THOUGHT YOU'D DIED, DEADLOCK.
I THOUGHT I'D BEEN ROBBED OF THIS PLEASURE.

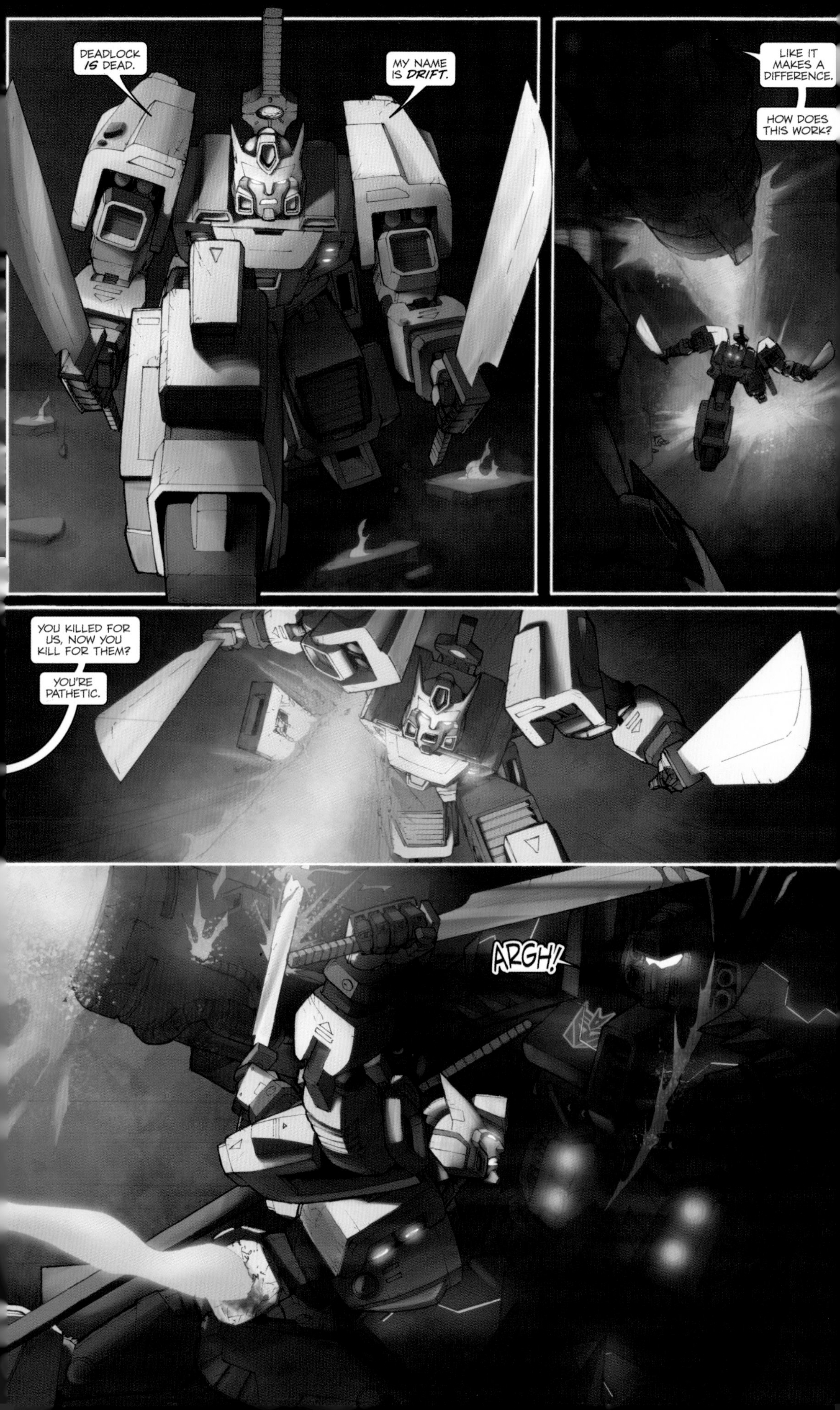
DEADLOCK IS DEAD.
MY NAME IS DRIFT.
LIKE IT MAKES A DIFFERENCE.
HOW DOES THIS WORK?
YOU KILLED FOR US, NOW YOU KILL FOR THEM?
YOU'RE PATHETIC.
ARGH!

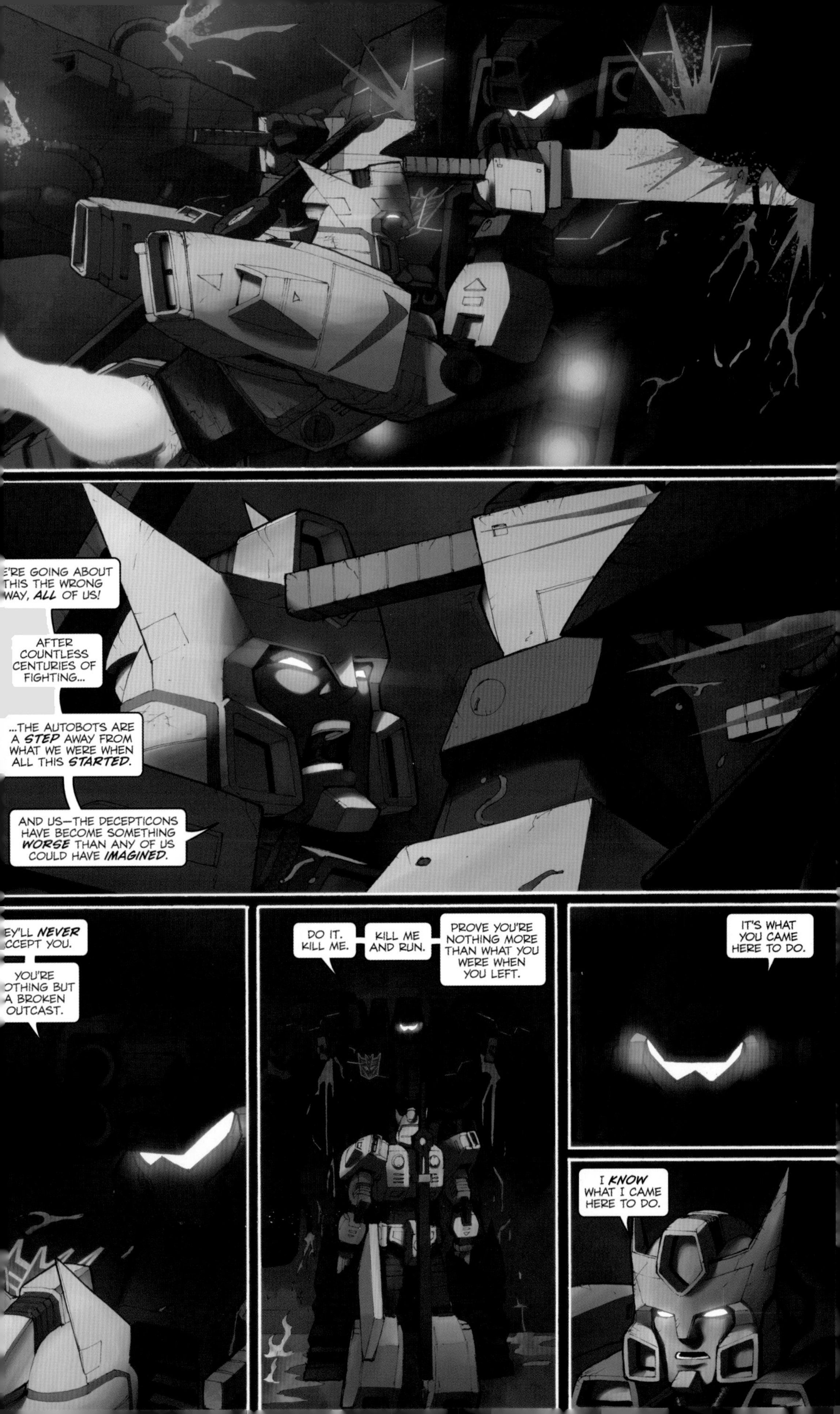

E'RE GOING ABOUT THIS THE WRONG WAY, ALL OF US!
AFTER COUNTLESS CENTURIES OF FIGHTING...
...THE AUTOBOTS ARE A STEP AWAY FROM WHAT WE WERE WHEN ALL THIS STARTED.
AND US—THE DECEPTICONS HAVE BECOME SOMETHING WORSE THAN ANY OF US COULD HAVE IMAGINED.
EY'LL NEVER CCEPT YOU.
YOU'RE OTHING BUT A BROKEN OUTCAST.
DO IT. KILL ME.
KILL ME AND RUN.
PROVE YOU'RE NOTHING MORE THAN WHAT YOU WERE WHEN YOU LEFT.
IT'S WHAT YOU CAME HERE TO DO.
I KNOW WHAT I CAME HERE TO DO.

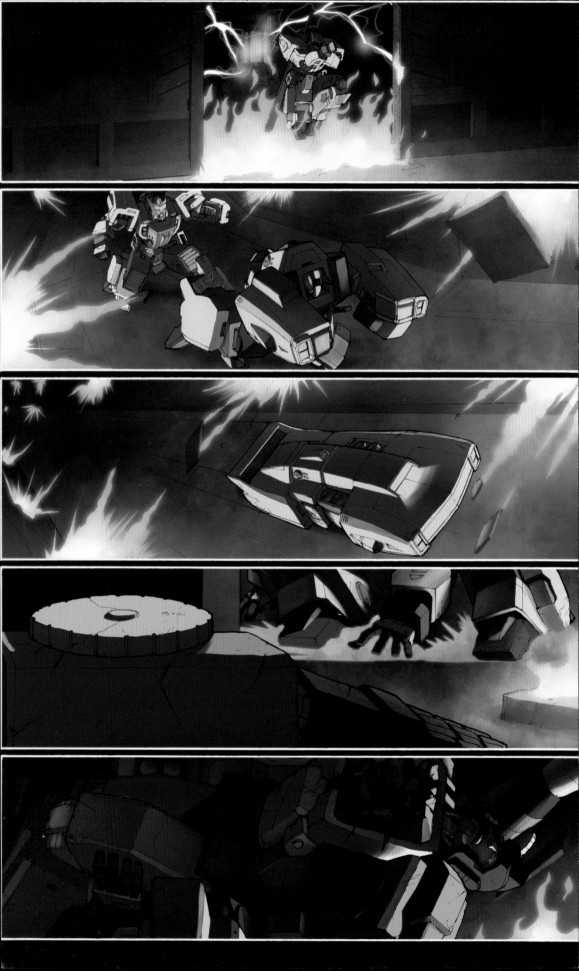

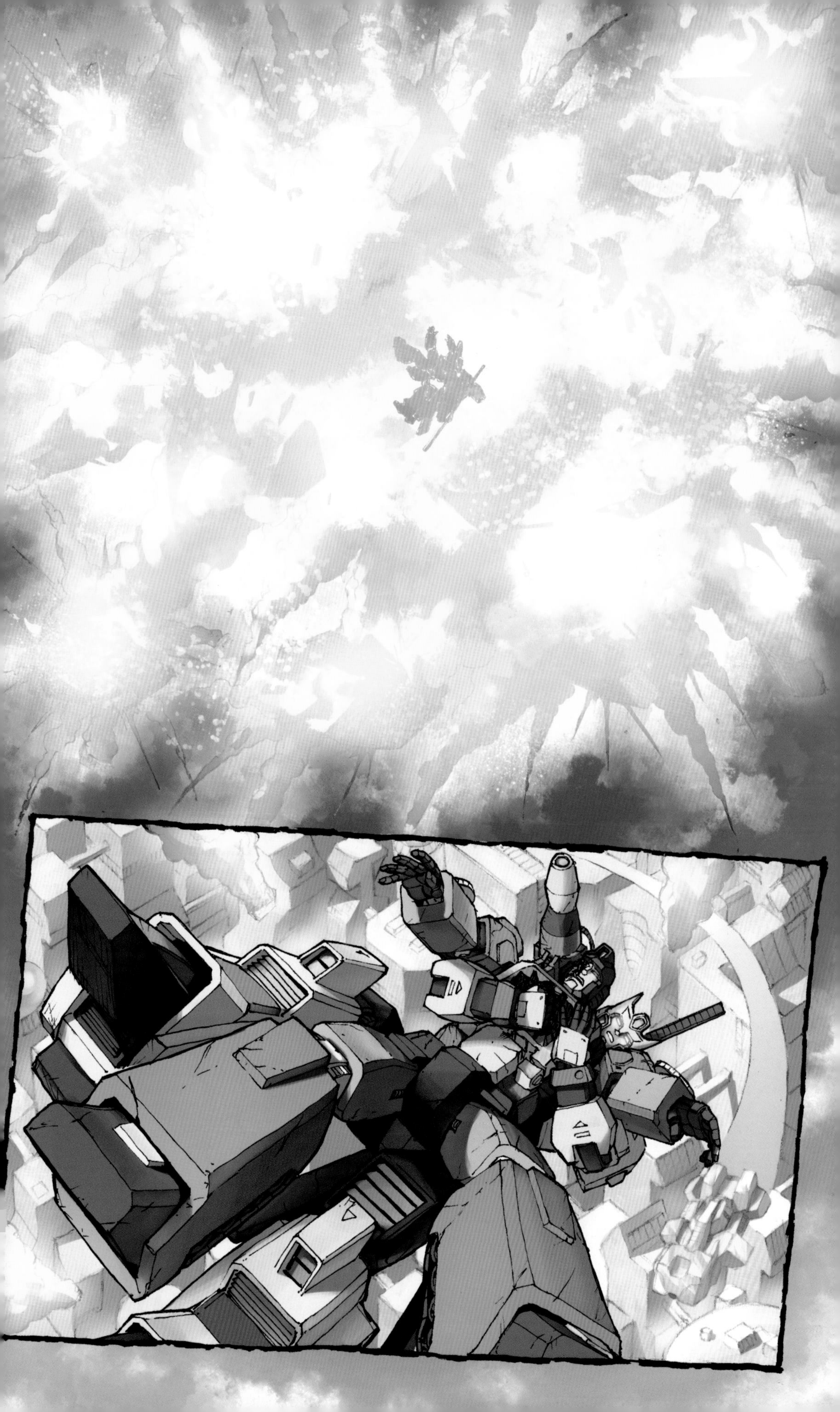

I'VE MADE CONTACT WITH THE TRION. WE'LL BE DOCKING SHORTLY.

THEY'VE BEEN INFORMED, ALL SIX AUTOBOTS RETRIEVED AND ACCOUNTED FOR.

SEVEN.

SEVEN?

I'M FORMING A NEW UNIT. I WANT YOU ON IT.

WHAT DO YOU SAY? WILLING TO WEAR THE BADGE?

KUP—

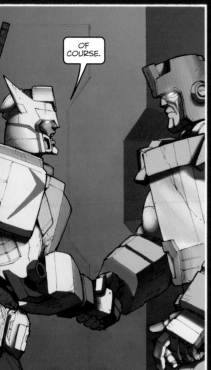

OF COURSE.

KUP, THIS ISN'T WISE...

HE PROVED HIMSELF DOWN THERE. YOU SAW IT.

THERE'S MORE TO FIGHTING THIS WAR THAN JUST BLOWIN' OFF HEADS.

BESIDES, YOU OF ALL PEOPLE SHOULD KNOW...

...EVERYONE DESERVES A SECOND CHANCE.

END.

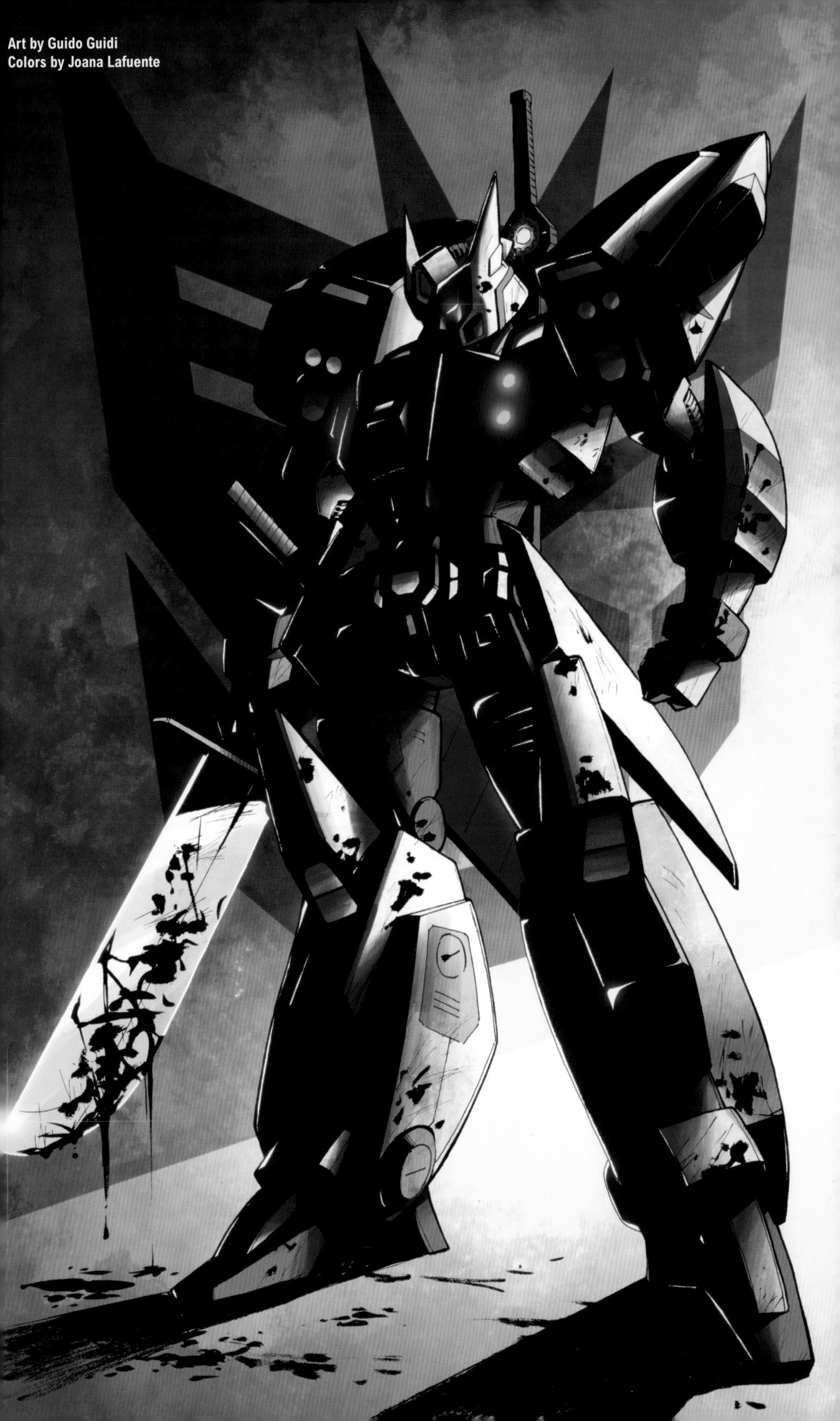

Art by Guido Guidi
Colors by Joana Lafuente

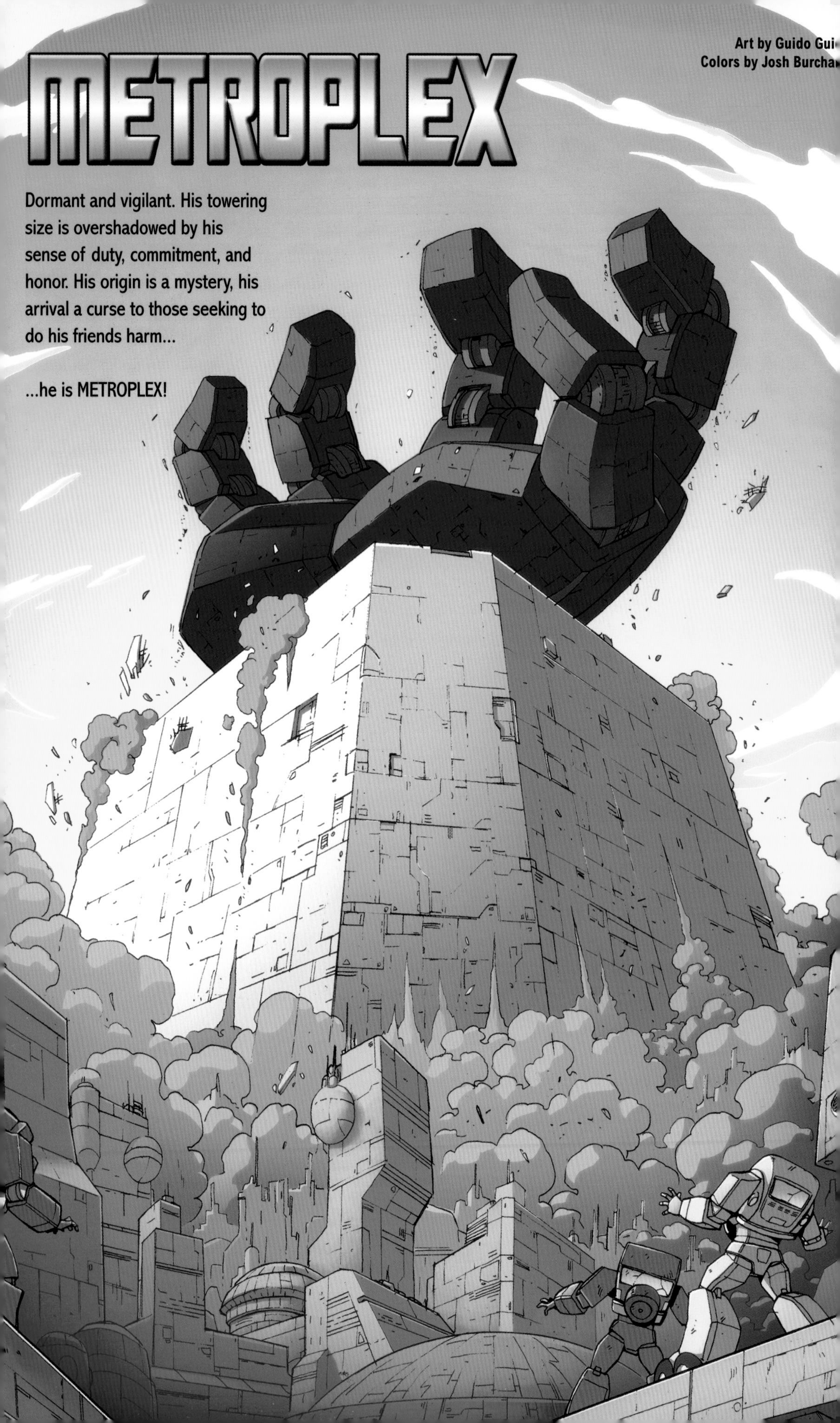
Art by Guido Gui
Colors by Josh Burcha
METROPLEX
Dormant and vigilant. His towering size is overshadowed by his sense of duty, commitment, and honor. His origin is a mystery, his arrival a curse to those seeking to do his friends harm...
...he is METROPLEX!

WE WERE STATIONED ON ORVUS BASE IN ORBIT OVER SALVATAN VI.

I KNEW THE LAB'S WORK WAS IMPORTANT BECAUSE THE OTHER *THROTTLEBOTS* AND I WERE THERE AS COURIERS TO KEEP THE WORK FROM FALLING INTO ENEMY HANDS.

THERE'S NO ONE FASTER AND BETTER AT EVADING THE ENEMY THAN US THIS SIDE OF THE BENZULI EXPANSE.

I CAN'T SAY WE WERE VITAL TO THE RESEARCH, THOUGH. WE WERE NEVER IN THE COMMAND CENTER, KEPT SEPARATE TO KEEP THE WORK SECRET.

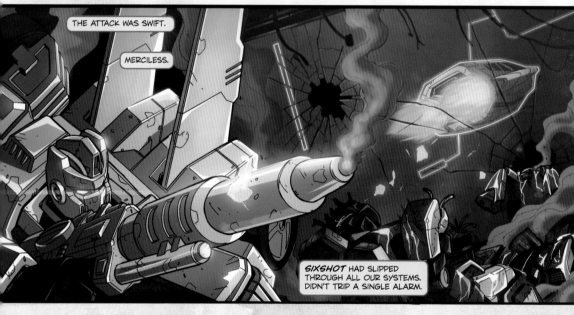

THE ATTACK WAS SWIFT.

MERCILESS.

SIXSHOT HAD SLIPPED THROUGH ALL OUR SYSTEMS. DIDN'T TRIP A SINGLE ALARM.

I SAID WE WERE FAST. BUT EVEN I'M SURPRISED WE WERE FAST ENOUGH TO GET OUT OF THE STATION. WE SHOULD BE DEAD. ALL OF US...

FREEWAY.

ROLLBAR.

CHASE.

SEARCHLIGHT.

WIDELOAD.

AND ME. I'M GOLDBUG. AND WE'RE THE ONLY SURVIVORS OF A MISSION I NEVER HAD CLEARANCE TO KNOW ABOUT.

WITHIN HOURS OUR DARKEST HOUR GOT A LITTLE BRIGHTER.

SALVVATAN VIII HAD SIGNS OF LIFE.

W-WE'RE GOING TO FALL APART!

HOLD STEADY! KEEP HER TOGETHER!

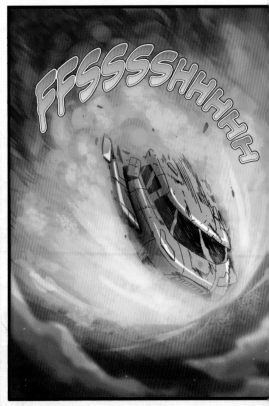

FFSSSSSHHHHH

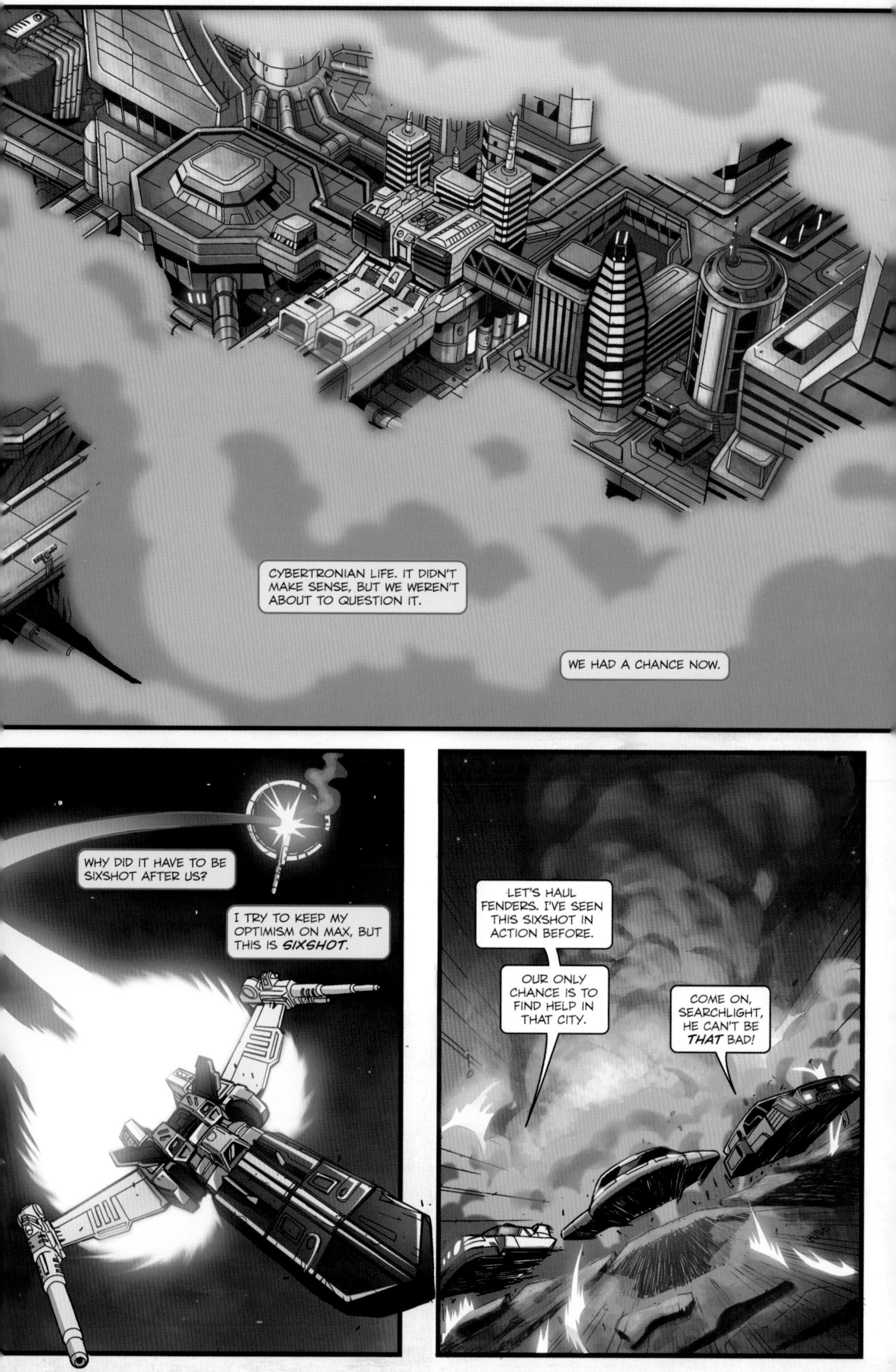
CYBERTRONIAN LIFE. IT DIDN'T MAKE SENSE, BUT WE WEREN'T ABOUT TO QUESTION IT.
WE HAD A CHANCE NOW.
WHY DID IT HAVE TO BE SIXSHOT AFTER US?
I TRY TO KEEP MY OPTIMISM ON MAX, BUT THIS IS *SIXSHOT*.
LET'S HAUL FENDERS. I'VE SEEN THIS SIXSHOT IN ACTION BEFORE.
OUR ONLY CHANCE IS TO FIND HELP IN THAT CITY.
COME ON, SEARCHLIGHT, HE CAN'T BE *THAT* BAD!

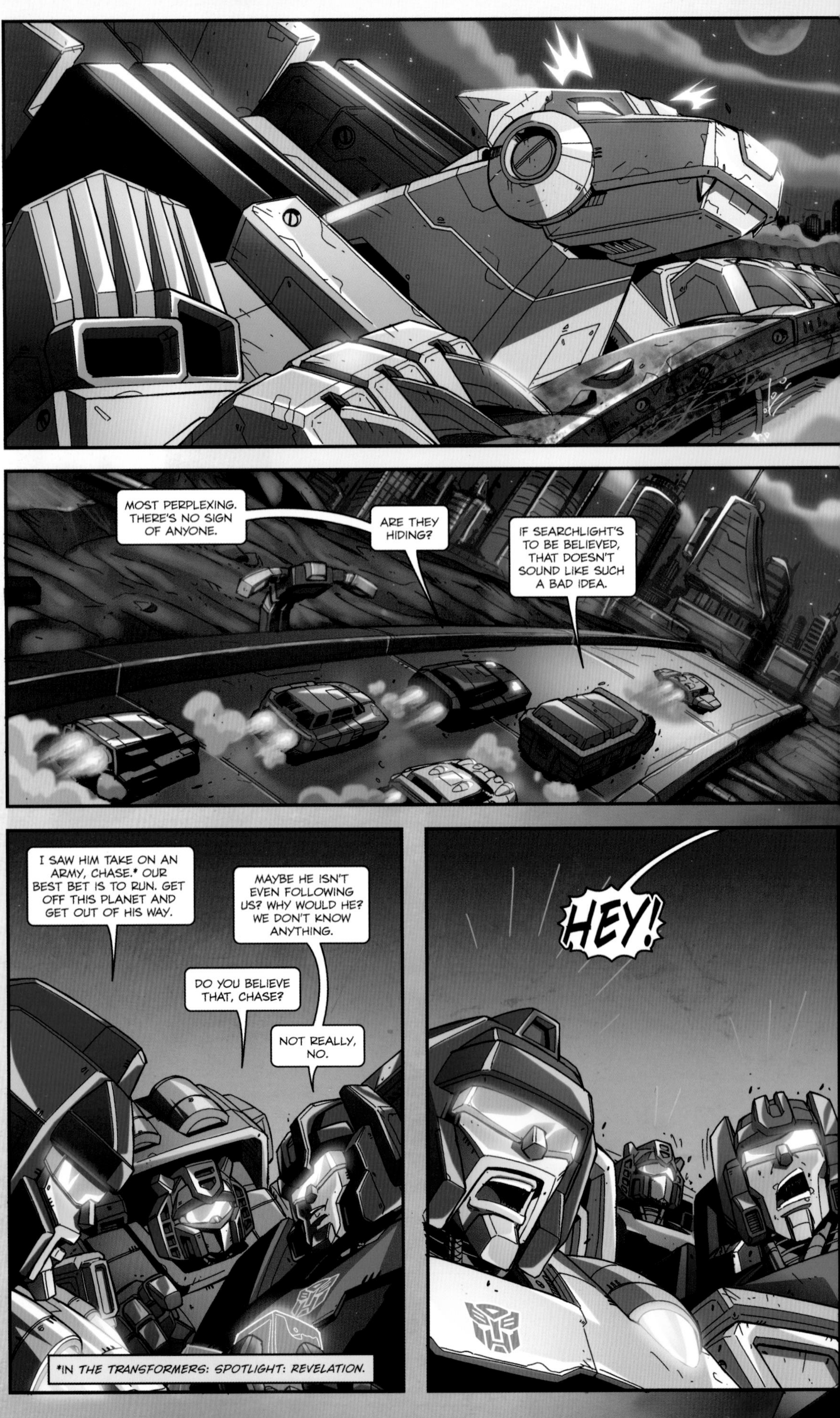
MOST PERPLEXING. THERE'S NO SIGN OF ANYONE.
ARE THEY HIDING?
IF SEARCHLIGHT'S TO BE BELIEVED, THAT DOESN'T SOUND LIKE SUCH A BAD IDEA.
I SAW HIM TAKE ON AN ARMY, CHASE.* OUR BEST BET IS TO RUN. GET OFF THIS PLANET AND GET OUT OF HIS WAY.
MAYBE HE ISN'T EVEN FOLLOWING US? WHY WOULD HE? WE DON'T KNOW ANYTHING.
DO YOU BELIEVE THAT, CHASE?
NOT REALLY, NO.
*IN THE TRANSFORMERS: SPOTLIGHT: REVELATION.
HEY!

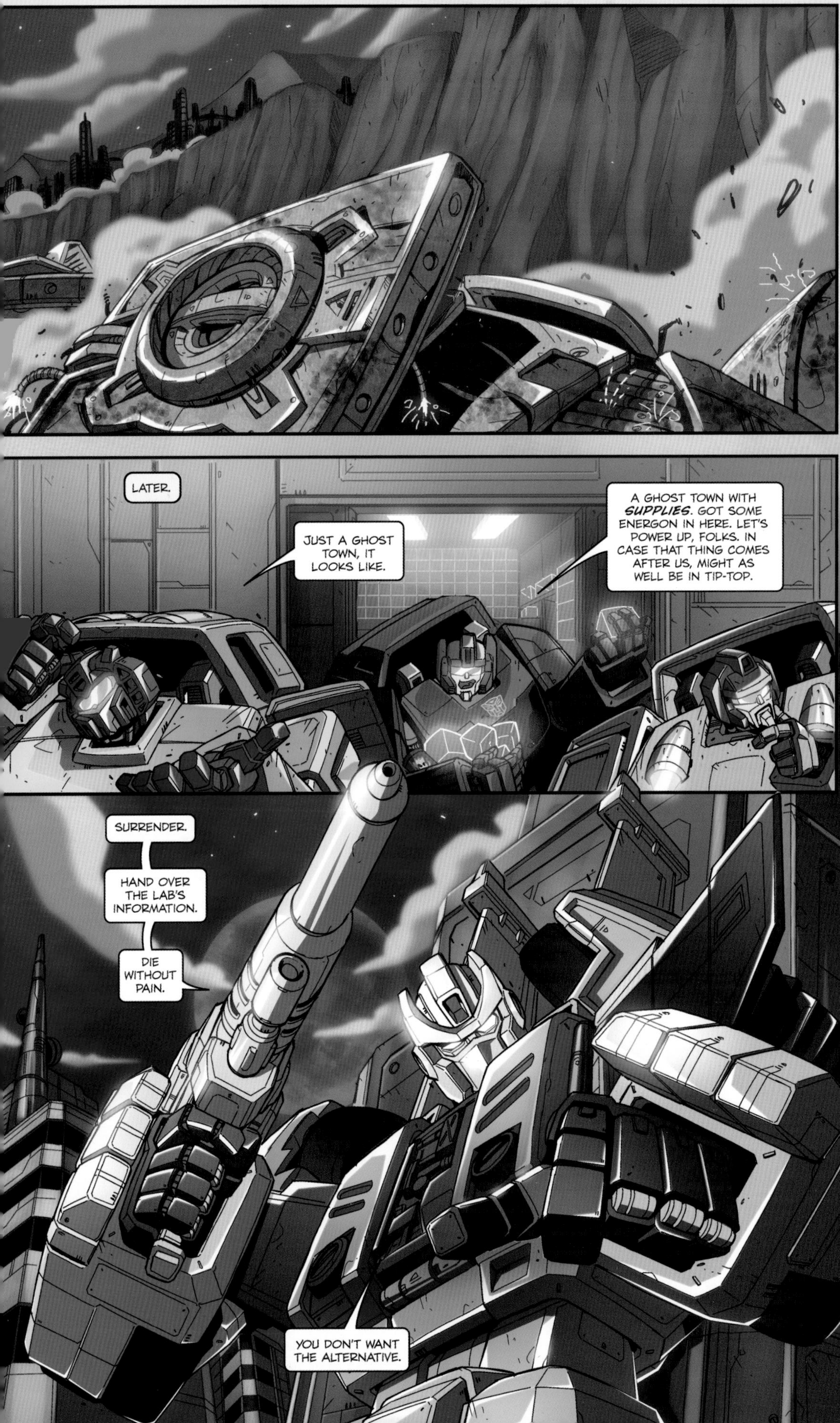
LATER.
JUST A GHOST TOWN, IT LOOKS LIKE.
A GHOST TOWN WITH SUPPLIES. GOT SOME ENERGON IN HERE. LET'S POWER UP, FOLKS. IN CASE THAT THING COMES AFTER US, MIGHT AS WELL BE IN TIP-TOP.
SURRENDER.
HAND OVER THE LAB'S INFORMATION.
DIE WITHOUT PAIN.
YOU DON'T WANT THE ALTERNATIVE.

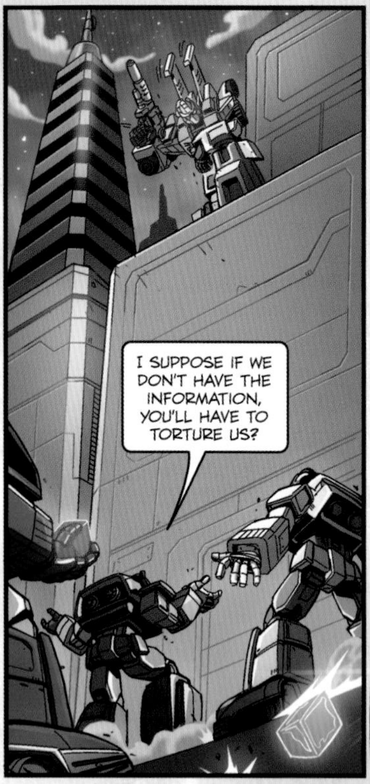
I SUPPOSE IF WE DON'T HAVE THE INFORMATION, YOU'LL HAVE TO TORTURE US?
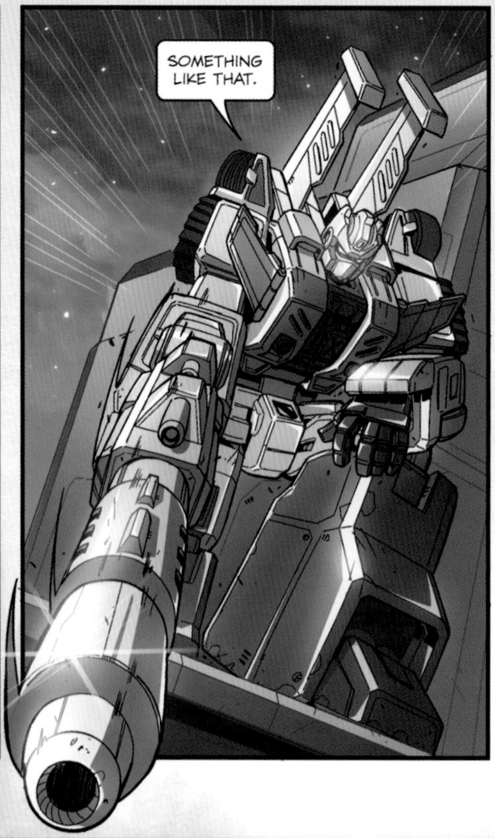
SOMETHING LIKE THAT.
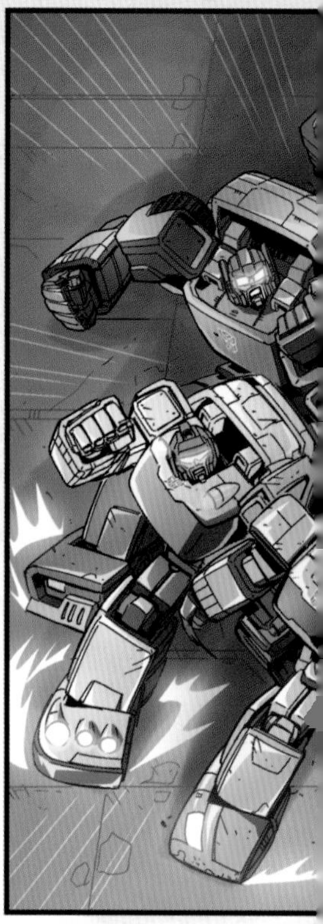
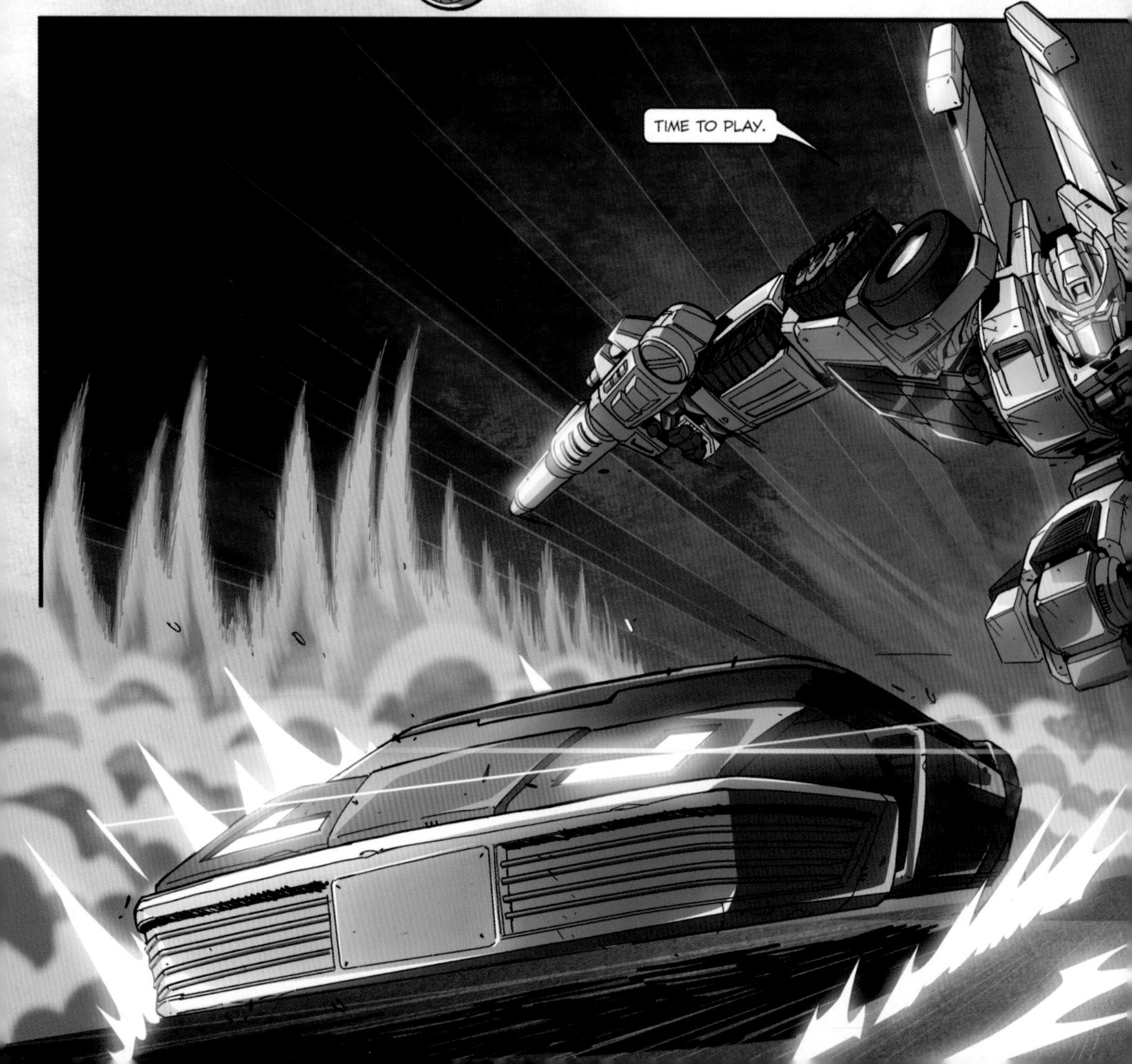
TIME TO PLAY.

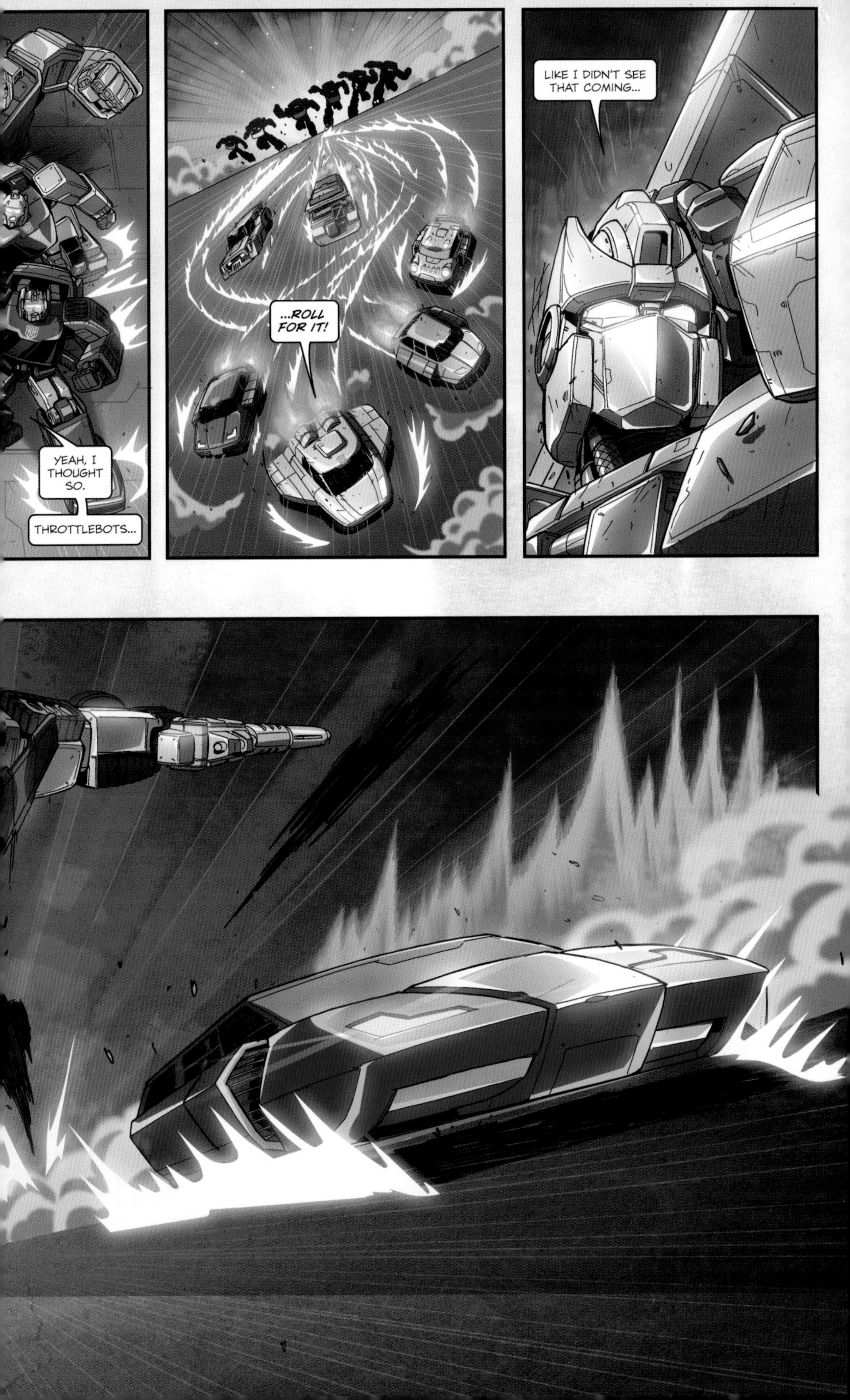

YEAH, I THOUGHT SO.
THROTTLEBOTS...
...ROLL FOR IT!
LIKE I DIDN'T SEE THAT COMING...

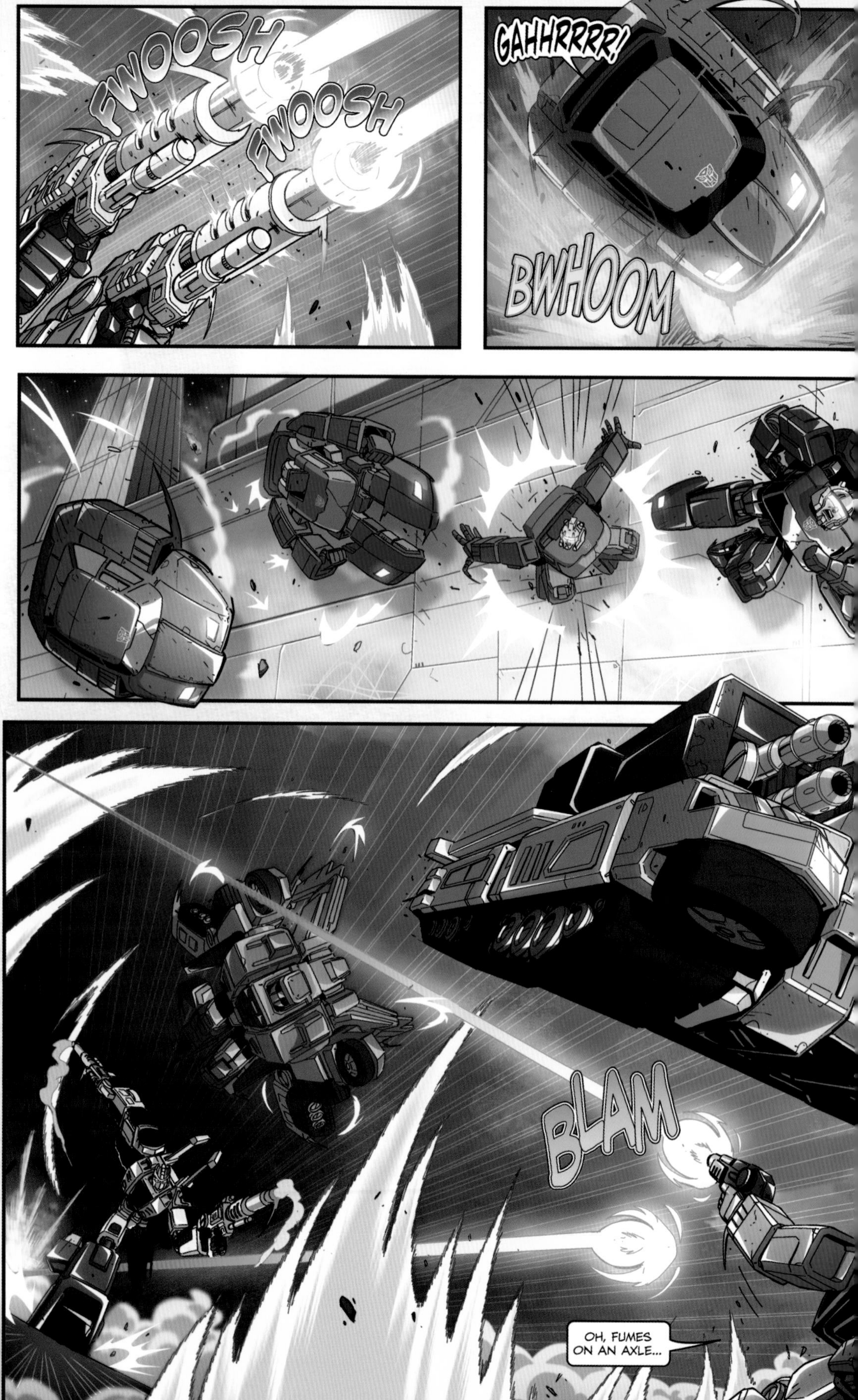
FWOOSH
FWOOSH
GAHHRRRR!
BWHOOM
BLAM
OH, FUMES ON AN AXLE...

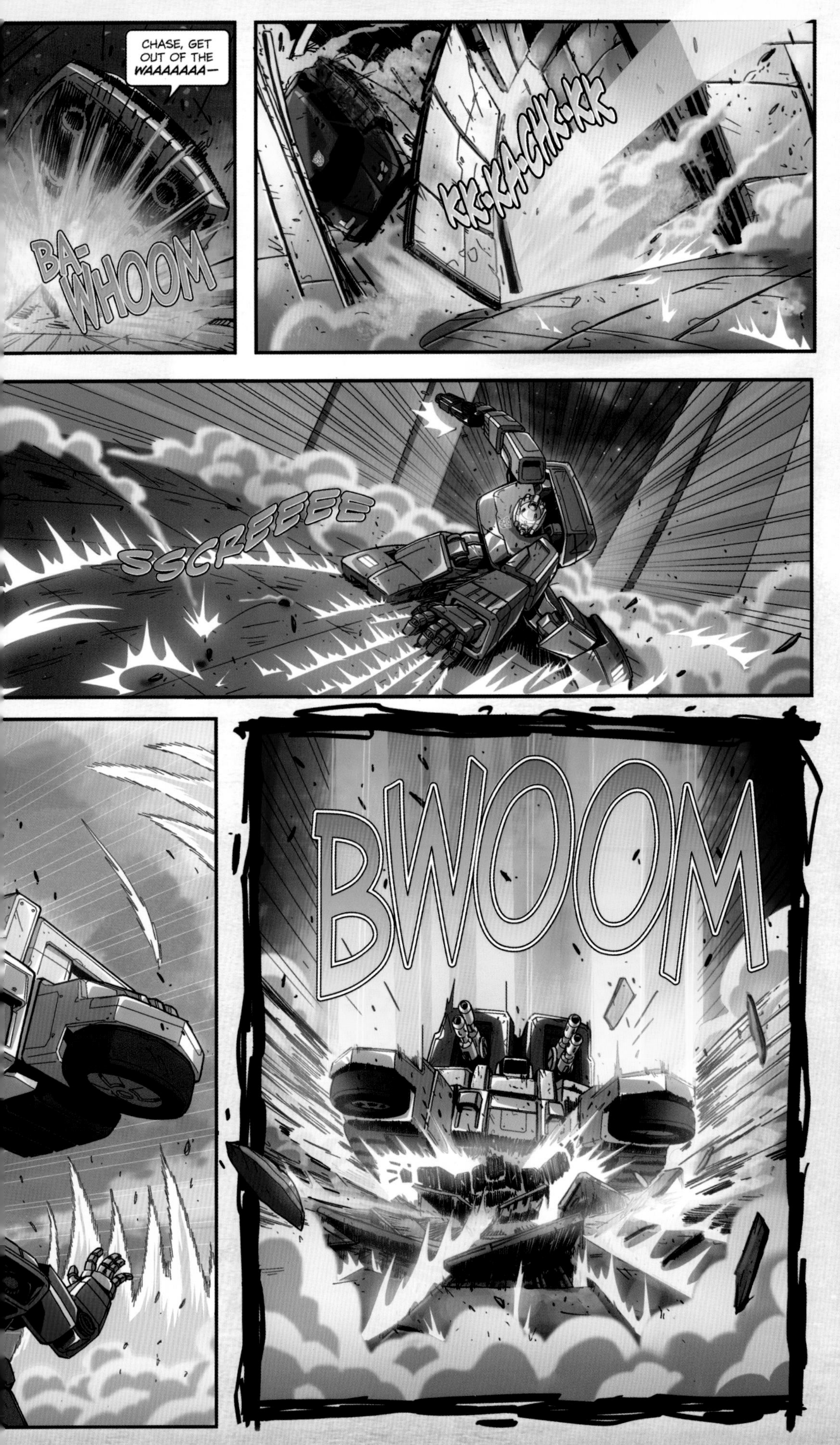
CHASE, GET OUT OF THE *WAAAAAAA*—
BA-WHOOM
KK-KA-CHK-KK
SSCREEEEE
BWOOM

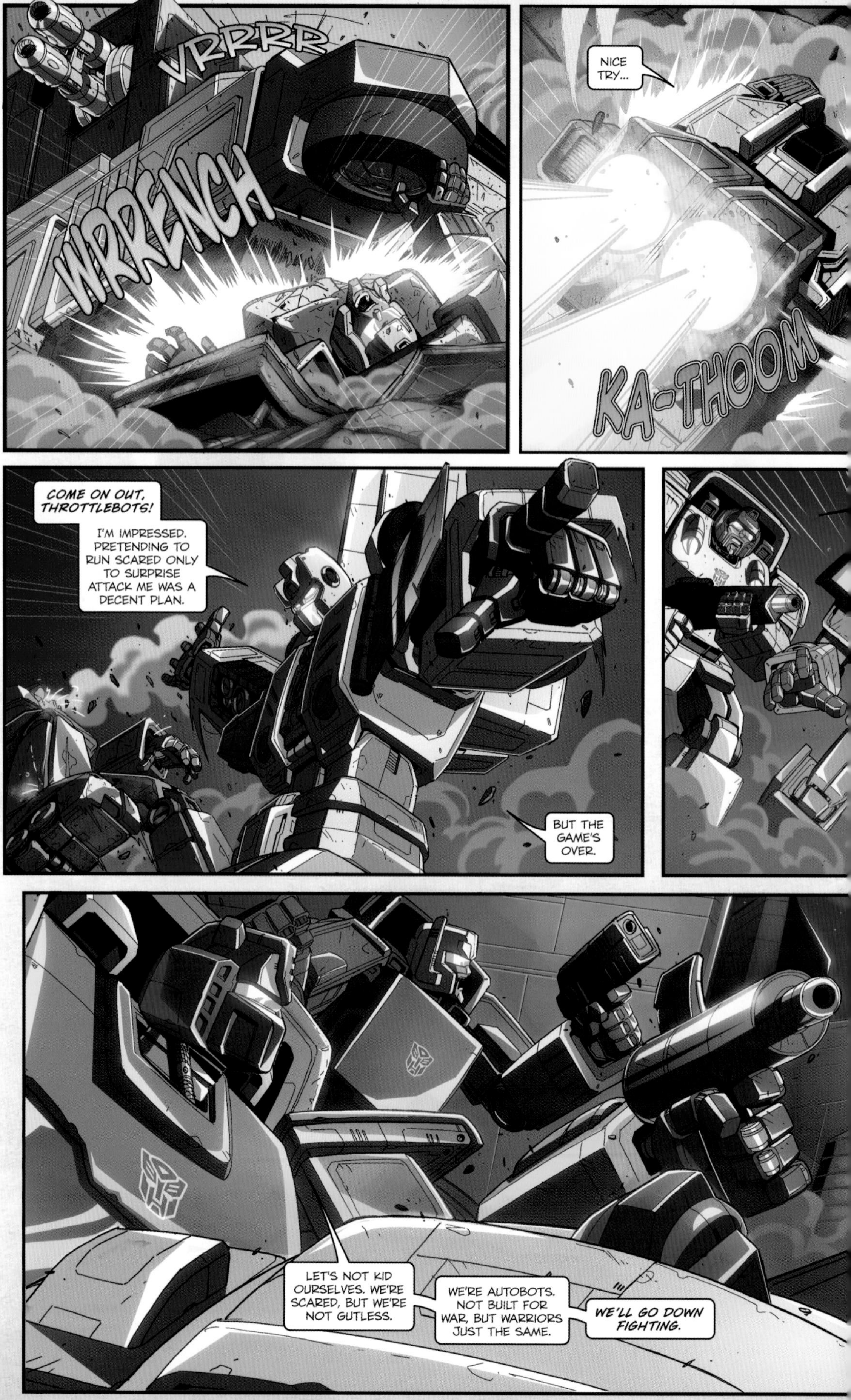

VRRRR
WRRENCH
NICE TRY...
KA-THOOM
COME ON OUT, THROTTLEBOTS!
I'M IMPRESSED. PRETENDING TO RUN SCARED ONLY TO SURPRISE ATTACK ME WAS A DECENT PLAN.
BUT THE GAME'S OVER.
LET'S NOT KID OURSELVES. WE'RE SCARED, BUT WE'RE NOT GUTLESS.
WE'RE AUTOBOTS. NOT BUILT FOR WAR, BUT WARRIORS JUST THE SAME.
WE'LL GO DOWN FIGHTING.

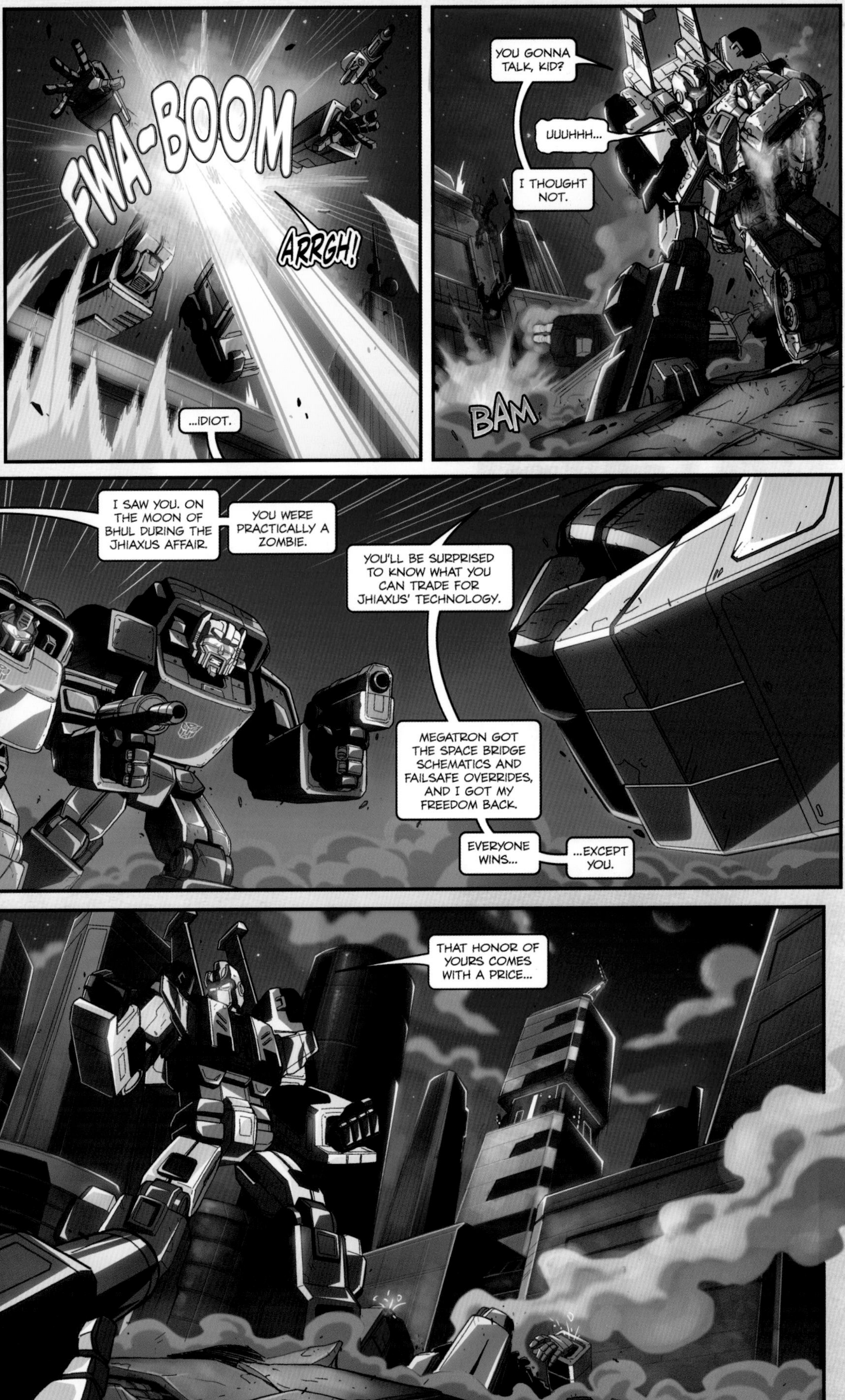
FWA-BOOM
ARRGH!
...IDIOT.
YOU GONNA TALK, KID?
UUUHHH...
I THOUGHT NOT.
BAM
I SAW YOU. ON THE MOON OF BHUL DURING THE JHIAXUS AFFAIR.
YOU WERE PRACTICALLY A ZOMBIE.
YOU'LL BE SURPRISED TO KNOW WHAT YOU CAN TRADE FOR JHIAXUS' TECHNOLOGY.
MEGATRON GOT THE SPACE BRIDGE SCHEMATICS AND FAILSAFE OVERRIDES, AND I GOT MY FREEDOM BACK.
EVERYONE WINS...
...EXCEPT YOU.
THAT HONOR OF YOURS COMES WITH A PRICE...

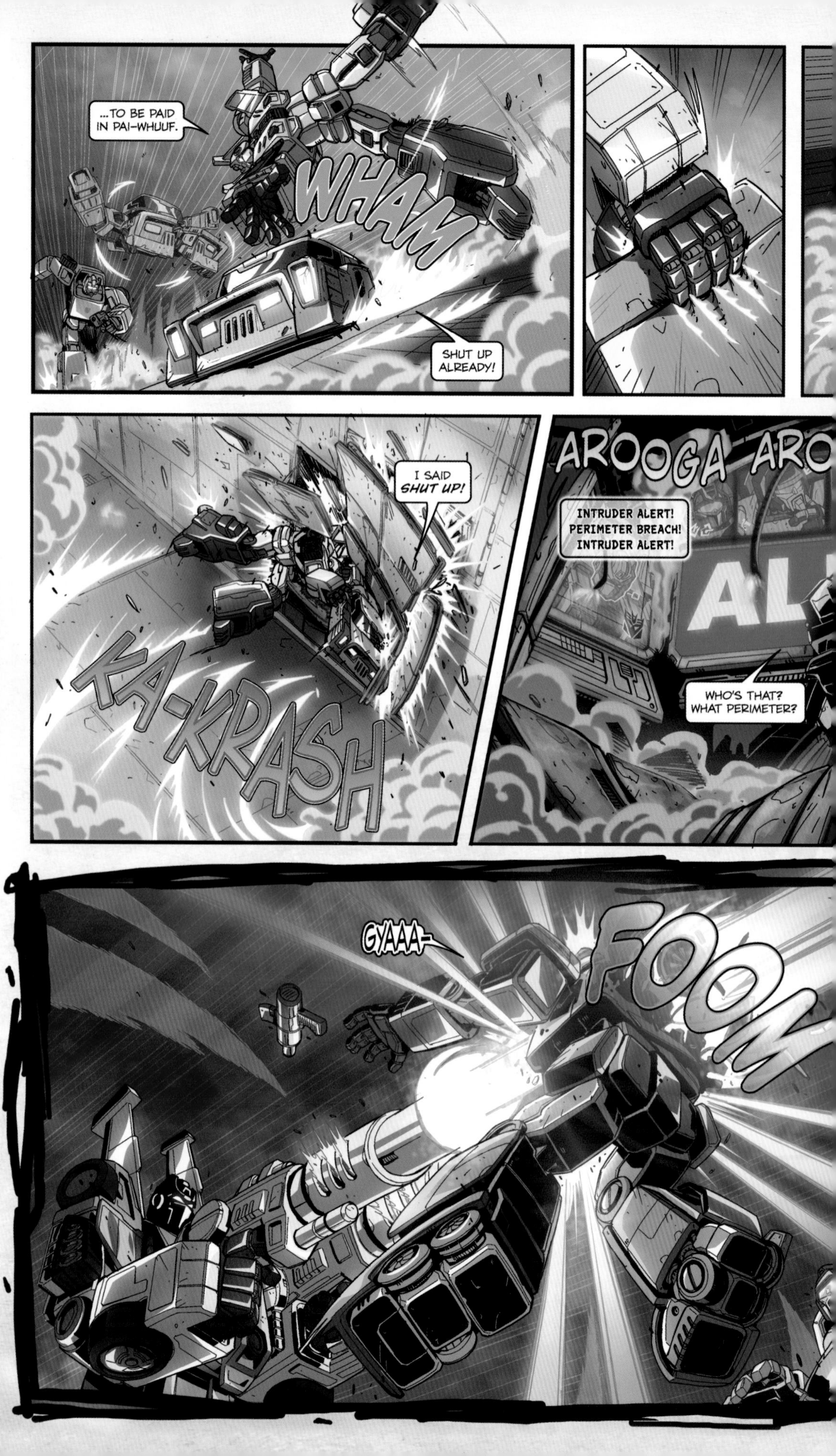
...TO BE PAID IN PAI-WHUUF.
WHAM
SHUT UP ALREADY!
I SAID *SHUT UP!*
KA-KRASH
AROOGA ARO
INTRUDER ALERT! PERIMETER BREACH! INTRUDER ALERT!
AL
WHO'S THAT? WHAT PERIMETER?
GYAAA-
FOOM

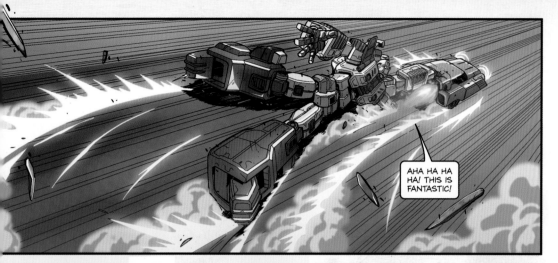

AHA HA HA HA! THIS IS FANTASTIC!

AROOGA

NOW, SEARCHLIGHT!

SERIOUSLY?

I'D KEEP YOUR OPTICS ON ME, IF I WERE YOU.

BY THE MATRIX. GOLDBUG.

BOOM

THUNK

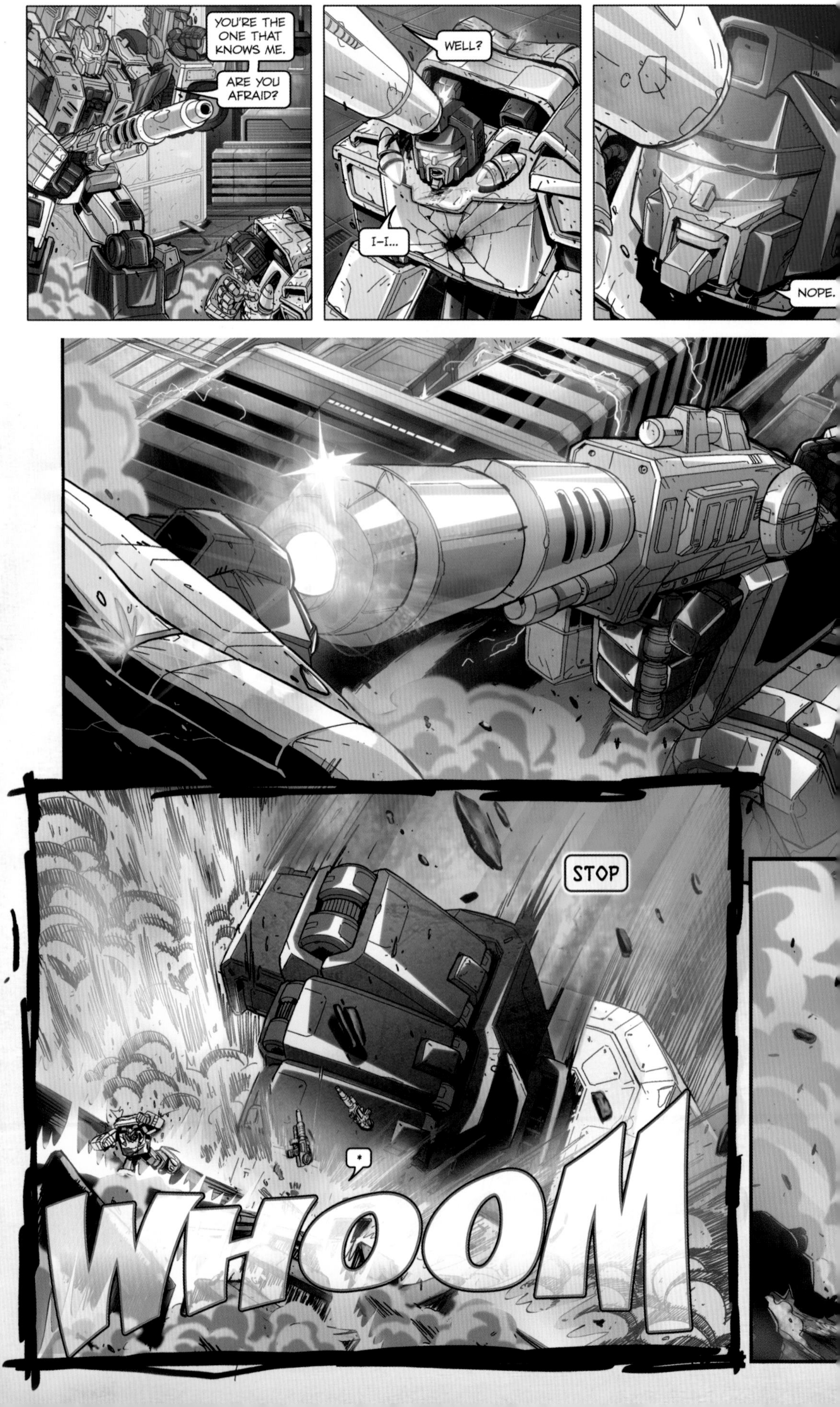
YOU'RE THE ONE THAT KNOWS ME.
ARE YOU AFRAID?
WELL?
I-I...
NOPE.
STOP
*
WHOOM

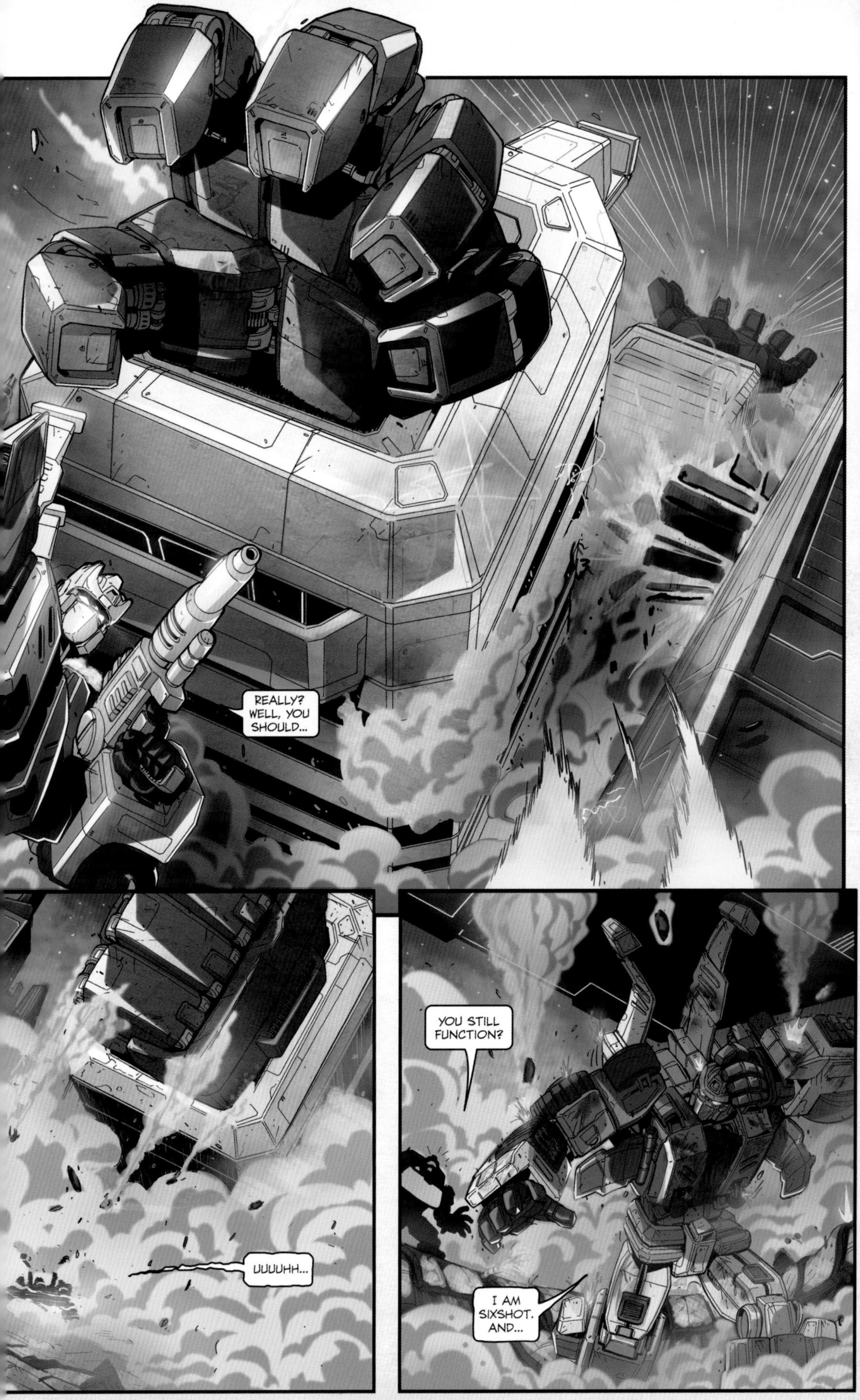
REALLY? WELL, YOU SHOULD...
UUUUHH...
YOU STILL FUNCTION?
I AM SIXSHOT. AND...

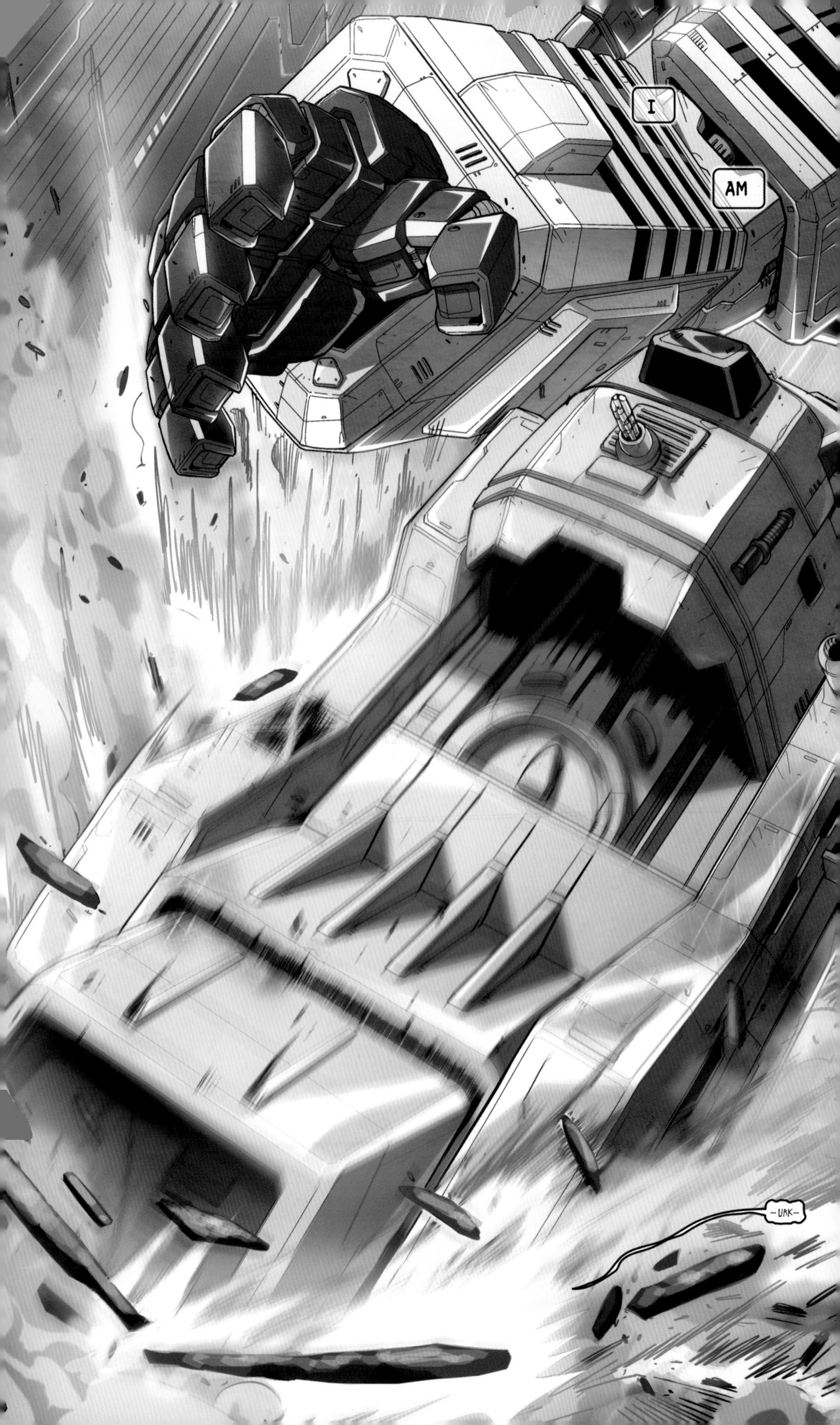
I
AM
—URK—

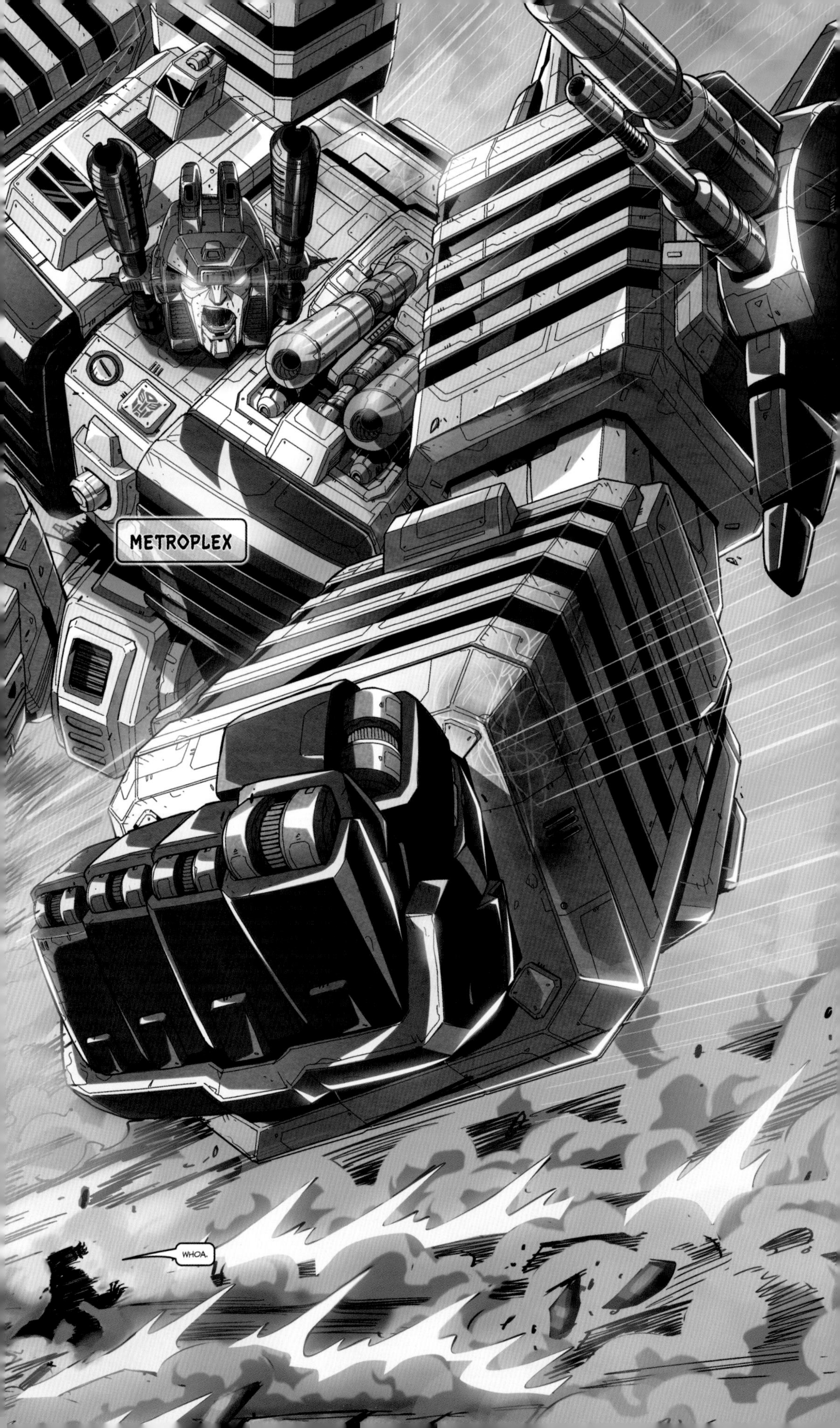
METROPLEX
WHOA.

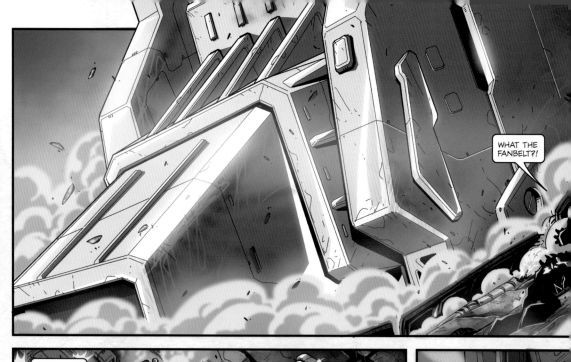

WHAT THE FANBELT?!

WHY DO WE HAVE TO LEAVE?

TO

HIDE

YOU'LL

FIND

SUPPLIES

INSIDE

SAVE

YOUR

FRIENDS

HIDE? YOU CAN'T HIDE! YOU HAVE TO JOIN US. THERE'S A WAR GOING ON!

YOU STOPPED *SIXSHOT—SIXSHOT*, FOR CYBERTRON'S SAKE!

HOW CAN YOU REFUSE?

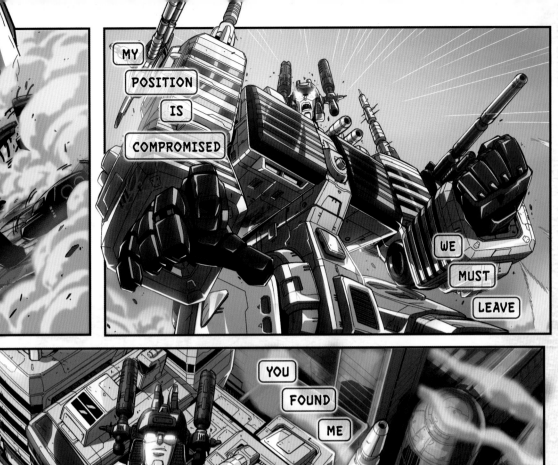

MY POSITION IS COMPROMISED

WE MUST LEAVE

YOU FOUND ME

SO WILL OTHERS

-KAKK- YOU'RE LEAVING US... TO DIE?

WHAT KIND OF -KAFF- AUTOBOT *ARE* YOU?

SHUTTLE IN HANGAR 205

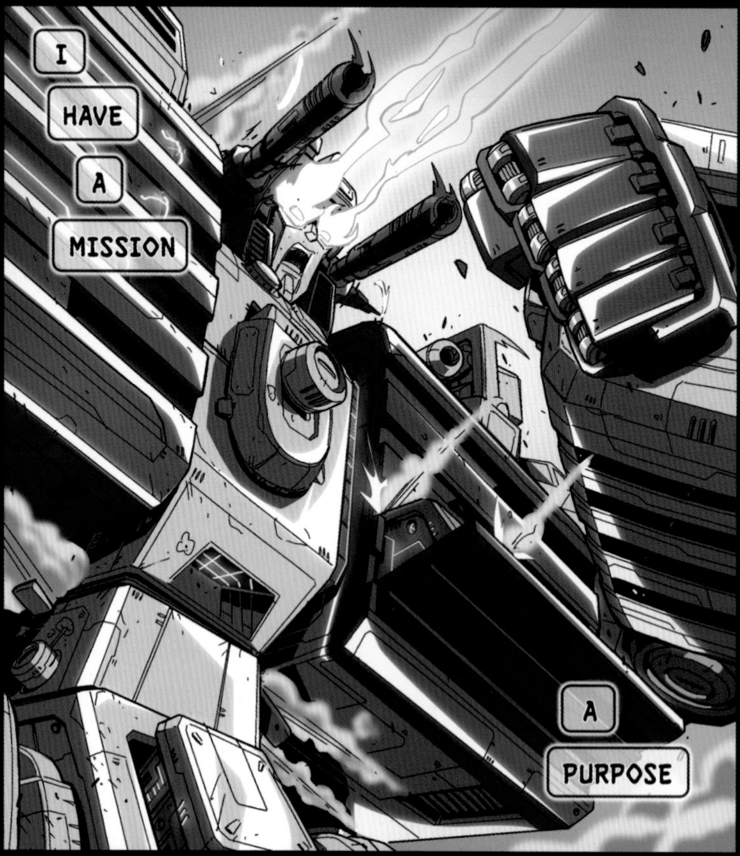
I
HAVE
A
MISSION
A
PURPOSE

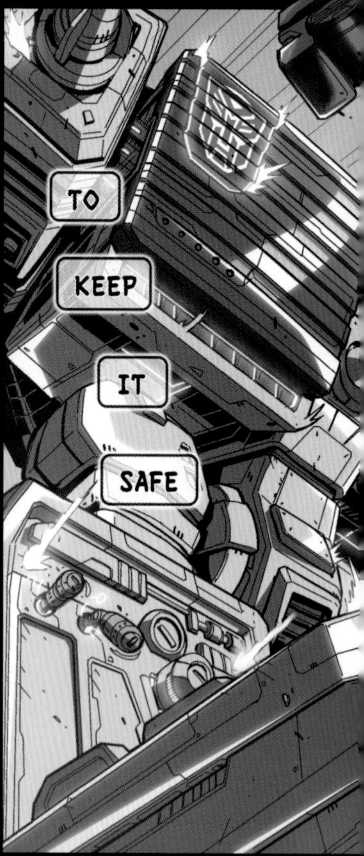
TO
KEEP
IT
SAFE

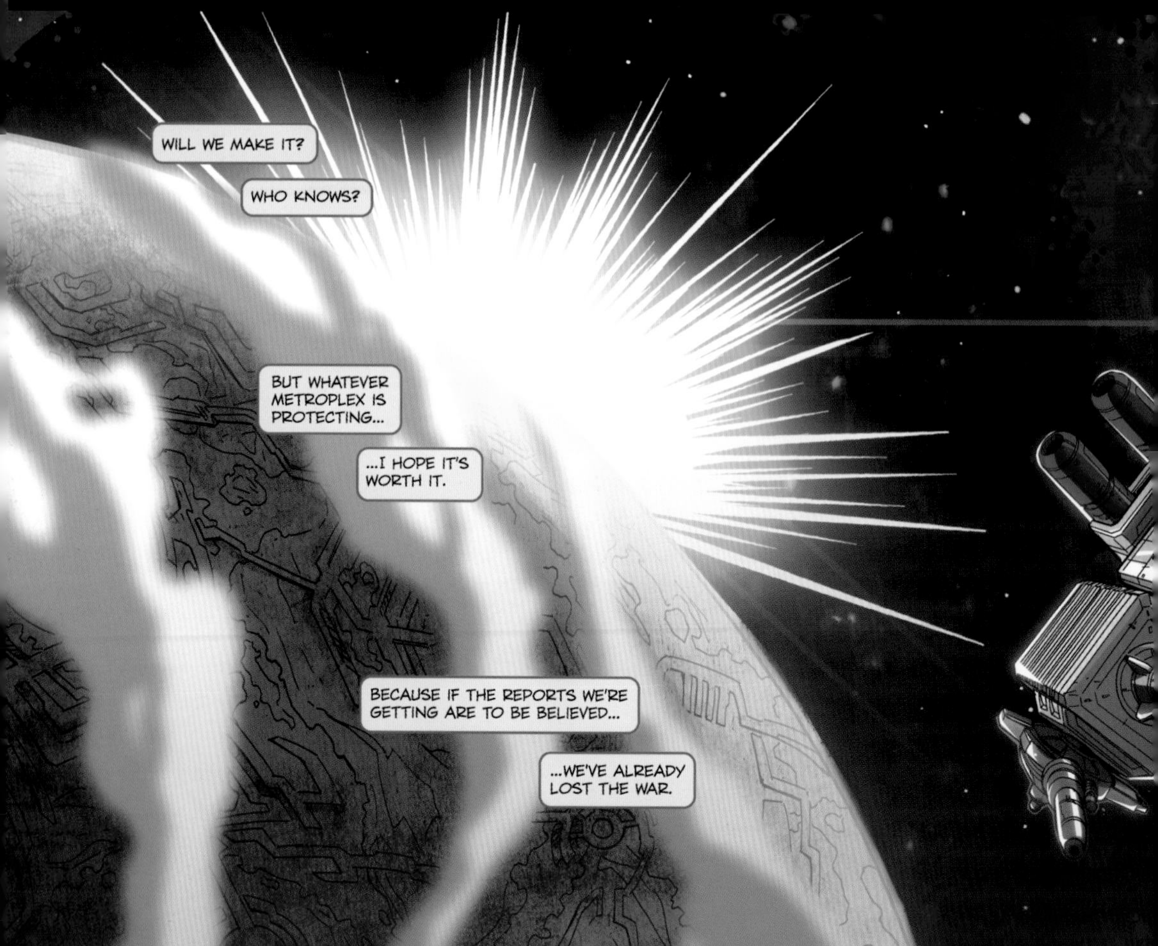
WILL WE MAKE IT?
WHO KNOWS?
BUT WHATEVER METROPLEX IS PROTECTING...
...I HOPE IT'S WORTH IT.
BECAUSE IF THE REPORTS WE'RE GETTING ARE TO BE BELIEVED...
...WE'VE ALREADY LOST THE WAR.

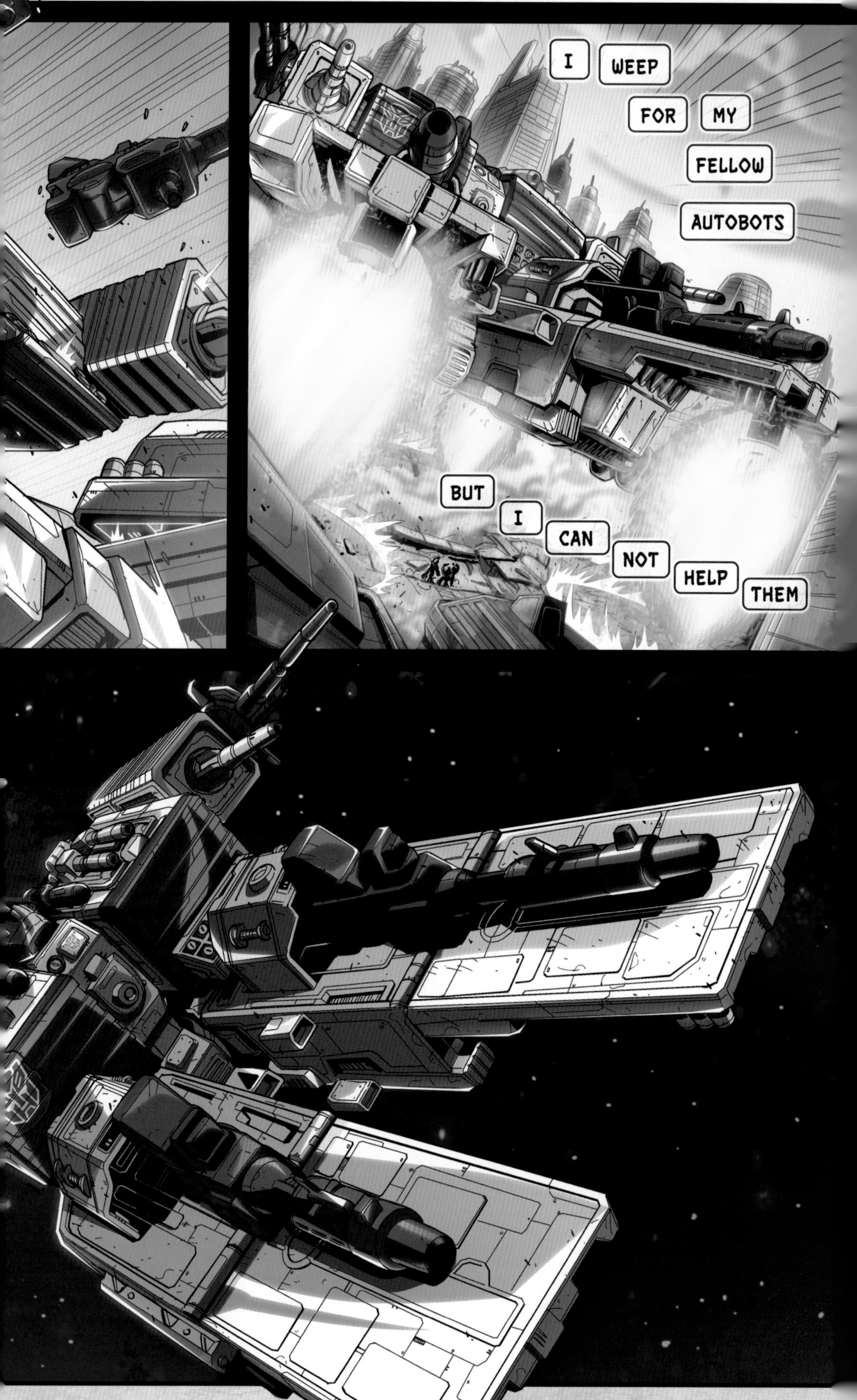
I
WEEP
FOR
MY
FELLOW
AUTOBOTS
BUT
I
CAN
NOT
HELP
THEM

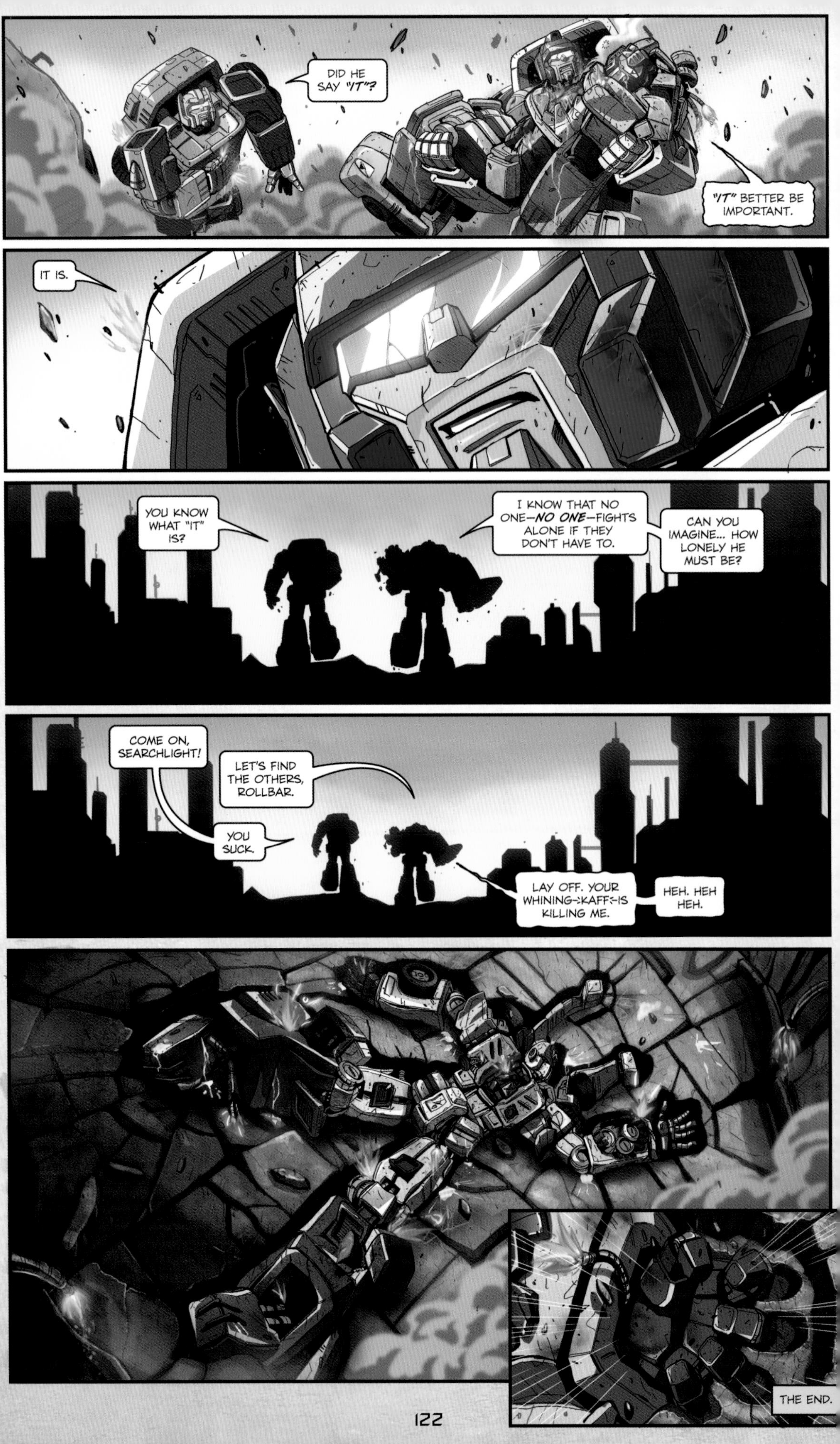
DID HE SAY "IT"?
"IT" BETTER BE IMPORTANT.
IT IS.
YOU KNOW WHAT "IT" IS?
I KNOW THAT NO ONE—NO ONE—FIGHTS ALONE IF THEY DON'T HAVE TO.
CAN YOU IMAGINE... HOW LONELY HE MUST BE?
COME ON, SEARCHLIGHT!
LET'S FIND THE OTHERS, ROLLBAR.
YOU SUCK.
LAY OFF. YOUR WHINING—KAFF—IS KILLING ME.
HEH. HEH HEH.
THE END.

rt and Colors by Marcelo Matere

Chase
Searchlight
Freeway
Wildload
Rollbar
Goldbug

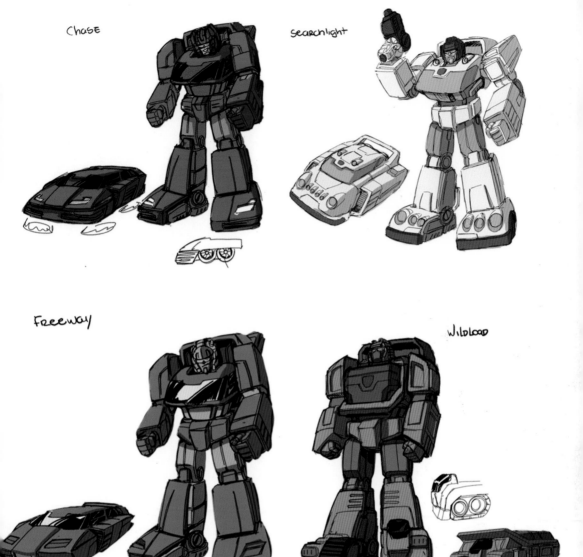

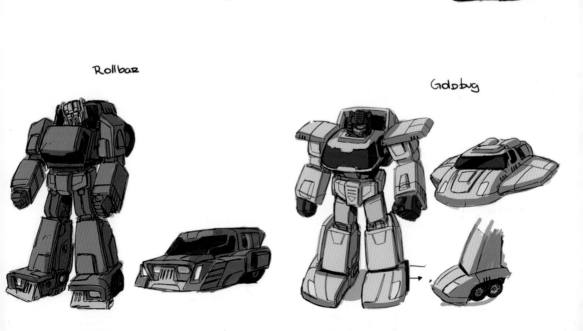

ART GALLERY

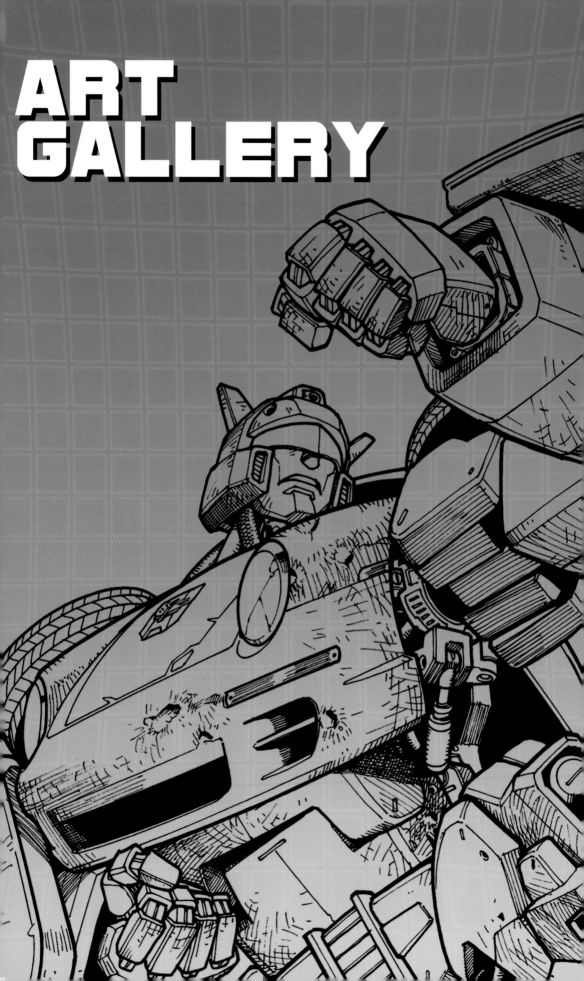

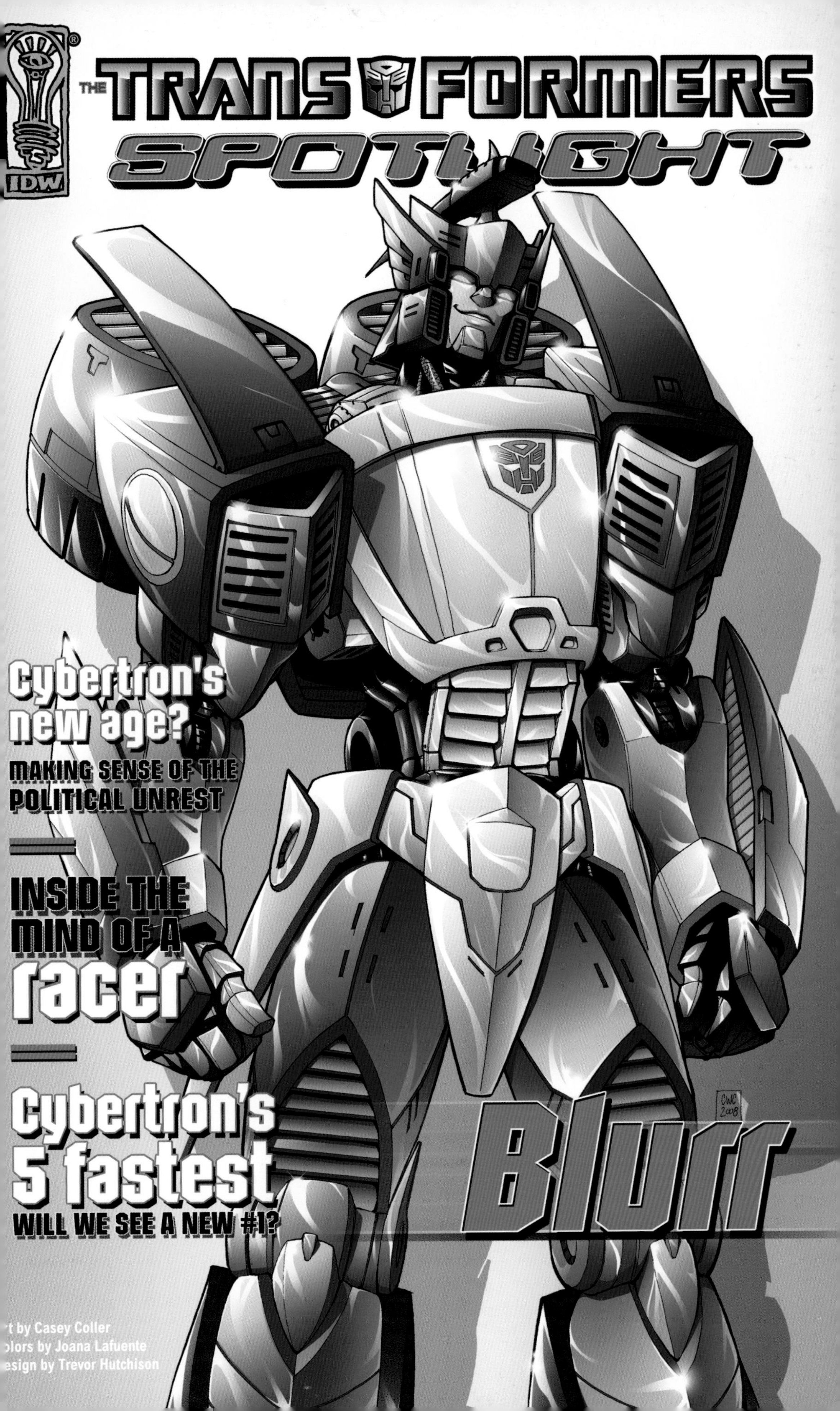
IDW
THE TRANSFORMERS
SPOTLIGHT
Cybertron's new age?
MAKING SENSE OF THE POLITICAL UNREST
INSIDE THE MIND OF A racer
Cybertron's 5 fastest
WILL WE SEE A NEW #1?
Blurr
CWC 2008
t by Casey Coller
olors by Joana Lafuente
esign by Trevor Hutchison

Art and Colors by Andrew Griffith

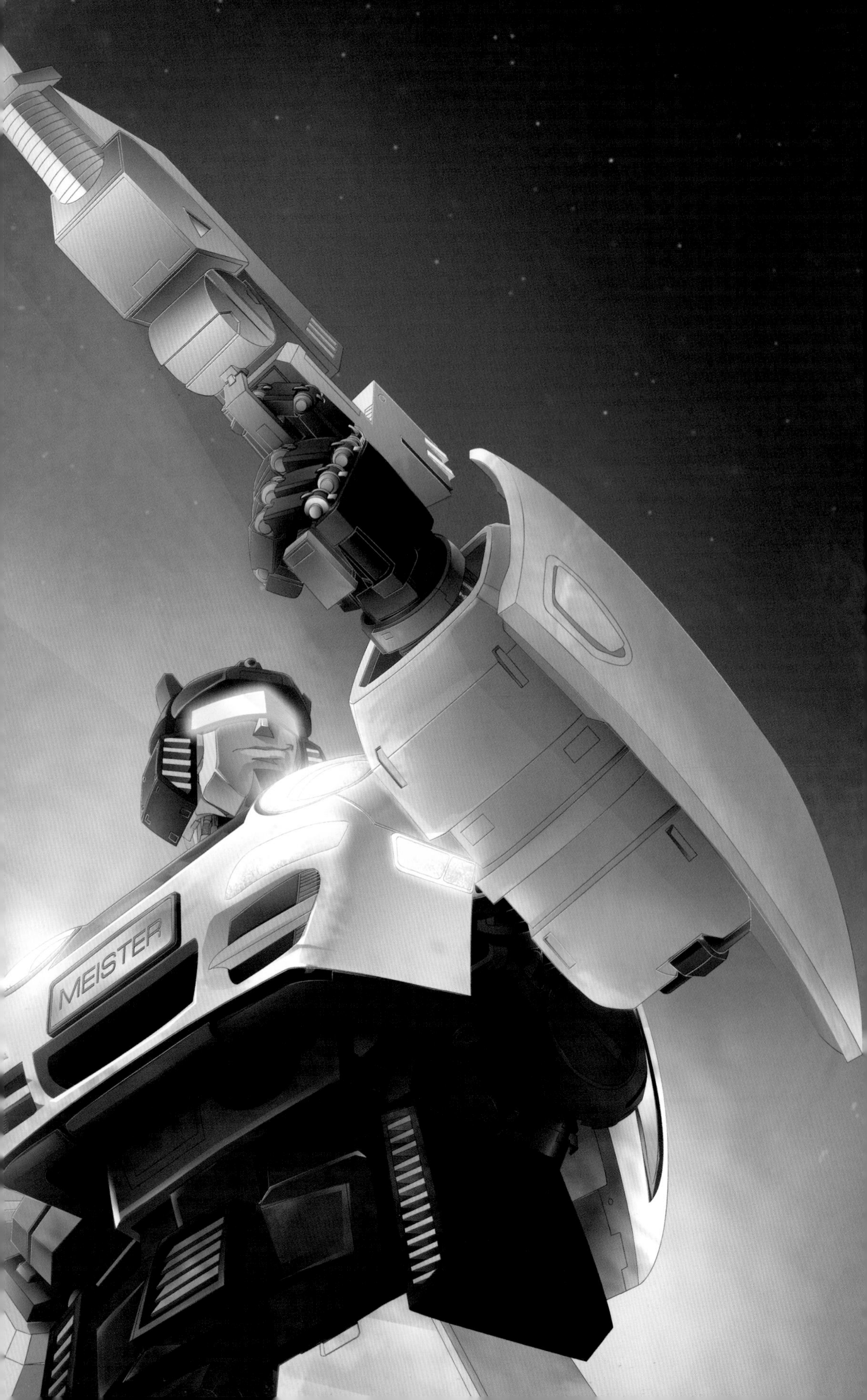
MEISTER

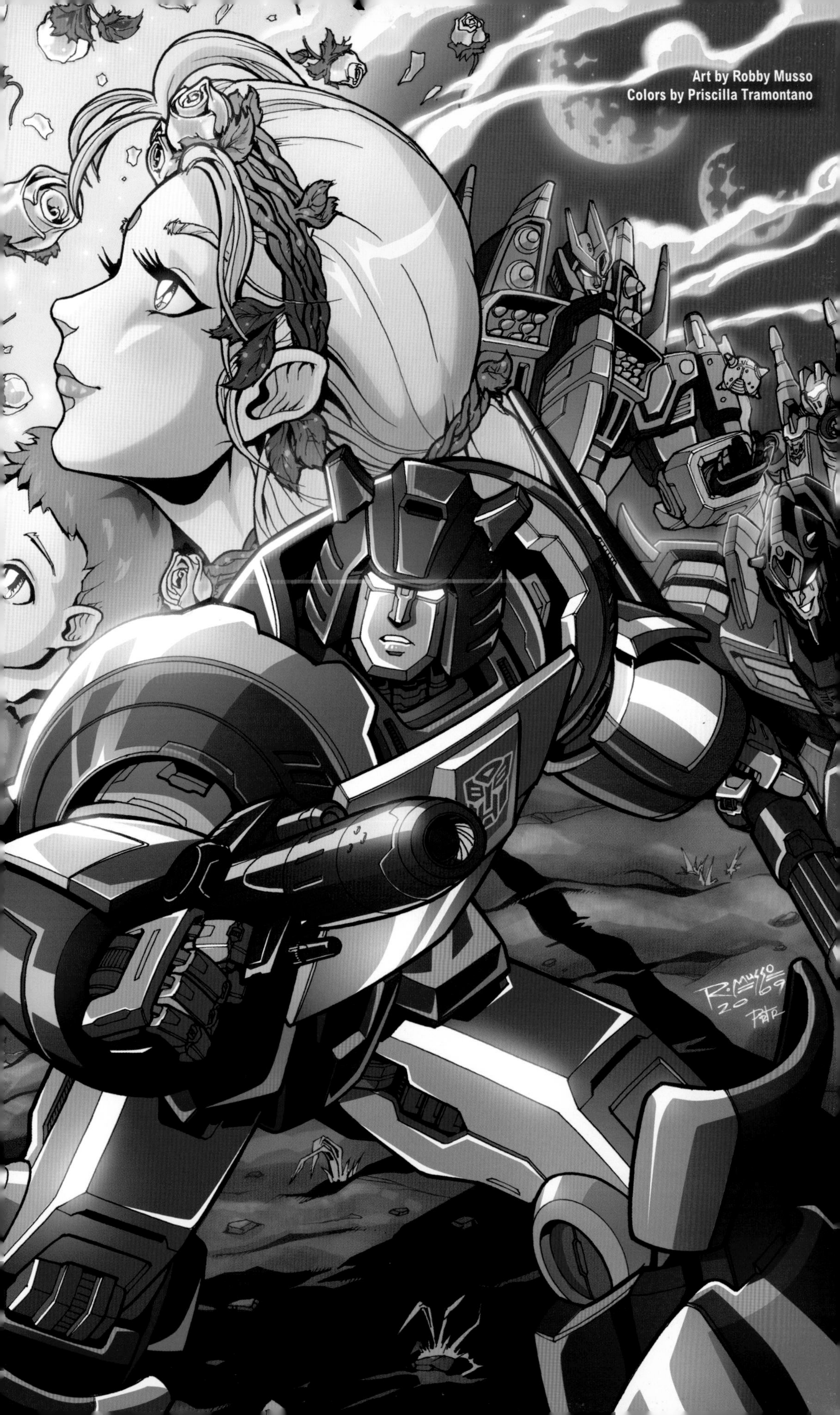
Art by Robby Musso
Colors by Priscilla Tramontano

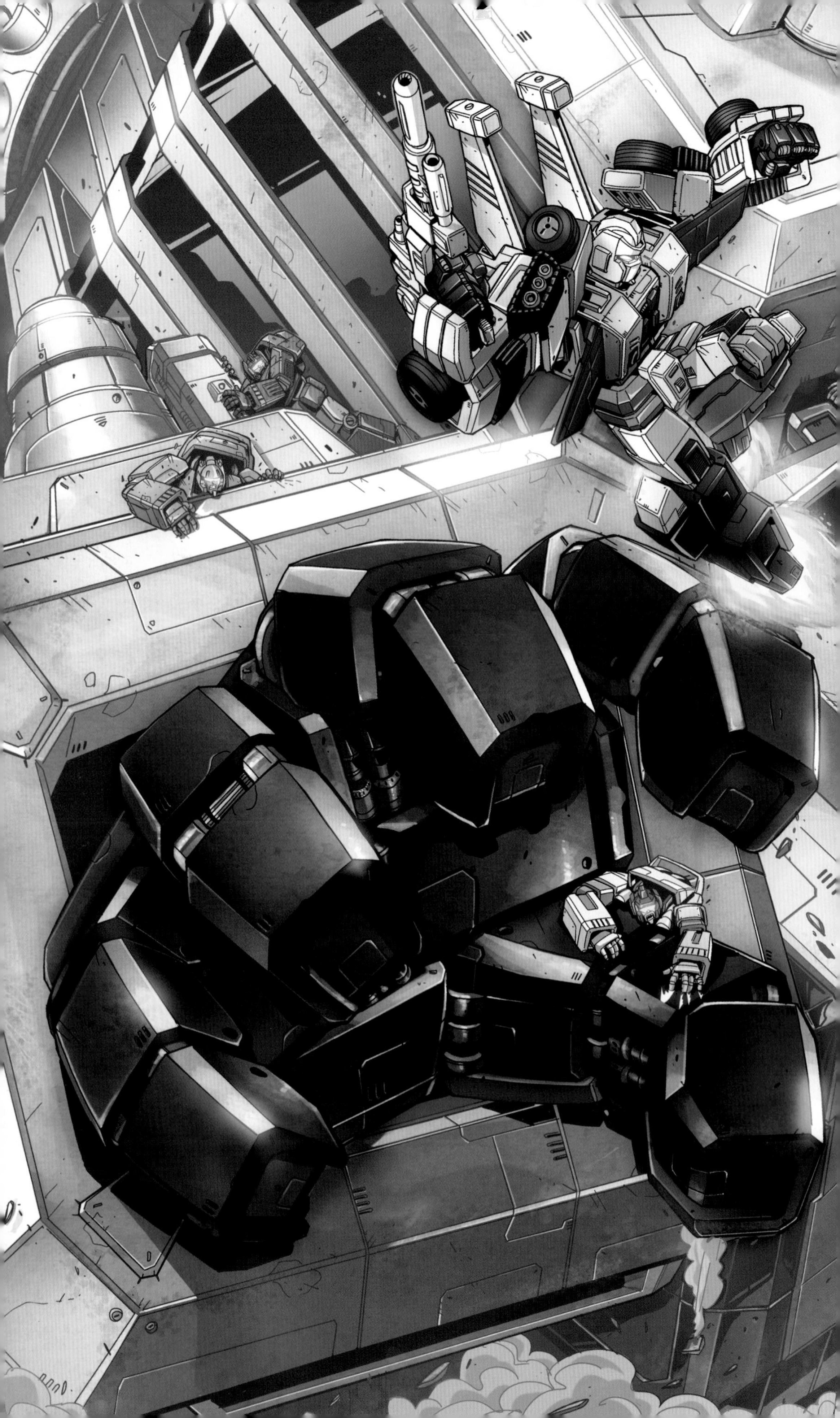

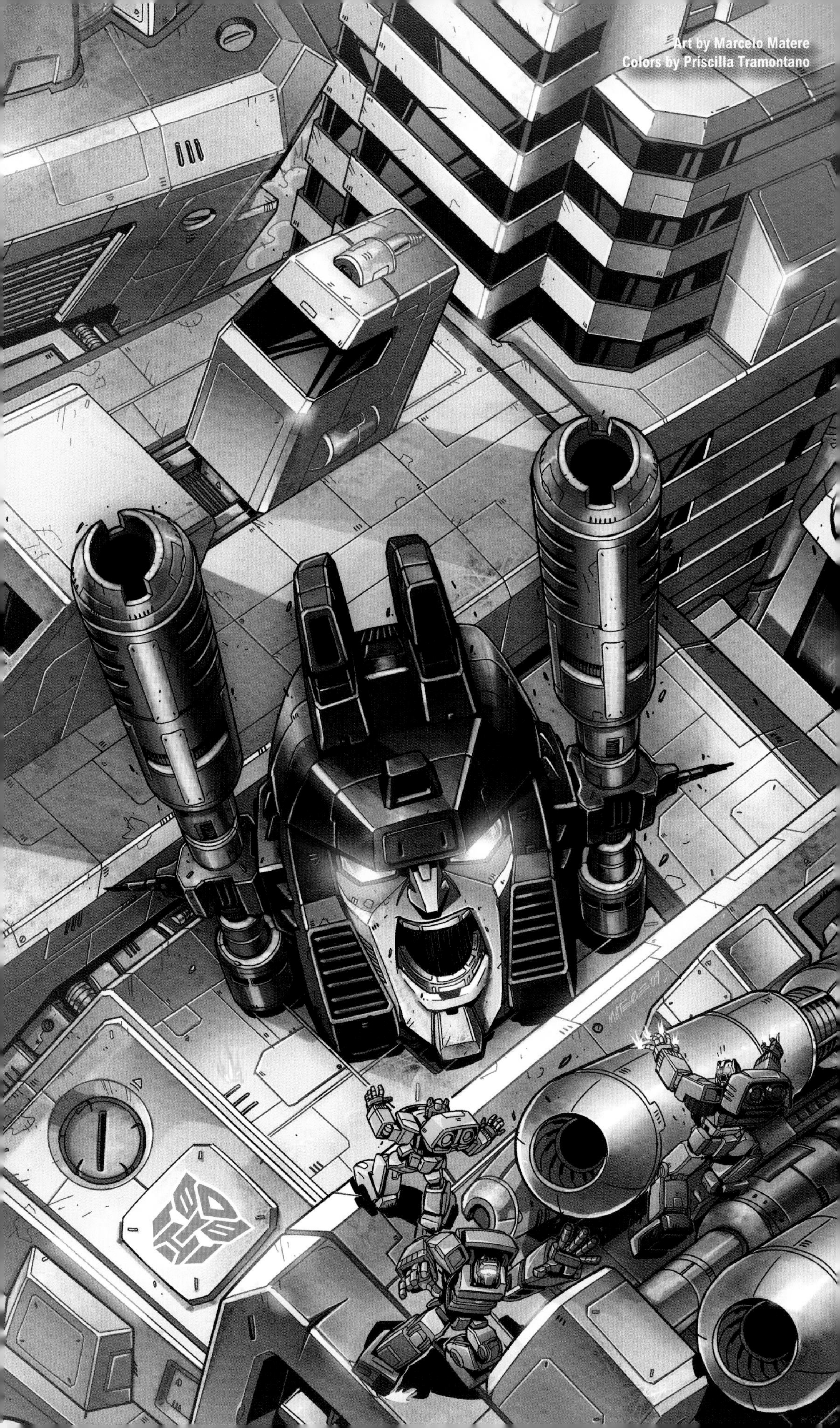

Art by Marcelo Matere
Colors by Priscilla Tramontano

Art by Casey Coller
Colors by Joana Lafuente

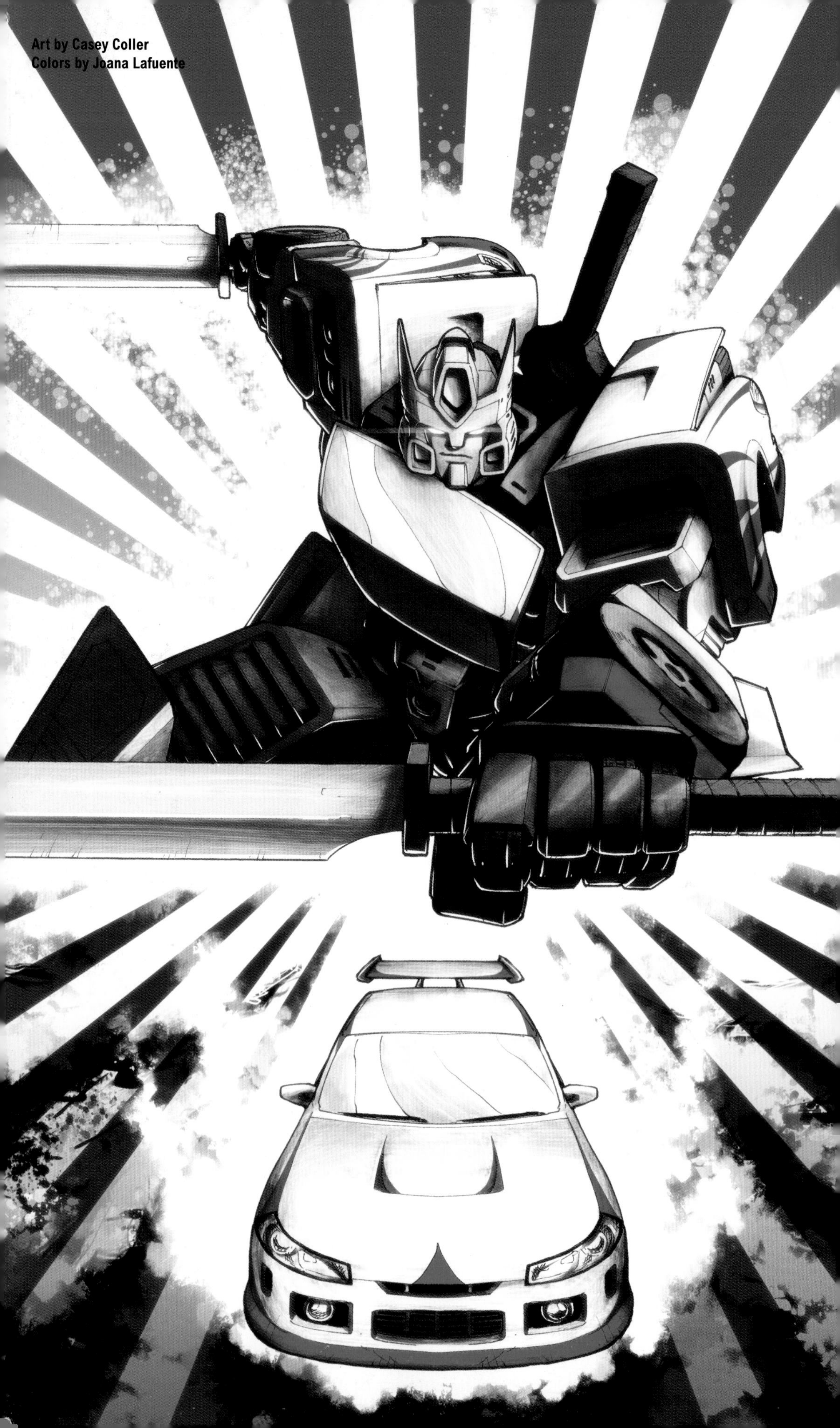

Appomattox Regional Library System
Hopewell, Virginia 23860
12/09
DIS